1. Scope and Purpose

This handbook is designed to assist joint task force commanders and staffs in planning, organizing, conducting, and assessing attack the network (AtN) activities in support of military operations. It describes the fundamental actions, analytical methodology (i.e., AtN framework) that forms the basis for identifying and exploiting threat network vulnerabilities, AtN roles and responsibilities of the joint task force staff, and contributions of civil organizations in the planning, execution and assessment of AtN activities.

2. Background

As the post Cold War political environment demonstrates, the United States and its partners continue to face an uncertain and unstable world. This inherent uncertainty and instability means the American military must be prepared to face the continuing potential challenges of large-scale combat and smaller scale contingency operations. While the most important mission of the American military has been to fight and win the nation s wars, the ability of US forces to deter conflict has risen to equal footing. The ability to deter adversaries depends on the capability and effectiveness of US forces to act across the range of military operations. Deterrence also depends on the adversaries belief that the United States will use its military power in defense of its national interests. Consequently, the US military roles and missions will continue to be: protection of the homeland; maintenance of the global commons; deterrence of adversaries; reassuring partners and allies; and when necessary, fighting and winning.

While states and other conventional powers remain the principal brokers of power, there is an undeniable diffusion of power to unconventional, non-state, or transnational organizations and individuals. These groups have rules of their own and exist and behave outside the recognized norms and conventions of society. Some transnational organizations seek to operate beyond state control and acquire the tools and means to challenge states utilizing terrorism against populations to achieve their aims. These unconventional transnational organizations possess no regard for international borders and agreements.

The increasing globalization of trade, finance, and human travel in the commercial world has facilitated the rise of these transnational threats. Criminal and terrorist networks are intermingling to construct their own "shadow globalization," micro markets, and trade and financial networks that has enabled them to coordinate nefarious activities on a global scale. The ubiquity and ease of access to these markets outside of legal structures attract shadow financing from a much larger pool, irrespective of geography. In these markets, rates of innovation in tactics, capabilities, and information sharing has accelerated and enabled virtual organizational structures that quickly coalesce, plan, attack, and dissolve. As they grow, these markets will allow adversaries to generate attacks at a higher rate and sophistication beyond law enforcement s capability to interdict. For example, Somali pirates have hired indigenous spotters to identify ships leaving foreign harbors as prime targets for hijackings. Shadow globalization is expected to encourage this outsourcing of criminality to interface increasingly with insurgencies, such that participants in local conflicts will impact with perhaps hundreds of groups and thousands of participants globally.

The line between insurgency and organized criminal activities likely will continue to blur. This convergence is already seen in the connections between the Colombian FARC and cocaine trafficking, Nigerian Movement for the Emancipation of the Niger Delta (MEND) and stolen oil, and the Taliban and opium production. This means that funding for violent conflicts will interplay and abet the growth of global gray and black markets. The current size of these markets is already $2-3 trillion and is growing faster than legal commercial trade; it has the potential to equal a third of global GDP by 2020. If so, violent insurgencies will have the ability to trade within this economic regime, amassing financial resources in exchange for market protection, and to mobilize those resources to rival state military capabilities in many areas. This gives them the increased ability to co-opt and corrupt state legal structures.

In this era of failed states, destabilized elements, and high end asymmetric threats; the military must be prepared to adapt rapidly to each specific threat across the range of military operations. Successful operations will require military forces to work closely with, provide support to, and receive support from civil United States Government (USG) agencies and US Allies. This is not a fight the military can win alone, but only through the application of all the instruments of national power. Identifying and defining specific threats will become increasingly difficult, but is absolutely necessary if the US and its partner nations aim to counter the threats those organizations pose to local and regional stability.

The majority of the threats facing the US and its regional partners are in fact organized networks with well established and identifiable infrastructures that are adapted to their operational environment and capable of surviving and accommodating substantial military and political changes. Neutralizing threat networks is not an easy task and requires an intense intelligence collection effort, patience, and an integrated, synchronized, cooperative effort on the part of numerous civilian governmental (and nongovernmental) organizations. By identifying a network's critical capabilities and requirements, friendly forces can develop a range of lethal and nonlethal options that disrupt or create critical vulnerabilities to neutralize these networks.

3. Content

a. The idea of AtN has emerged from experiences gained during US military operations in Iraq and Afghanistan. As a result, the research and the examples used throughout this handbook will draw primarily from those experiences, but will propose solutions that will be of value to the JFC in any operational area.

b. Specifically, this handbook provides:

(1) Fundamental background information on AtN, its objectives, and required capabilities;

(2) Considerations to guide the planning, conduct and assessment of AtN activities in support of the overarching campaign plan; and

(3) A discussion of the whole-of-government contribution to AtN activities and the importance of the role of DOD and non-DOD organizational enablers in the AtN fight.

4. Application

This handbook is not approved joint doctrine, but is a non-authoritative supplement that can assist commanders and their staffs in planning, organizing, executing, and assessing AtN activities in support of their operations. The information herein also can help the joint community to further develop the application of AtN techniques to the conduct of military operations and mature AtN concepts for possible transition into joint doctrine. This handbook should be treated as a guide and not as a template. It is important to understand the dynamic nature of AtN in a joint context and not as a step-by-step "how-to" manual.

5. Contact Information

Comments and suggestions on this important topic are welcomed. United States Joint Forces Command, J7 Joint Warfighting Center points of contact are LTC James Di Crocco, 757-203-6243, james.dicrocco@jfcom mil; and Dr. Theodore Dyke, 757-203-6137, theodore.dyke.ctr@ jfcom mil

FREDERICK S. RUDESHEIM
Major General, U.S. Army
Director, J7/Joint Warfighting Center

Intentionally Blank

TABLE OF CONTENTS

FIGURES

CHAPTER I
FUNDAMENTALS

Attack the Network - A focused approach to understanding and operating against a well-defined type of enemy activity—such as terrorism, insurgency, and organized criminal actions—that threatens stability in the operational area and is enabled by a network of identifiable nodes and links.

SECTION A. CONTEXT

1. Background

a. One of the major lessons learned from Operation IRAQI FREEDOM was the nature of the threat had significantly changed. Coalition forces were facing an insurgency armed with improvised explosive devices (IEDs) and supported by internal and international resources. It was an insurgency that learned to quickly adapt its use of IEDs, turning an improvised weapon into a tool of strategic influence and using information operations (IO) and intimidation to maximize its secondary and tertiary effects. The coalition also realized that it was facing a particular type of networked threat that would rapidly adapt its operations to offset friendly force advantages in numbers and technology. Over time the coalition realized that attacking a networked threat was more than just a counter-IED (C-IED) or counterinsurgency (COIN) challenge and that networked threats were a world-wide phenomena operating across the range of military operations.

b. Consequently, it was necessary to have a common understanding of how threat networks operated, their strengths and vulnerabilities, and what actions the joint force commander (JFC) could take to neutralize them. This involved focusing the analysis of the operational area provided through joint intelligence preparation of the operational environment (JIPOE) to identify and examine, in detail, the pertinent threat network(s); use of that analysis to refine the commander's intent and develop guidance that focused on the threat network(s); and the identification, integration, and employment of military and civil partners' counter-network capabilities.

"AtN activities never stand alone. They must be integrated into full spectrum operations in such a way that they reinforce and support the overarching campaign plan of the engaged force."

"Attack the Network: An Operational Approach"
US Army Training and Doctrine Command
January 2011

2. Attack the Network in Joint Operations

a. **General.** The JFC and staff develop plans and orders through the application of operational art, operational design, and the joint operation planning process (JOPP). They combine art and science to develop products that describe how (ways) the joint force will employ its capabilities (means) to achieve the military end state (ends). Operational art is the application of creative imagination by commanders and staffs—supported by their skill, knowledge, and experience—to design strategies, campaigns, and major operations and organize and employ forces. Operational design supports commanders and staff in their application of operational art with tools and a methodology to conceive and construct operations and campaigns. Operational design results in the commander's operational approach, which broadly describes the actions the joint force needs to take to reach the military end state. Finally, JOPP is an orderly, analytical process through which the JFC and staff translate the broad operational approach into detailed plans and orders.

(1) **Operational art** provides the vision that links tactical actions to strategic objectives. More specifically, the interaction of operational art and operational design provides a bridge between strategy and tactics, linking national political aims to tactical combat and noncombat operations that must be executed to accomplish these aims. Likewise, **operational art promotes unified action** by helping JFCs and staffs understand how to facilitate the integration of other civilian agencies and multinational partners toward achieving strategic and operational objectives.

(2) **Operational design** supports operational art with a general methodology and *elements of operational design*. The methodology helps the JFC and staff reduce the uncertainty of a complex OE, understand the nature of the problem or challenge facing them, and construct an operational approach to create achieve the desired end state. The elements of operational design are individual tools, such as *center of gravity* and *line of operations*, which help the JFC and staff visualize and describe the broad operational approach.

(3) **Joint Operation Planning**. Operational art, operational design, and JOPP are complementary elements of the overall planning process. The JFC, supported by the staff, gains an understanding of the environment, defines the problem, and develops an operational approach for the joint operation/campaign through the application of operational art and operational design during the initiation step of JOPP. Commanders transmit their operational approach to their staff, subordinate and supporting commanders, agencies, and multinational/nongovernmental entities as required in their initial planning guidance so that their approach can be translated into executable plans. As JOPP is conducted, commanders refine their initial operational approach so the staff understands the basis for COAs and an eventual CONOPS.

For a detailed discussion on operational art and design in the joint operation planning process, see JP 5-0, Joint Operation Planning.

b. **Commander's Intent**. The commander provides a summary of his current understanding of the OE and the problem, along with his visualization of the operational approach to his staff and to other partners through commander's planning guidance. At a minimum, the commander issues planning guidance, either initial or refined, at the conclusion of mission analysis, and provides refined planning guidance as his understanding of the OE and of the problem and visualization of the operational approach mature. The planning guidance will also include the commander's initial intent – describing the desired end state (strategic and military), identifying operational risks and what risks are acceptable, his intent for integrating all instruments of national power and the employment of interorganizational and multinational partners in achieving strategic success. In articulating their intent and providing on-going guidance to the staff, commanders should be aware of the importance of the various networks interacting in their operational area and the need to influence those networks (positively or negatively) to achieve the desired end state. A detailed JIPOE will assist in framing the problem, identifying the key networks (enemy and friendly), their potential vulnerabilities (and strengths), and potential approaches to attack or exploit those vulnerabilities.

c. **Attack the network (AtN) activities are nested within the broader joint operation/ campaign planning, execution, and assessment processes (e.g., JIPOE, operational art/ design, JOPP, targeting)**. The AtN methodology, discussed in paragraph 3 below and illustrated in Figure I-2. is designed to enable a commander, joint task force (CJTF) and staff to fine tune its understanding of how a threat network operates and neutralize its ability to efficiently and effectively conduct its activities. It should be noted that merely neutralizing or destroying a portion of the threat network does not guarantee lasting success. Many networks reconstitute or move to a new location. Lethal and nonlethal engagements against the conditions within the operational environment (OE) that allow the enemy to operate sets the conditions that render the enemy irrelevant and achieves the commander's intent. In COIN operations, for example, successful lethal and nonlethal engagements to clear the enemy from an area allow friendly forces to hold and build. This provides the host nation (HN) government with the opportunity to restore rule of law, provide necessary infrastructure, and reduce support for the enemy's activities; thereby fundamentally altering the OE in favor of friendly forces. Ultimately, **AtN activities are designed to neutralize the threat network, create the conditions that enable friendly networks to effectively function with the support of the local population, and establish the conditions that will allow the disengagement of friendly forces.**

SECTION B. FUNDAMENTAL ACTIONS

AtN involves more than the focused use of ISR assets, analytical methodologies, and dynamic or deliberate targeting means. If AtN is to make a contribution to the success of the overall joint operation/campaign, it must be a part of a broader, command wide effort to: 1) Build a better friendly network, 2) Empower information exchange, 3) Employ all enablers, and 4) Exploit all opportunities with IO. These fundamental actions leverage the lethal and nonlethal capabilities of the military force and participating United States Government (USG), multinational, and HN partners.

1. Build a Better Friendly Network

a. **Unified action is employed to shape and strengthen the friendly network** to the benefit of friendly forces and the detriment of the threat network. The CJTF and staff must first design a joint operation/campaign that reflects their understanding of the OE in order to "build a better network." This sets the conditions for a fully partnered AtN planning and execution that can effectively support rapid decision-making and synchronize military and civil actions. This also enables units and commanders to take advantage of fleeting opportunities and quickly identify and take educated tactical risks.

b. **Provide Commander's Guidance**. The CJTF will initially conduct a brief evaluation of the mission and provide initial planning guidance to the staff. **At a minimum, very early in the mission analysis process, the intelligence staff must ensure that the CJTF is aware of the capabilities and intent of threat networks, current status of friendly networks, and current posture of the neutral networks.** This will assist the CJTF in formulating initial commander's guidance, which normally initiates the mission analysis and planning process. Key elements that result from mission analysis and the planning process include a draft mission statement, commander's intent, and concept of operations (CONOPS).

(1) The **mission statement** should be a short sentence or paragraph that describes the organization's essential task (or tasks) and purpose — a clear statement of the action to be taken and the reason for doing so.

(2) The **commander's intent** is a clear and concise expression of the purpose of the operation and the military end state. It serves to drive the targeting process.

(3) The **CONOPS** describes how the actions of the JTF components and supporting organizations will be integrated, synchronized, and phased to accomplish the mission, including potential branches and sequels. The CJTF and staff must ensure that AtN considerations are woven throughout the products of the planning guidance.

c. **Conduct Operational Design**. Operational design enables the CJTF and staff to outline a strategy for reaching a sustainable end state in the operational area. An outcome is development of LOEs that are further developed into intermediate objectives and desired effects with supporting measures of effectiveness (MOE) and measures of performance (MOP). This ensures commanders and staffs at each echelon are planning and executing operations across all LOEs that support achieving the same overall end state. **Continuous assessment is required to identify and adapt to changing conditions.** Additionally, linkages between unit plans' defining intermediate objectives for all LOE and the commander's critical information requirements should be established to focus units on collecting information that commanders at all levels will use to make timely and accurate decisions.

For a detailed examination of the operation design and planning process, see JP 5-0, "Joint Operation Planning."

d. **Establish and Standardize Targeting Processes**. The CJTF identifies the focus for the targeting cycle and promulgates this in the commander's initial guidance and commander's intent. The targeting process is designed to transform intent into reality through the identification of the human, material, or other capital which the enemy need for the successful execution of their operations. The targeting process is designed to ultimately identify the high-payoff targets (HPTs) that must be executed to achieve friendly success and the high-value targets (HVTs) the loss of which would seriously degrade the threat network. The process is directly related to the find-fix-finish-exploit-analyze-disseminate (F3EAD) methodology that helps the commanders and staffs at all echelons to organize their targeting efforts. Targeting is a complex process that requires detailed analysis and input from multiple staff entities to integrate, synchronize, and focus combat power. Ideally, the staff is organized in a way that facilitates the analysis of these problem sets and develops solutions in the form of targeting recommendations. The standard targeting staff development process includes:.

(1) **Assessment Working Group**. The assessment working group analyzes unit/ staff assessments and commander's intent in order to identify and prioritize target sets for development. This meeting is crucial because it sets conditions for the rest of the targeting cycle by focusing collective efforts on developing the target sets identified at this meeting. Additionally, the CJTF and staff and receive critical bottom up refinements in the form of unit assessments that provide the team with a clear understanding of the OE. Key inputs to the group are the overall joint operations/campaign plan assessment, unit and staff assessments, battle damage assessments, and commander's guidance. Inputs help the team clearly describe the OE so commanders can then visualize and direct ongoing planning and operations.

(a) The **joint operation/campaign plan assessment** assists in ensuring the component's are moving forward in each LOE and can identify any course corrections as required.

(b) **Unit assessments** are critical because they drive the targeting cycle by describing the environment for commanders, enabling them to visualize and provide guidance for each cycle. **Unit assessments** need to cover at minimum battle damage assessments (BDA), target nominations, and an overall assessment with respect to all mission variables in the assigned AO.

(c) The **BDA assessment** can result in three outcomes: the target needs to be closed out, re-attacked, or changed or updated.

The assessment is the holistic view of the OE and covers both lethal and nonlethal aspects. The commander's guidance when combined with the assessment will enable the CJTF and staff to identify target sets requiring development. **The end state for the assessment working group is a prioritized target set established for further development at each of the specialized working groups.**

(2) **Specialized working groups** are temporary groupings of staff representatives who meet to coordinate and provide recommendations for a particular course of action. They synchronize the work of multiple cells and develop detailed courses of actions for identified periods of time. Specialized working groups such as the asymmetric warfare group, the lethal and nonlethal targeting working groups, and the targeting working group are responsible for developing the overall targeting plan; however, if a specific problem set arises that requires additional focus, the CJTF may convene additional specialized working groups (e.g., C-IED; intelligence, surveillance, and reconnaissance [ISR]; interagency; HN) to address other special areas.

A detailed discussion of the AtN Boards, Centers, Cells and Working Groups is contained in Chapter V, "Organize for the Fight."

(3) **Decision Brief**. The decision brief presents the fully resourced and synchronized LOE and targeting actions to the CJTF for decision and approval. The primary input for this meeting are the fully developed mission statement, commander's intent (with the military end state), and CONOPS

2. Empower Information Exchange

> "DoD responds to the IED problem from the military perspective, but we have increasingly recognized that interagency cooperation and cooperation with foreign governments are essential in addressing this complex issue. Active coordination with US Government diplomatic, economic, intelligence, and military resources, as well as cooperation from foreign governments, is the key to a successful effort to defeat IED networks. We rely heavily on the Department of State to assist in this area."
>
> **David S. Sedney**
> **Deputy Assistant Secretary of Defense for Afghanistan,**
> **Pakistan and Central Asia**
> **November 2010**

a. **Vertical and horizontal collaboration and knowledge sharing in planning and execution is essential**. Sharing operational knowledge and intelligence simultaneously across the entire friendly network to create a common understanding of the OE, and specifically the threat network, enables the friendly network to outmaneuver the threat network through information dominance. This shared understanding and information dominance also enhances the friendly network's ability to adapt to emerging trends in the OE. While elaborate communications architectures have been developed to facilitate information sharing and database access, the challenge is to avoid information overload and find the relevant, useable information that supports decision making. To be useful, information must be collected, stored, and searchable in digital form that can be rapidly translated into formats (visual or hard copy) to facilitate unit planning, decision making, and execution.

b. **Collaboration**. Collaboration is key to effective attack the network activities. It enhances planning and execution; intelligence collection, analysis, and reporting; and targeting.

(1) **Military-Civil Collaboration During Planning and Execution**. All participating military and civil organizations should be integrated into AtN planning to develop a shared understanding of their priorities and capabilities. They also should be included in execution. Inclusion of HN security forces in COIN operations, for example, demonstrate the competence of the security force to the populace and effectively increase their legitimacy in the eyes of the populace. Developing an effective collaborative environment requires the joint force to engage these multinational force and civil organization partners and share information. A methodology for attaining this level of cooperative exchange includes:

(a) Establish communications (face-to-face meetings are preferred with exchange of liaisons).

(b) Determine missions, tasks, and mutual goals. Identify and discuss points of divergence.

(c) Determine and discuss the information requirements that support these missions/tasks. Identify the specific types of information that needs to be exchanged to facilitate mutually supporting operations and the timelines for providing that information to decision makers and planners.

(d) Discuss methods for establishing a communications architecture for ongoing information exchange. Challenges to communication might be extensive, given differences of culture, language, and technologies.

(e) Determine respective battle rhythms and decide when/were to meet. Liaisons should attend and participate in appropriate meetings.

(2) **Intelligence Collaboration**. The JTF must establish a communications architecture that supports operations by facilitating the exchange of relevant intelligence information among all the AtN participants. In addition to hardware, the command's internal information management (IM) policies and practices must be crafted to facilitate the timely delivery of information (analyzed or raw) from collector to decision maker in a useable format. AtN activities are inherently dynamic and involve fleeting targets with short windows of opportunity for exploitation. In order to work, the system requires detailed and continuous coordination between collectors and customers.

(3) **Collaborative Targeting**. Establishing a collaborative targeting process is critical because it provides current unit troop to task, assessments of the operational area, and allows for the exchange of information real time. This decreases the time required to plan and execute operations and speeds decision making. Collaboration must occur not only vertically between the echelons (joint force to components to maneuver units), but also horizontally across staff sections and the HN's security forces. Through the use of digital collaborative systems the team can collaborate at echelon to develop resource and synchronize the force's targeting efforts across all LOEs.

c. **Knowledge Sharing**. US forces have multiple high-speed networks, video teleconferencing, digital mapping, satellites, and tons of high-tech gear designed to make information instantly available to those who need it; however, the enemy also has a highly adaptable communications network utilizing cell phones, video cameras, Internet access, and e-mail. The goal of a knowledge sharing process is to create, facilitate, and manage a horizontally based, vertically integrated knowledge transfer system designed to harness emerging enemy and friendly information to create a competitive advantage against a networked threat through technological innovation and cultural engagement. Many joint commands designate a knowledge management officer (KMO)who works with the communications staff officer, who normally also acts as the information management officer (IMO), and representatives from the intelligence and operations staff to craft the command's knowledge sharing processes. The IMO works closely with the KMO on content, staging, portal design, development of staff management processes, and automatic processes to ensure relevant information is delivered to the right person at the right time. The IMO focuses on helping commanders to develop situational understanding and disseminate decisions faster than the enemy. He provides the necessary technical guidance and direction to ensure digital systems operate seamlessly throughout the command and with other contributing participants – interagency, multinational, and HN. A well integrated communications architecture is built from the bottom up, since most of the information that serves as a basis for AtN comes from the small unit level. Such architecture would include the use of the following systems (or their equivalent):

(1) **Tactical Ground Reporting Network (TiGRNet)**. TiGRNet is a web based system that centers on events and places and is primarily used at the company level. Media such as photos, documents, video, and drawings may be added to amplify the descriptions of the event or place. The system has the ability to position events and places into reports to summarize a patrol or mission. TiGRNet is searchable from the distributable common ground system – Army (DCGS-A) and has the capability to display Combined Information Data Network Exchange (CIDNE) SIGACTs; but it is also web based and therefore can be accessed from any computer at every echelon. TiGRNet entries are made by the company intelligence support teams (for US Army units) or their US Marine Corps equivalent when operating a TiGRNet like system. A complete report will include a patrol debrief, a storyboard (if an attack occurs), and pictures.

(2) **Command Post of the Future (CPOF)**. The CPOF is a visualization and collaboration system which supports visualization and information interaction in a single, integrated environment that ultimately helps commanders and decision makers analyze information, share thoughts, and evaluate courses of action. The CPOF system is typically employed at battalion and higher headquarters. CPOF also provides commanders and key staff with the means to implement their own approach to viewing, organizing, distributing, and collaboratively creating information to achieve objectives. CPOF provides the building blocks for collaborative IM processes across many of the staff sections.

(3) **Combined Information Data Network Exchange (CIDNE)**. CIDNE serves the primary bridge between disparate communities who might not otherwise share data by providing a standardized reporting framework across intelligence and operations disciplines. This common framework allows structured operational and intelligence information to be shared vertically and horizontally as part of flexible, user-defined workflow processes that collect, correlate, aggregate, and expose information as part of the end-user's individual information lifecycle requirements. While CIDNE was initially designed and is primarily used to provide an end-to-end IM solution in support of C-IED operations, its capabilities support AtN from initial threat reporting through exploitation, target development, and tracking. CIDNE is interoperable with a number of Army Battle Command and Intelligence systems, including DCGS-A. The information in CIDNE is collected across the operational area; ensuring that mission-critical information doesn't slip through the seams. It provides a robust framework that includes full search, geospatial visualization, workflow, and report production capabilities with customizable reports to meet evolving war fighter needs.

d. **Intelligence Reachback**. While a bottom up approach to developing a working picture of the OE is essential to AtN, commanders at all levels also should leverage the resources of national, joint, foreign, and other military organizations and units. Requestors can acquire information through push and pull of information, databases, homepages, collaborative tools, and broadcast services. Requestors may also use reachback to fill intelligence gaps and requirements and answer requests for information (RFIs). This technique can preclude unnecessary tasking or risk to limited ISR assets, share the information derived from intelligence reach with subordinate, lateral, and higher echelons, and ensure follow-on forces have all information as well. Using DCGS-A, the SECRET Internet Protocol Router Network (SIPRNET) and the Joint Worldwide Intelligence Communications System (JWICS) communications network backbones, intelligence analysts can leverage collaborative tools and access specialized enablers databases, analysis centers, service providers and web sites that process, analyze, assesses and disseminate general military intelligence (GMI) including tailored intelligence reports, graphics and imagery to the supported commander. Use of specialized enablers provides niche intelligence collection and analytical ability that are not normally resident at unit level.

3. Employ All Enablers

To conduct effective AtN , it may be necessary to augment the JTF and select unit level headquarters with teams of specialists (e.g., analysts and subject matter experts (SMEs) such as law enforcement, C-IED technicians, human environment teams) to facilitate the gathering, interpretation, and processing of information; assist in understanding the OE (i.e., culture, religion, politics); report and collect signatures to provide trends, TTPs, and predictive analysis; and assist in the targeting process. **These enablers** provide niche intelligence collection and analytical abilities not normally resident in the JTF to maximize the JTF's capabilities. Inclusion in the staff and the targeting process allows the enablers to understand the context of the operation, visualize the commander's intent, and provide the best advice and support to the commanders and staff members. Additionally, fully integrated enablers are able to serve as advocates for support requests to parent and supporting organizations through direct communication or intelligence reachback.

4. Exploit All Opportunities with Information Operations

a. AtN requires the application of a mix of lethal and nonlethal means to successfully neutralize the threat network. While lethal means are often emphasized, in the long term, nonlethal options have a greater cumulative effect, especially when it comes to turning the local population against the enemy. For most threat networks, experience has shown that eliminating key individuals has only a limited disruptive effect; individuals are quickly replaced. Alternatively, IO have enduring effects in setting conditions (shaping), exploiting mission success, and mitigating the effects of negative events. Planners must design an agile and flexible IO plan that can quickly respond to dynamic situational developments and targets appropriate audiences. Being first with the truth counters enemy propaganda and reduces local population support. IO shape all operations by assisting to secure the populace, explain the operational rationale, and demonstrate the results of the operation. Initially, the detailed JIPOE will identify those societal elements (leaders and general population groups) whose support, or neutrality, will be the focus of friendly IO. JIPOE also will determine the interests and objectives of those individuals and groups (Figure I-1) that can be the basis for developing themes.

b. **Information Operations**

> "One company commander tasked to conduct information operations in OIF (OPERATION IRAQI FREEDOM) identified two major purposes for company-level information operations: "First, you must distribute information to the people.....You must inform them of your goals and actions. Second, information operations involve not only passing out information; it requires the collection of information. The development of an informed populace and involvement of community leaders by a commander leads to information about hostile threats and benevolent projects."
>
> **CPT Dan Morgan, USA**
> **2005**

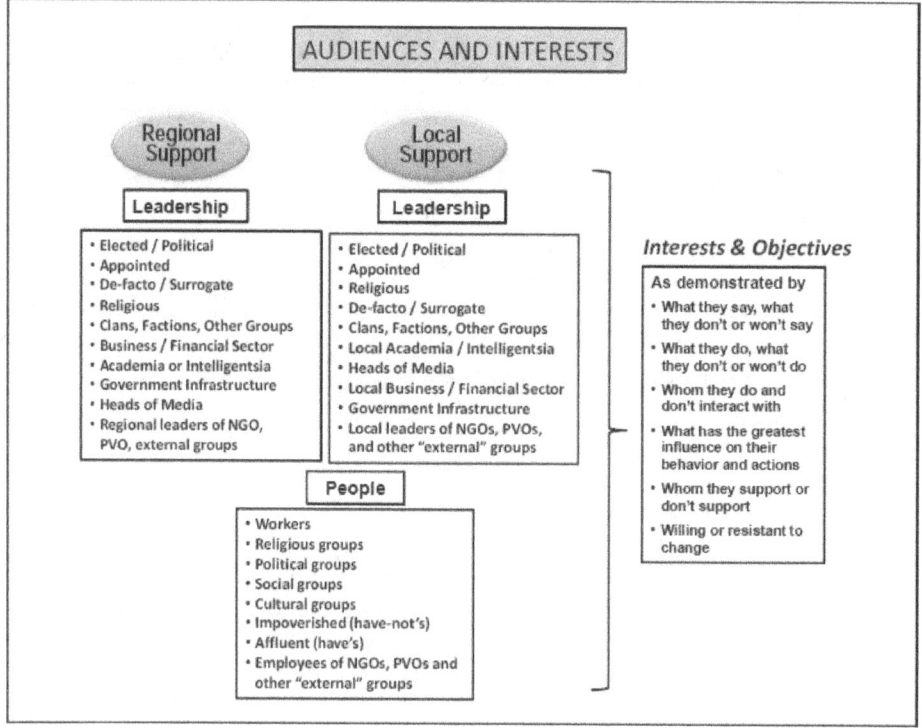

Figure I-1. Audiences and Interests

(1) Synchronized, integrated, multi-level IO are critical to AtN because they can help shape the OE, multiply the effects of friendly success, mitigate negative actions, and counter enemy IO. IO also can directly affect the perceptions of the threat network leadership. IO capabilities such as military information support operations (MISO) public affairs (PA), and civil affairs (CA); human environment teams (HET) (also referred to as tactical counterintelligence/HUMINT teams); and the provincial reconstruction teams

(PRT) provide a variety of IO options to commanders and staffs. Leveraging the HET and its social network analyses assists in understanding the human terrain and the causes of instability in the operational area. The PRTs, through their work with local civil governments, facilitate the development of the local economy and assist in legitimizing HN government. MISO, CA and HET cooperatively develop messages for the commander's key leader engagements (KLEs); plan for the use of media to publicize current and future security efforts; develop wanted posters and MISO products to assist in influencing the population, and obtain assistance in support of friendly force and local government efforts. During planning, the command IO staff officer develops IO exploitation options for each course of action by phase. The command IO staff officer also plans, synchronizes, and resources IO and the employment of enablers during the targeting process.

(2) **Setting Conditions**. The principle of isolating adversaries from their cause and support requires changing environmental conditions within and beyond the boundaries of the engagement area IO provide a potential mechanism for shaping or changing the environment that supports continued enemy activity by attacking the legitimacy of the group's actions. IO can be used to positively (rewards) or negatively (punishments) influence the target audience. Additionally, information products can be developed to support an environment of improving conditions as a result of visible security measures taking place in the area. The products provide a mechanism for engagement with the population and are distributed while active (usually offensive) operations are conducted to reduce the engagement area. In setting conditions, the friendly force at all echelons should conduct a series of KLEs to provide local leaders with information on upcoming operations and how they will affect and improve security in the operational area. For example, in COIN operations, engagement can be conducted with local shop owners and businessmen in the area to explain actions underway and solicit support in reducing violence in the area. These interactions set conditions by managing local leaders and the population's expectations and assist in illustrating to the populace the positive actions the government and security forces are taking to secure their safety.

(3) **Shaping**. Once conditions are set in the targeted area, unit IO staffs will participate in execution. This can take a number of forms depending on the unit capabilities and whether the command is executing "hard" or "soft" IO options or a mix thereof. Soft options are aimed at influencing the enemy's OE to turn against them. They include supplying the messages, print products (leaflets, handbills, etc) that are broadcast on various friendly media. Assisted by the IO staff, unit commanders should employ local leaders and governmental, security, and religious personnel to disseminate the messages who use radio, TV, and loudspeakers. Hard options include offensive exploitation of enemy communications means (cell phones, land lines, couriers) by jamming, exploiting for intelligence, or co-opting the systems or individuals. At operational and strategic levels, IO can include computer network attack by disrupting or corrupting the enemy's use of the Internet.

(4) **Post Combat IO Activities**. IO does not terminate with the conclusion of the" Dominate" phase of a joint operation. It continues well beyond in order to exploit success or mitigate negative consequences. The joint operation and subordinate plans must ensure that post combat IO are appropriately planned, prepared and resourced. Soft options include the IO staff preparing messages for the friendly force leadership (US,

multinational, HN security forces) to deliver at press events or through interaction with local leaders in the immediately affected area and throughout the operational area. HETs and MISO teams perform continuous assessments to determine the population's view of the operation and how it impacted their situation. This can include something as simple as claims forms for damaged property. For hard options, the command's intelligence resources are focused on the enemy's reactions to include determining how they rebuild their capacity.

See Appendix A, "Information Operations" for a more detailed discussion on information operations.

See also, the US Joint Forces Command publication, Commander's Handbook for Strategic Communications and Communications Strategy" for a more detailed discussion on communications strategies.

SECTION C. ATTACK THE NETWORK FRAMEWORK

1. Overview

a. The AtN tasks, illustrated in Figure I-2 and described in Chapters II-VI, are designed to guide the planning, execution, and assessment of AtN. It represents the next level of JIPOE analysis, operational design, mission execution, and assessment that helps planners focus the specialized assets required to identify the threat network's key operating nodes and links and applies the lethal and nonlethal capabilities that will

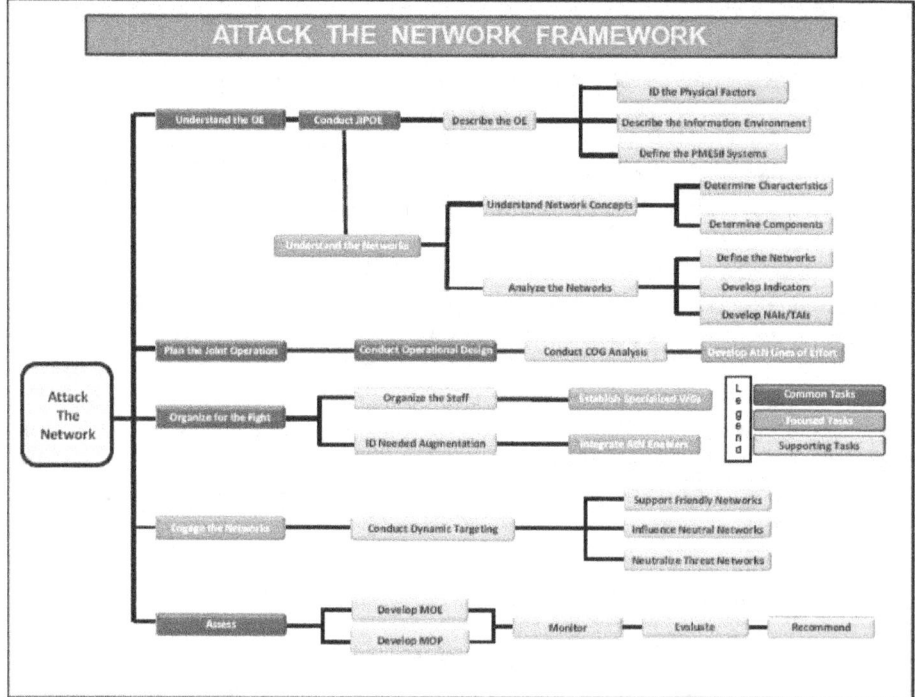

Figure I-2. Attack the Network Framework

have the greatest effect on that network's ability to operate. It leverages the lethal and nonlethal capabilities of the military force and civilian partners to attack and disrupt the threat network nodes and links. These activities occur continuously, in parallel, and in coordination with one another. Figure I-2, and Chapters II through VII, depict and describe only the top level tasks; Appendix B, "Attack the Network Framework" provides greater detail

2. Application

a. **Attack the Network Methodology in Joint Operation Planning**. Networks operate in inherently complex environments that are often difficult to understand and which often defy coherent joint operation planning. The tasks illustrated in Figure I-2 supports joint operation/campaign planning by focusing the CJTF and staff on challenges inherent in the systems perspective of the OE and how they impact mission accomplishment. It facilitates the joint staff's planning for the employment of limited resources against critical vulnerabilities in the threat network; and, enables the employment of civilian resources to reach the desired end state. The task outcomes also assists in the development of the commander's intent by focusing the description of the major components (friendly, adversary, and neutral) of the OE during JIPOE; defining the problem confronting the joint force, and identifying the opportunities that can be exploited. The AtN essential task outcomes also can assist in identifying centers of gravity and decisive points; focusing the employment of intelligence resources on identifiable threat activities; and prioritizing potential targets for lethal or nonlethal exploitation. **AtN planning activities are nested within the broader JOPP and its supporting activities; they normally are not conducted independently.**

b. **Successful AtN planning and execution normally is accomplished by working with USG, multinational, and HN partners to conduct a complimentary and coordinated mix of lethal and nonlethal actions focused on specific nodes and links in the threat network.** Successful AtN operations will blend actions that directly degrade threat network capabilities while increasing the friendly network capabilities. Although the threat network likely will never disappear, it is neutralized when its capabilities are marginalized or sufficiently degraded and friendly network capabilities have improved to the point where they can manage any residual threat independently over time.

c. The AtN activities described in this handbook primarily apply to joint operations that do not involve state-sponsored, conventional military forces. While it is most applicable to threat networks during stability operations, it can also be applied to a wide variety of irregular, networked threats – transnational criminal organizations, terrorists, piracy, etc. – that threaten our national interests or those of our partner nations.

Intentionally Blank

CHAPTER II
UNDERSTANDING THE OPERATIONAL ENVIRONMENT

"We believe the global trends portend several decades of persistent conflict in which local and regional frictions, fueled by globalization and other emerging trends, are exploited by extremists to support their efforts to destroy our way of life. They will increasingly confront the United States and our friends and allies with combinations of complex, dynamic and unanticipated challenges to our national and collective security. Future conflicts will occur in many forms as violence ebbs and flows across the spectrum of conflict—ranging from stable peace to general war and all points in between—and in each of the physical domains—in the air, at sea and on land."

Gen George W. Casey,
"America's Army In an Era of Persistent Conflict"
October 2008

1. Joint Intelligence Preparation of the Operational Environment

a. A comprehensive, multidimensional assessment of the OE will assist commanders and staffs in uncovering the underlying drivers of instability and root causes that facilitate threat network activities; develop focused operations to attack threat vulnerabilities; better anticipate the second and third order effects of AtN activities; and MOE. A detailed JIPOE is the first step in identifying the essential elements that constitute the OE and is critical to the planning and conduct of AtN activities.

b. JIPOE is the analytical process used by joint intelligence organizations to produce intelligence assessments, estimates, and other intelligence products in support of the JFC's decision-making process. It is a continuous process that involves four major steps: (1) defining the total OE; (2) describing the impact of the OE; (3) evaluating the adversary; and (4) determining and describing adversary potential courses of action (COAs), particularly the adversary's most likely COA and the COA most dangerous to friendly forces and mission accomplishment. The process is used to analyze the physical domains (air, land, maritime and space), and the information environment (which includes the cyberspace domain); political, military, economic, social, information, and infrastructure (PMESII) systems; and all other relevant aspects of the OE to determine an adversary's capabilities to operate within that environment.

c. The OE is the composite of the conditions, circumstances, and influences that affect the employment of capabilities and bear on the decisions of the commander. Understanding this environment requires a holistic view that extends beyond the adversary's military forces and other combat capabilities within the operational area. A holistic view of the OE encompasses physical areas and factors (of the air, land, maritime, and space domains) and the information environment (which includes cyberspace). Included within these are the adversary, friendly, and neutral PMESII systems and subsystems that are relevant to a specific joint operation. Understanding the OE is fundamental to identifying the conditions required to achieve stated objectives; avoiding the effects that may hinder mission accomplishment (undesired effects); and assessing the impact of friendly, adversary, and other organizations and individuals, as well as the local populace, on the commander's CONOPS and progress toward attaining the military end state.

d. An understanding of the systems in the OE and their interaction can help the CJTF and staff visualize and describe how military actions can affect other agency and coalition partners as well as how those partners' actions can affect the CJTF's operations. Visualizing and describing the interaction of PMESII systems and subsystems can facilitate the CJTF's collaboration with counterparts from other agencies and organizations and help influence actions that are beyond the CJTF's directive authority. JIPOE analysts develop a systems perspective of the OE through the identification and analysis of all major elements within friendly, adversary, or neutral PMESII systems and subsystems that are potentially relevant to the success of a joint operation. Based on understanding strategic objectives, the joint force's mission, and the CJTF's intent, objectives, conditions required to achieve objectives, and tasks, the J-2 identifies PMESII systems and their subordinate components that are relevant to the mission and operation. Understanding the interaction of these systems with each other and how their relationships will change over time can help the CJTF visualize how joint force actions on one system can affect other systems.

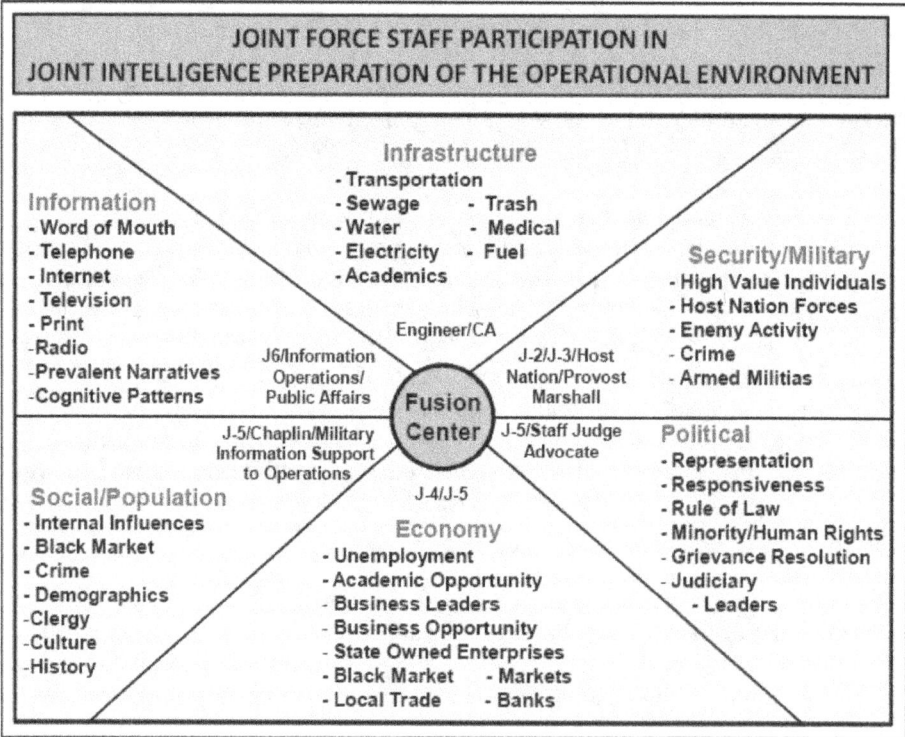

Figure II-1. Joint Force Staff Participation in Joint Intelligence Preparation of the Operational Environment

e.   The entire joint force staff participates in JIPOE development (Figure II-1); contributing according to their area of expertise. An in-depth analysis is required to identify threat, neutral, and friendly network members, their functions within the network, and relationships between network members. Defining the OE with sufficient detail to support operations requires the joint force to seek input from all the participants in the operation – multinational forces, HN and USG agencies, nongovernmental organizations, and private entities.

f.   Using information derived from a properly focused JIPOE, the CJTF and staff can identify the threat network's nodes and links, direct intelligence collection to further refine the critical requirements and capabilities that sustain and direct the threat network, identify the effects that must be created to (positively or negatively) influence that the threat network, and identify the appropriate resources that will create those effects. The following discussion examines the range of threats found in the current global environment that can become the focus of an operational JIPOE.

2.   Current Challenge

While US forces, through superior technology and training, have achieved dominance in the conduct of conventional warfare, they increasingly face irregular threats that employ asymmetric means to counter those advantages. Our experience in recent crisis response and limited contingency operations indicate that coalition forces likely will increasingly face an enemy that displays the characteristics of irregular forces; using terrorism, unconventional warfare, and even criminality. Thus, in addition to being prepared to face conventional forces, the near term OE will require US forces to be prepared to face a diverse and dynamic combination of irregular forces as well as criminal elements that are unified to achieve mutually benefitting effects. From the narco-terrorists in Colombia with their global cocaine market to the Movement for the Emancipation of the Niger Delta insurgents in Nigeria attacking oil supplies, the worldwide impact of these blended groups can no longer be ignored. A further disturbing development can be derived from the Israeli experience in Lebanon in 2006 and US experience against Iraqi *fedayeen* where state organizations adopted the characteristics of irregular forces. Future adversaries (states, state sponsored, or non-affiliated groups) may very well exploit access to modern weaponry and communications systems and combine their inherent capabilities with insurgent methods – ambushes, IEDs, and assassinations. The exploitation of modern information technology also will enhance the learning cycle of irregular adversaries, improving their ability to transfer lessons learned and techniques from one theater to another. These opponents will remain elusive, operate in a highly distributed manner, and rapidly adapt to environmental change. Defeating them and maintaining global stability to protect US and allied interests will require the United States and its global partners to comprehensively define the OE (globally and in each theater), develop integrated strategies, and conduct a coordinated campaign.

3.   Threats to Stability

a.   **Overview**. The threats to regional and local stability vary greatly across the globe. They include traditional state-on-state rivalries and traditional leftist insurgencies.

They also include the growing challenge posed by violent Islamic jihadists and international organized criminals. International organized criminals are threatening US interests by forging alliances with corrupt government officials, undermining competition in key global markets, perpetrating extensive cyber crimes, attempting to co-opt legitimate networks, and expanding their narco-trafficking networks. The nexus between international criminal organizations and terrorist and insurgent groups also present continuing dangers. With its long history of promoting global political and economic stability, it is in the US's best interests to confront these threats. The geographic combatant commanders (GCCs) have what is often the largest and best organized arm of the USG in any part of the world and are in the front lines of this fight. Each of the GCCs confronts real challenges to regional stability.

    b.   **Global Threat Summary**. With the end of the Cold War, conflicts sponsored by various nations have significantly declined only to be replaced by a wider variety of threats (Figures II-2 to Figure II-5) including networked international criminal organizations, Islamic insurgents, violent global jihadists, insurgents combining with transnational criminal gangs (narco-terrorists), and human smugglers. These new threats highlight the need to adapt our traditional methodologies for threat analysis to determine the most effective means of disrupting, neutralizing, or defeating them. Conventional arms alone will not defeat these new and emerging threats. As our adversaries have adopted irregular warfare, the United States must learn to adopt a comprehensive global approach in cooperation with its interagency (Figure II-6), multinational, intergovernmental, nongovernmental, and even private sector partners to answer the challenge. The US military's responsibilities range from enabling our friends and Allies through intelligence sharing, providing specialized training for partner nation forces, to the actual conduct of combat operations.

Figure II-2. Global Islamist Threat

Figure II-3. National Islamist Threat

Figure II-4. National Separatist Threat

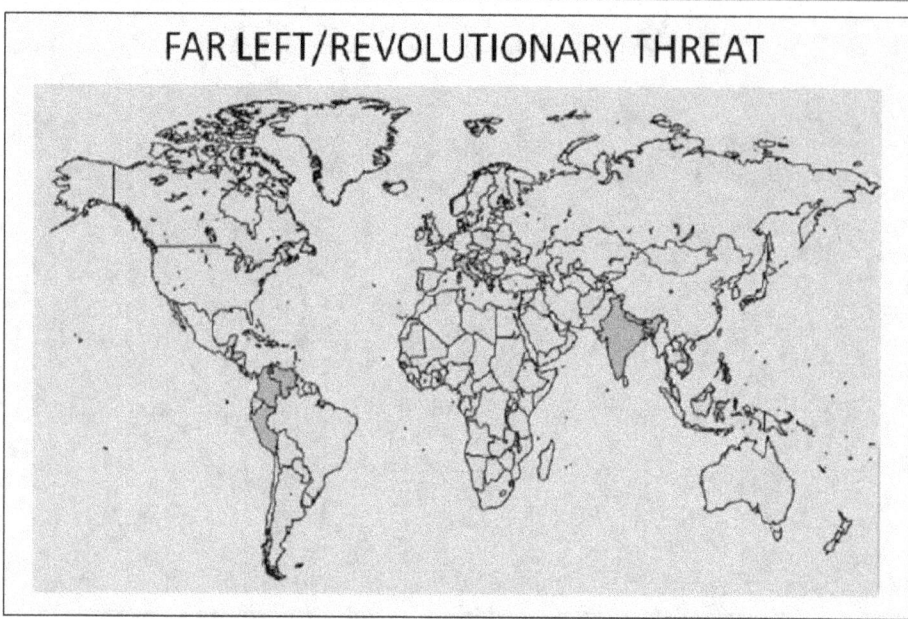

Figure II-5. Far Left/Revolutionary Threat

US INTERAGENCY PARTNERS IN GLOBAL SECURITY INITIATIVES	
Department of State	Department of the Treasury
Agency for International Development	Federal Bureau of Investigation
Immigration and Customs Enforcement	Department of Energy
Department of Homeland Security	Customs and Border Protection
Drug Enforcement Administration	

Figure II-6. US Interagency Partners in Global Security Initiatives

c.   **Regional Threat Summaries**

    (1)   **US Southern Command (USSOUTHCOM)**

    d.   Illicit trafficking (e.g., drugs, weapons, money, people), transnational terrorism, crime, and transnational criminal organizations (TCOs) pose the principal security challenges for the region. The military supports the lead federal agencies and partner nations in meeting these threats. TCOs and the illicit trafficking they conduct continue to be the primary threat to regional security. These groups construct flexible, resilient networks which use multiple paths to support illicit activity.

> *"In countering this international threat, working with our partners, we must attack TCOs in a broad, coordinated manner, to include demand reduction; eradication and regulation of source materials; suppression of money laundering; interdiction of shipments; and ultimately the disruption and dismantling of TCOs operating in the region. However, TCO's are increasingly*

sophisticated and have proven resilient and adaptive to attempts to disrupt their operations. They are innovative.... TCOs support and use a spectrum of destabilizing activities to conduct their operations, to include corruption, intimidation, kidnapping, targeted violence and terror tactics. Confronting this spectrum requires a sophisticated, orchestrated strategy that both guides efforts to meet current challenges as well as sets a frame work for disrupting future TCO adaptations."

**General Douglas M. Fraser, USAF
Testimony Before the 112th Congress, Senate Armed Services Committee
5 April 2011**

e.   There is also a continuing leftist insurgency in Colombia by the Revolutionary Armed Forces of Colombia (FARC) and the Sendero Luminoso (Shining Path) in Peru. While the government of Colombia has had considerable success in combating the guerrillas, by virtue of their affiliation with the region's criminal elements, they remain a well funded threat. In recent years, the Central American corridor has seen a dramatic increase in illicit trafficking activities and brutal violence and is now the most violent region in the world outside of active war zones. Rising crime and corruption in El Salvador, Guatemala, Jamaica and Honduras has challenged the ability of local governments to provide for basic security and the rule of law. The more sophisticated gangs operate regionally and globally with deep reach back into the US and Europe. Regional stability is further complicated by Venezuela's support of the guerrillas in Colombia.

See Appendix C, "Transnational Criminal Gangs" for a detailed examination of the threats posed by these organizations in the USSOUTHCOM area of responsibility.

(1)   **US Africa Command (USAFRICOM).** Sub-Saharan African nations continue to show progress in developing more democratic political institutions and pursuing policies that encourage economic growth and development and improve living conditions. Nevertheless, economic and political progress in Africa remains uneven, varies greatly from nation to nation, and is still subject to sudden reversal or gradual erosion. The most visible regional threats are from Al-Shabaab insurgents in Somalia and the militants in Nigeria's river delta region. Al Shabaab, which provides protection for regional al-Qa'ida elements, has expanded its operations beyond Somalia and is capable of attacking worldwide targets. The Nigerian militants threaten the flow of oil to Western clients and the stability of the Nigerian government. Both groups have effectively thwarted the best efforts of local and regional powers to curtail their activities. Failed states, such as Somalia, have also seen the rise of opportunistic criminal gangs (the pirates) whose activities directly impact the world's economy by increasing the cost of shipping and the shipment of oil from the Middle East to Europe. There are also a number of potential interethnic problems, such as in Guinea, that could descend into fighting and destabilize the region. Lastly, transnational gangs dealing in narcotics use East and West Africa as major transshipment points between South America and Europe, and Afghanistan/Pakistan and Europe. The wholesale values of the cocaine alone exceed the gross domestic products of several of the affected West African states.

See Appendix D "Regional Threats: Somalia and Piracy" for a more detailed examination of the complexities of the challenge facing USAFRICOM.

(2) **US European Command (USEUCOM).** While most of the current and potential flashpoints involve rivalries between states (Russia-Georgia, Armenia-Azerbaijan, Serbia-Kosovo), there is a growing threat to local governments from Islamic militants in Kyrgyzstan, Tajikistan, and Turkmenistan. Islamic militants pose a continuing terrorist threat in Western Europe. Terrorist networks use Europe principally to recruit fighters, garner financial and logistic support, and provide sanctuary. There is also a reverse flow of foreign fighters out of Iraq and Afghanistan to Europe which increases the overall risk of attack. These terrorists cooperate closely with criminal networks and engage in numerous illegal activities as fund raising mechanisms. Of concern is a growing nexus in Russian and Eurasian states among government, organized crime, intelligence services, and big business figures.

(3) **US Pacific Command (USPACOM).** Countries in the USPACOM area of responsibility face a full range of potential threats. These include state on state rivalries in the Koreas, India and Pakistan, and China and Japan; Islamic militants in Thailand, the Philippines and Indonesia; a leftist insurgency in Nepal; Islamic jihadist terrorist attacks throughout the region; and a number of transnational criminal organizations smuggling drugs and people on a global basis.

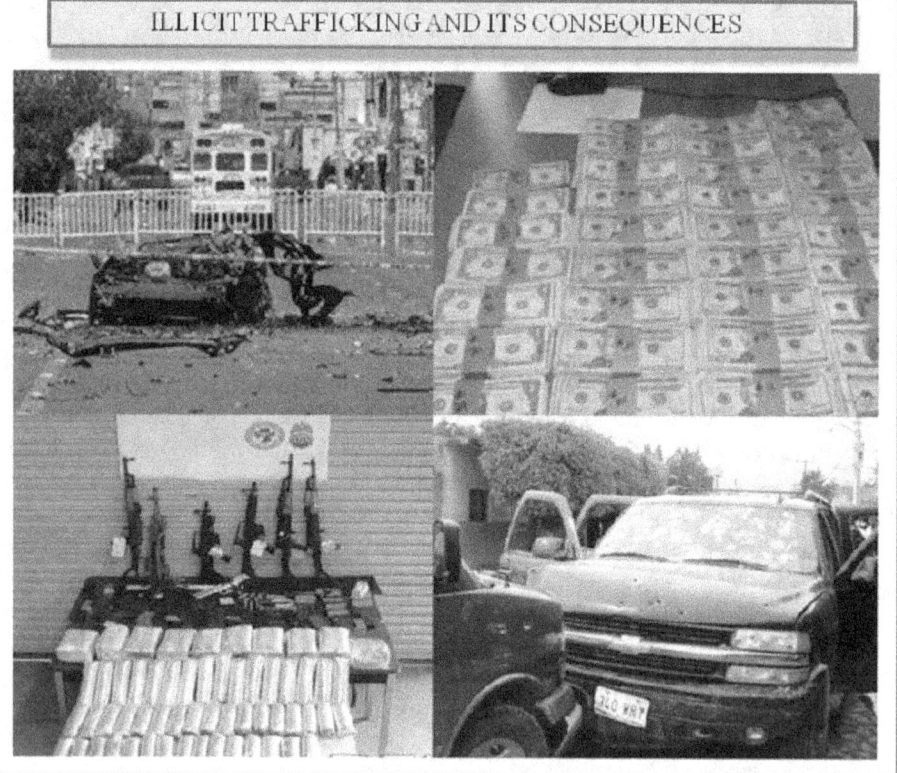

ILLICIT TRAFFICKING AND ITS CONSEQUENCES

Figure II-7. Illicit Trafficking and Its Consequences

(4) **US Northern Command (USNORTHCOM)**. With primary responsibility for the air, land, and maritime defense of the US homeland, USNORTHCOM focus is on countering state sponsored military threats. However USNORTHCOM, in support of various lead federal agencies, also responds to a variety of asymmetric threats. These threats (Figure II-7) include narco-trafficking which has reached levels that threaten the stability of regional governments, such as Mexico. Presently, the level of violence in Mexico's northern states has become a major threat to the security of the US border region and provides unlimited opportunities for the smuggling of arms, terrorists, and narcotics through the border region. Because of statutory limitations on domestic operations, USNORTHCOM is in a support role when it comes to dealing with most asymmetric threats. To assist in countering the on-going narcotics trafficking challenge, USNORTHCOM employs surveillance assets to monitor ground, air, and maritime approaches for drug trafficking; provides information and intelligence sharing among law enforcement agencies;, and supports Federal law enforcement with transportation, tunnel detection capabilities, and training. On a regional basis, USNORTHCOM's engagement with regional partners includes providing military hardware and training, and developing the ability to analyze and share the information that will facilitate the regional government's (Mexico and the Bahamas) ability to identify and target drug trafficking networks.

(5) **US Central Command (USCENTCOM)**. The USCENTCOM area of responsibility has a number of active insurgencies, is home to various transnational extremist organizations that threaten the US homeland, and has a high level of criminal activity of all types to include narcotics production, money laundering, and arms smuggling. In many cases, there are close working partnerships between the local and transnational extremists and the criminal organizations. Weak local governments throughout the region are generally unable or unwilling to take the actions necessary to fight these threats and thereby imperil the stability of their neighbors. There is also the challenge of Iranian financial, training and material support to extremist elements in Iraq, Afghanistan, Lebanon, and Gaza. USCENTCOM, in order to promote regional stability, is a major participant in programs (material assistance, training, intelligence sharing) with the Department of State and other federal agencies designed to assist local governments in gaining the initiative in countering these threats.

4. The Networked Threat

a. While threats to the USG and its partners posed by nation states seemingly has declined in recent years, a wide range of local, national, and transnational asymmetric challenges to the stability of the international system has emerged. Although some threats, such as insurgencies and powerful criminal gangs, have been around for years exploiting weak or corrupt governments, the rise of the transnational extremists and their active cooperation with the more traditional threats has changed the global dynamic. Successful deterrence of these non-state groups is more complicated and less predictable than in the past.

b. Neutralizing these threats is a complex task because it involves the tailored application of lethal force and nonlethal options in a comprehensive approach that includes USG agencies, partner nations, intergovernmental and nongovernmental organizations, and the private sector. It requires the US to develop a detailed understanding of how that threat operates – identifying their constituent elements, understanding how their internal processes work to carry out their activities, and understanding how these elements interact as their process unfolds. Basically, there is a need to examine how a specific threat network operates. From that point vulnerable individuals or activities that can be exploited (to further refine our understanding of the network) or disrupted (to observe how the network reacts).

c.   All networks have vulnerabilities that can be exploited, but only through a comprehensive understanding of how that network operates can the CJTF and staff pick the effective junction and methods to conduct that exploitation. A detailed joint JIPOE by specialists familiar with the underlying principles of networking is the first step in establishing control over the threat network. However, while it is simple to state the theory of network analysis and exploitation, in reality, these are not simple tasks. Networked threats are highly adaptable adversaries, who have the ability to select from the whole menu of tactics and technologies and blend them in innovative ways to meet their own strategic culture, geography, and aims.

5.   Networks in the Operational Environment

Targets are also categorized by their relation to the friendly war effort and objectives. For the sake of clarity in tracking information, this relation is assigned a color code. This system serves as a guideline for general target categorization in order to manage the target set. It is not a rigid or inflexible construct; rather, a target may fall into more than one category by definition, but the targeting board will have to determine which category is most appropriate based upon its objectives. The system is as follows:

- *Red for threat elements.*
- *White for general population.*
- *Green for host nation government entities (security, government).*
- *Black for malign actors, such as criminal entities.*

These designations are generally self explanatory, with the exception of "black." There may be elements within an area of operations that are not directly hostile to friendly forces but potentially serve as threat facilitators. For example, narcotics transportation might include IED components. The amount of money generally associated with narcotics makes it a corrupting force and undermines the coalition's attempts to establish a legitimate local government. These actors are designated as "black" and must be targeted in an appropriate manner to achieve coalition objectives. Often, narcotics operations that are steeped in violence, such as those in Latin America, may receive a red designation.

MAGTF Counter-Improvised Explosive Device Operations
24 January 2011

a.   An operational-level JIPOE will seek to identify and define all the networks that impact the OE, how they interact, and what actions must be taken to influence those networks to achieve the objectives contained in the operations plan. While the focus normally is on the challenges posed by threat (red) networks, the CJTF and staff must also be aware of the impacts of other networks ("White," "Blue," "Green," and "Black") on mission execution. Factually, the threat network will have a relationship with the much larger society in which it operates. Elements in that society (the "White" network in Figure II-8) actively favor the enemy, actively support the government, or are neutral and by their ambivalence allow the threat network to operate. At a minimum, the CJTF must be prepared to undertake actions to ensure that support for the government is maintained (and grows) while shrinking support for the enemy. Successfully influencing public opinion is a major challenge for multinational forces. (Note: Criminal networks that support whatever side provides them with the greatest advantage can be designated separately as "Black" even when they are operating on behalf of the "Red" network.)

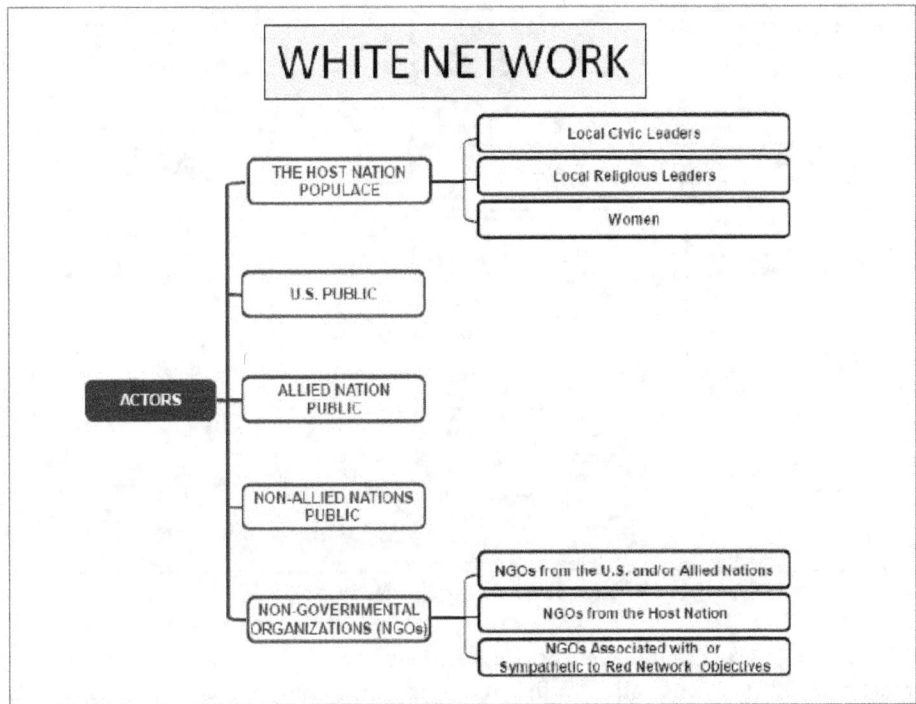

Figure II-8. White Network

    b. In addition to the civil society that lives in the operational area and/or participates in providing resources to support coalition operations, there is the equally complex military-governmental agency environment that is a characteristic of modern irregular warfare (Figure II-9). At a minimum, the CJTF must be prepared to undertake actions to ensure that these participants (multinational partners and the HN) are conducting mutually supporting operations that are integrated and designed to achieve the overall strategic end state. Successfully managing the impact of disparate organizations is another major challenge for multinational forces.

    c. "Black" or criminal networks. Are found in every society on the planet and, while generally a nuisance, do not normally rise to a point where they threaten the stability of that society. They are profit driven and will work for both sides in a conflict. Personal loyalties and ties are essential to the maintenance of the network and are key determinants of relationships. It should be noted however that various individuals within the network do not carry the same weight and the network is generally formed around a key series of individuals (or nodal points) through which most of the network connections run. They are generally of two types:

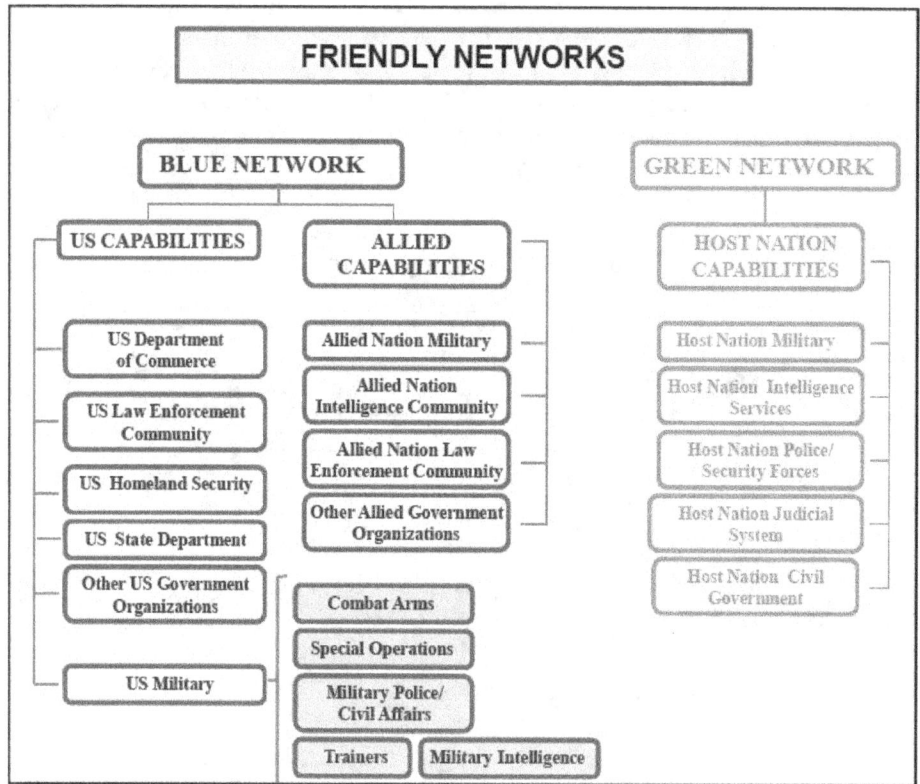

Figure II-9. Friendly Networks

(1) Petty criminal networks. These networks are normally localized, poorly organized and easily controlled (with some effort). Examples of their activities include auto theft, robbery, localized prostitution, etc.

(2) Gangs and Organized Crime Networks. These networks include recognizable organized gangs and criminal syndicates. Their activities may include narcotics distribution, human trafficking, larger black market networks, and other structured and highly organized criminal activities. Financial market manipulation and racketeering, operation of prostitution rings or other vice networks are additional examples.

d. Lastly the focus of the overall operation is in neutralizing the threat network(s) (Figure II-10) whose activities threaten stability. These threat networks take many forms and will usually be deeply rooted throughout the fabric of the local society. They are resilient and adaptable with multiple redundant support systems. They are hard to neutralize. Threat networks will often form (temporary) alliances in order to gain advantage over their competitors. Successful friendly operations will require an integrated and synchronized whole of government approach by all participants.

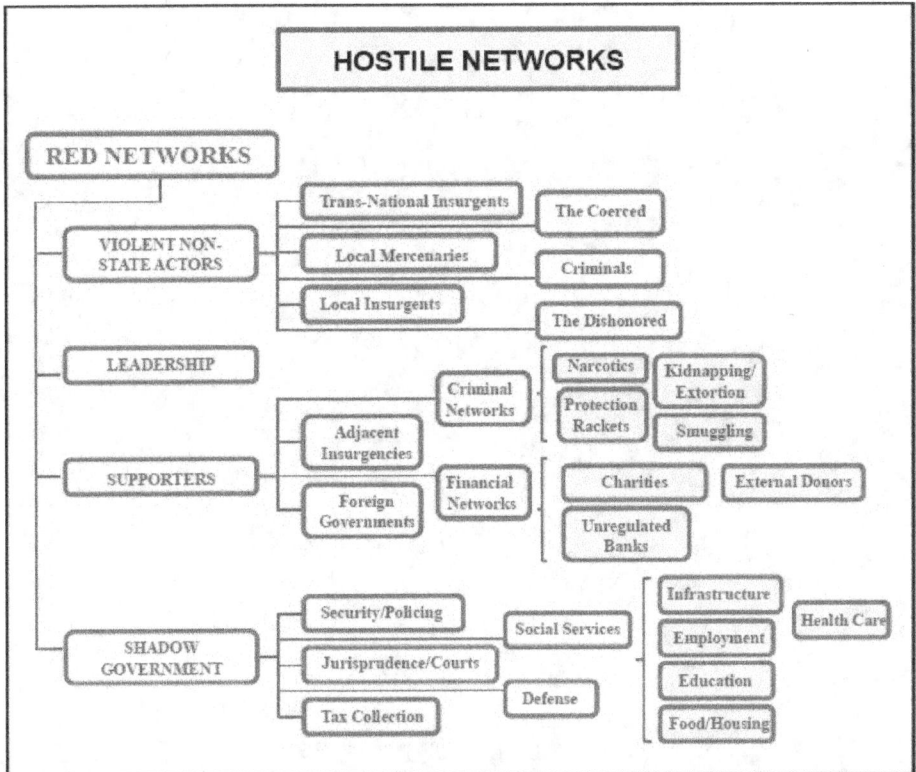

Figure II-10. Threat Networks

Intentionally Blank

CHAPTER III
UNDERSTAND THE NETWORKS

1. Introduction

Understanding the threat network requires a basic appreciation of the nature of adaptive networks; their structure and components, characteristics, attributes, and purpose. Although different from conventional military threats, once these differences are understood, the analytical process for describing the threat network and predicting its behavior remains largely the same. Pattern analysis, link analysis, social network analysis, and forensics are the foundational analytic methods that enable intelligence analysts to begin templating the threat network, focusing ISR capabilities, and providing intelligence support to targeting. Available intelligence is fused and simplified to create a model of how the threat network generally operates. This activity model can be further refined into a narrative and graphic template of the network. The network activity model and template support critical factors analysis, a detailed functional decomposition of the network activities to identify its critical capabilities, critical requirements, and critical vulnerabilities.

2. Threat Network Characteristics

a. **Types and Components**. There are many **types** of networks – insurgent, criminal, social, or conventional military networks, e.g., computer, air defense etc. While they take many forms, **networks are comprised of people, processes, places, and material – components that are identifiable, targetable, and exploitable**.

b. **Forms and Purposes**. **Networks vary in basing, size, shape, membership, cohesion, and purpose**. Successful networks are well integrated into their operating environment; they are hard to locate and even harder to effectively attack. Some networks are territorially based, such as the FARC in Colombia, while others have little physical presence in their target countries and their members are spread across the globe. Transnational networks make full use of the interconnected global environment to direct operations, raise money, obtain and train recruits, and freely exchange technological information. Networks can be large or small, local or global, domestic or transnational, cohesive or diffuse, centrally directed or highly decentralized, purposeful or directionless. Networks facilitate the flow of information, knowledge, and communication as well as more-tangible commodities. A specific network can be narrowly and tightly focused on one goal or broadly oriented toward many goals, and it can be either exclusive or encompassing in its membership. For example, A human network is an alliance of socially connected individuals who are involved in activities to achieve some form of social, political, monetary, religious, or personal common goal.

c. **Attributes**. In order for the network to survive in an environment while being hunted, the enemy must continuously respond to changing environmental pressures, e.g., political, economic, social, and military. Survival and success are directly connected to adaptability and the ability to compete for resources – financial, logistical, and human.

While threat networks possess many attributes, among the ones important to their success are:

(1) **A flexible command and control (C2) structure**. Some networks are flat and decentralized while others are centralized and hierarchical but they are all designed to facilitate the attainment of the network's goals and continued survival.

(2) **Shared identity** among the membership normally based on kinship, ideology, religion, and personal relations that bonds the network and also facilitates recruitment (Figure III-1).

(3) **Knowledge, skills, and abilities of group leaders and members**.

(4) **Resources** in the form of arms, money, social connectivity, and public recognition.

(5) **Adaptability,** including the ability to learn and adjust behaviors and modify TTP in response to friendly initiatives.

(6) **Sanctuary** to conduct planning, training, and logistic reconstitution.

NETWORK BONDS

Family Network: Some members or associates have familial bonds. These bonds may be cross-generational.

Cultural Network: The network shares bonds due to a shared culture, language, religion, ideology, country of origin and/or sense of identity. Some of these networks may evolve over time from being culturally to proximity based.

Proximity Network: The network shares bonds due to certain geographical ties of its members (ex. Past bonding in correctional or other institutions, or living within specific regions or neighborhoods). Members may also form a network with proximity to an area strategic to their criminal interests (ex. A neighborhood or key border entry point). There may be a dominant ethnicity within the group, but they are primarily together for other reasons.

Virtual Network: A criminal network that may never physically meet but work together through the Internet or other means of communication (ex. Networks involved in online fraud, theft or money laundering).

Specialized Network: Individuals in this network come together to undertake criminal activities primarily based on the skills, expertise or particular capabilities they offer.

Figure III-1. Network Bonds

---

d. **Network Strengths and Weaknesses**

(1) **Strengths**. The ability to adapt over time is a fundamental requirement for any network to survive. Core strengths required to maintain an effective network may include:

(a) The ability to blend into the OE making it difficult to separate the enemy from the local population.

(b) The ability to rapidly replace personnel losses by recruiting new members, usually through personal relationships.

(c) The relative insularity of threat networks makes it difficult to gain intelligence on them. This impenetrability is based primarily on the bonds of kinship, religion, and purpose that tie members together.

(d) Ability to establish a cellular organization which limits the friendly force's ability to roll up sizable portions of the network.

(e) Networks can be highly connected both internally in terms of their members and to the respective country's social structure. Individuals can be connected to one another and their leaders in multiple ways, including kinship, religion, former association, and history, among other factors. This layering of affinity creates densely internally connected networks and supports their cohesiveness. Through their membership, these networks are also connected to major social structures —the tribal system and their respective religious structure—giving them opportunities to acquire both resources and support.

Network - That group of elements forming a unified whole, also known as a system.

Node - An element of a system that represents a person, place, or physical thing.

Cell – A subordinate organization formed around a specific process, capability, or activity within a designated larger organization.

Link – A behavioral, physical, or functional relationship between nodes.

---

(2) **Weaknesses**. While threat networks have inherent strengths, they also have exploitable inherent weaknesses. These may include:

(a) Competition for resources, including the loyalty of the population, often leads to one group working against the other.

(b) Connectivity among cells. Although the cellular structure is a highly secure one, the links between cells can be identified and exploited over time.

(c) The need to surface to take action. Detection, especially during the preparation/planning/reconnaissance phases prior to an attack, exposes some cells and network key functions to attack.

(d) The natural tendency to replicate previous successful actions and hence unwittingly set patterns.

3. Defining a Network

a. **Macro Analysis**. To develop a threat network profile, the staff needs to first identify the network that poses the greatest threat. For example, in a COIN environment where population protection is paramount, insurgents attacking the populace might be a higher priority than those merely attacking friendly forces. Consequently, friendly forces analyze and exploit threat network tactics, techniques, and procedures. They determine which threat network poses the highest threat. Once the network is identified, a more detailed analysis is conducted with the help of specialized resources (such as the analysts of the COIC). This initial **macro analysis** seeks to identify threat network critical capabilities and requirements, activities, and operational areas; and, using COG analysis, its critical vulnerabilities. This enables the staff to identify potential targets and the target area. During macro analysis, analysts will assist the staff in determining which members of the targeted network can be identified with actionable intelligence and which of those network members represent the most lucrative targets for achieving the desired effects.

b. **Critical Factors**. A holistic approach to understanding the critical capabilities and requirements of a particular network's operations assists commanders and their staffs in identifying the critical vulnerabilities and points of exploitation for lethal and nonlethal attack. In order to continue to exist, a mature network usually possesses certain **baseline critical capabilities and requirements** (Figure III-2) to ensure the network functions. Many of these are subject to discovery and exploitation – thereby becoming critical vulnerabilities. Figure III-3 is an example of an IED network's critical capabilities and requirements.

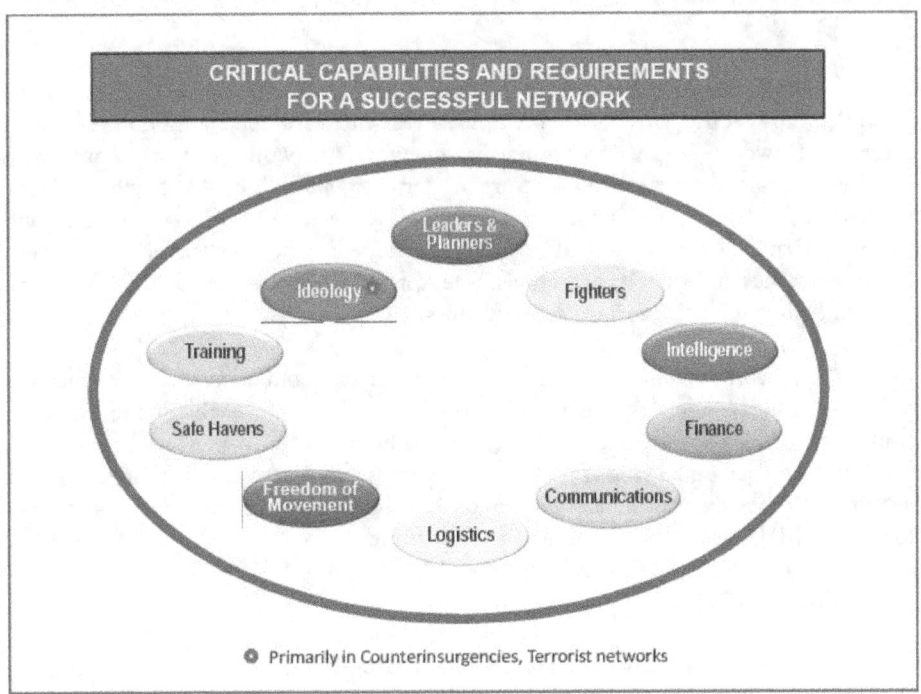

Figure III-2. Critical Capabilities and Requirements for a Successful Network

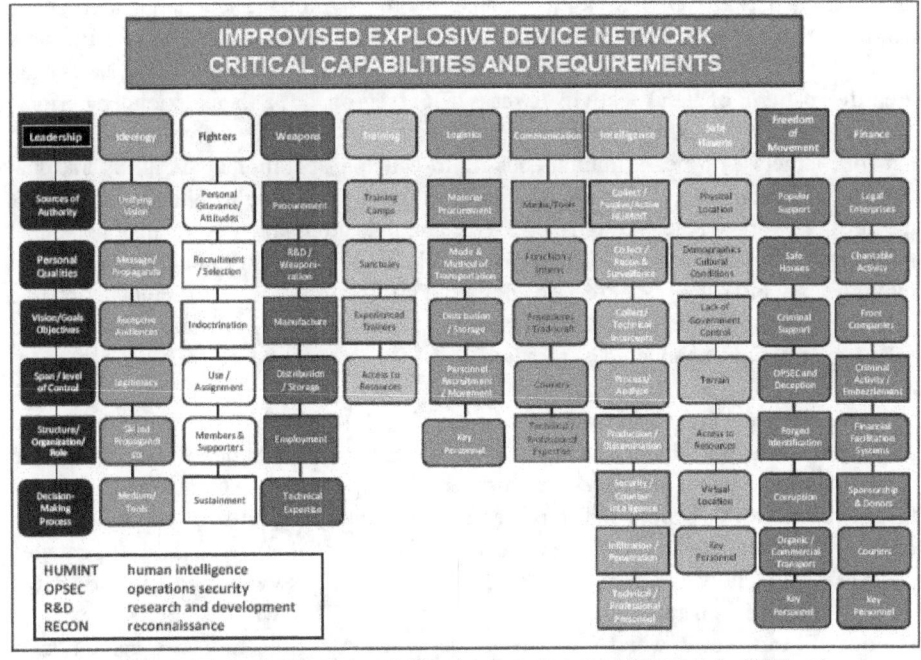

Figure III-3. Improvised Explosive Device Network Critical Capabilities and Requirements

c. **Activities**

(1) While the baseline critical capabilities and requirements are common to all networks, the specific activities that employ them will vary depending on the type of network. However, it is worth noting that many IED network tasks are shared with activities that are supporting other insurgent, terrorist, and criminal behaviors such as drug trafficking and money laundering. Often; through detecting, tracking, and exploiting general activities; US and multinational forces can identify how a network is structured and sustains and carries out its operations. See Appendix E, "Enemy Finance," for a more detailed examination of threat network finances.

(2) Networks enhance their survivability by carrying out many of their supporting tasks on an independent, simultaneous basis. Participants in each function may be completely unaware of the others existence. This limits the network's vulnerability to a handful of key personnel who are orchestrating the network's overall activities. Not all network activities are critical, but information derived from non-critical activities can lead to the identification and exploitation of vulnerabilities.

d. **Micro Analysis**

(1) Once the initial macro analysis is accomplished, the staff and supporting analysts can then produce **micro network** data by leveraging all source information (to include information derived from the exploitation of enemy activities). This effort includes synchronizing specialized analytical resources (COIC for IED, ORSA) and ISR resources and reaching back to CONUS-based resources in order to produce actionable intelligence against threat network personnel, functions, and activities in order to find additional actionable targets. The staff analyzes adversaries in named areas of interest (NAIs) and identifies patterns of enemy activity to mass ISR assets on the NAIs for extended periods. Massing ISR assets further refines targetable data and facilitates the attack of multiple network targets with near simultaneous multi-echelon operations. As an operational technique, the joint force can conduct a series of small-scale shaping operations to cause the threat network to react through increased communications and movement of personnel – activities carefully monitored by signals and human intelligence, and GMTI (ground moving target indicator) radar to gain additional information. Once sufficient actionable intelligence has been developed, operations will be conducted, the results exploited, and follow-on missions conducted as required.

(2) **Templating** allows analysts to graphically represent those functions and activities, overlaying what we know and what we don't know in order to refocus PIR and create opportunities for learning. Network templating enables the commander and staff to map the network's people and activities on the ground using all-source intelligence in order to "fix" the enemy. A basic template indentifies potential HVIs, NAIs, TAIs, detailed processes, and how we can detect them through the development of indicators (observables and signatures) the "what we know" part. The "what we don't know" part informs PIR refinement, which is then used to optimize AtN collection gaps; collection on already known NAIs, HVIs, and processes, as well as collection to expand what we know.

(3) When analyzing a threat network, it's useful to ask some basic questions that assist in understanding how the network functions and the complexities of the relationships between and among its critical capabilities and requirements. Answering these questions can often reveal potential critical vulnerabilities that can be exploited by lethal and nonlethal means. Figure III-4 is an example of typical questions about a network's regional leadership that, when answered, can form the basis of part of the threat network analysis. If the answers to these questions are not known, they should be treated like any other intelligence requirement and tasked for collection.

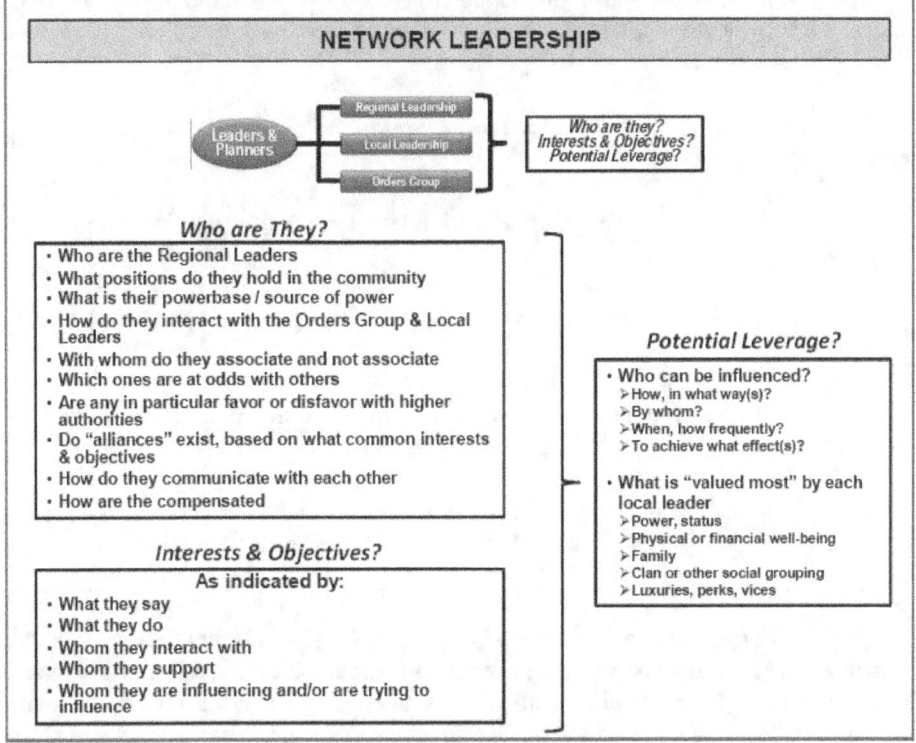

Figure III-4. Network Leadership

4. Intelligence, Surveillance, and Reconnaissance Support

a. ISR assets are employed to gain greater situational awareness and fill intelligence gaps regarding the threat network. ISR supports AtN by tracking key or vulnerable nodes within a network. Employing all ISR capabilities — air and ground, manned and unmanned, tactical through theater, and national technical means — to answer priority intelligence requirements (PIRs) has a synergistic effect. However, AtN related ISR operations are conducted in a blended environment (where the network exists and operates throughout the operational area and beyond) and finding a low signature target is a difficult problem. Attempting to employ limited ISR assets without a specific focus leads to analysis overload. Thus, when planning ISR support to AtN, a detailed preliminary analysis of the network's structure and activity must be undertaken to provide preliminary focus for ISR employment. Over time, as the picture of the network is refined, ISR assets can be more tightly focused in time and space. NAI are tied to PIRs. Detection assets and HUMINT are applied to NAIs to create target areas of interest (TAIs) for exploitation. Over time, an overview of the network should be established with sufficient detail to commence targeting of individuals and activities.

(1) Organizing and allocating ISR resources for AtN requires a coordinated, synchronized, and integrated effort beginning at the tactical level and often involving the use of national level resources. Intelligence personnel at all echelons must be prepared to employ traditional and non-traditional intelligence sources to build the picture of the enemy's infrastructure and share it across the joint force. A detailed and continuous JIPOE of the network and its OE will provide a:

(a) Detailed knowledge of the network's patterns of activity and related processes;

(b) Detailed knowledge of network related observables resulting from those patterns;

(c) Detailed knowledge of the network's signatures produced by the observables; and,

(d) Common understanding of how such signatures present themselves, in what sequence, in what duration, and in what combination.

By quantifying the signatures associated with the network, collection managers at all echelons can specifically focus ISR resources to develop targetable, actionable intelligence.

(2) Modern technology (Figure III-5) provides the CJTF with unprecedented abilities to maintain near-constant surveillance over specific geographic areas using a wide variety of ISR resources. When combined with the real time imagery down-link provided systems, such as ROVER [remote operational video enhanced receiver], aerial surveillance assets can provide AtN analysts and targeteers with vital information on enemy activities. This support is also capable of detecting and tracking individuals to their safe houses and caches. Once these support sites are located, they can be further exploited to identify and locate other network functions.

(3) When these enhanced visual surveillance capabilities are combined with SIGINT means and HUMINT resources (media exploitation, informers, volunteer HN information sources, "every soldier a sensor"), the AtN analysts and targeteers can develop an accurate picture of the critical nodes of the various networks operating in their operational area. Gathering basic "street level" information is an essential part of AtN. Whether we are looking at individual soldiers on patrols, or information derived from meeting local leaders, or even conversations with local workers, all of these are information sources. While interactions with the local population and their observations of the physical environment may be considered a tactical concern, when aggregated, they can provide

an operational level picture of enemy activities. Over time this information can be refined sufficiently to produce targetable intelligence and further opportunities for exploitation.

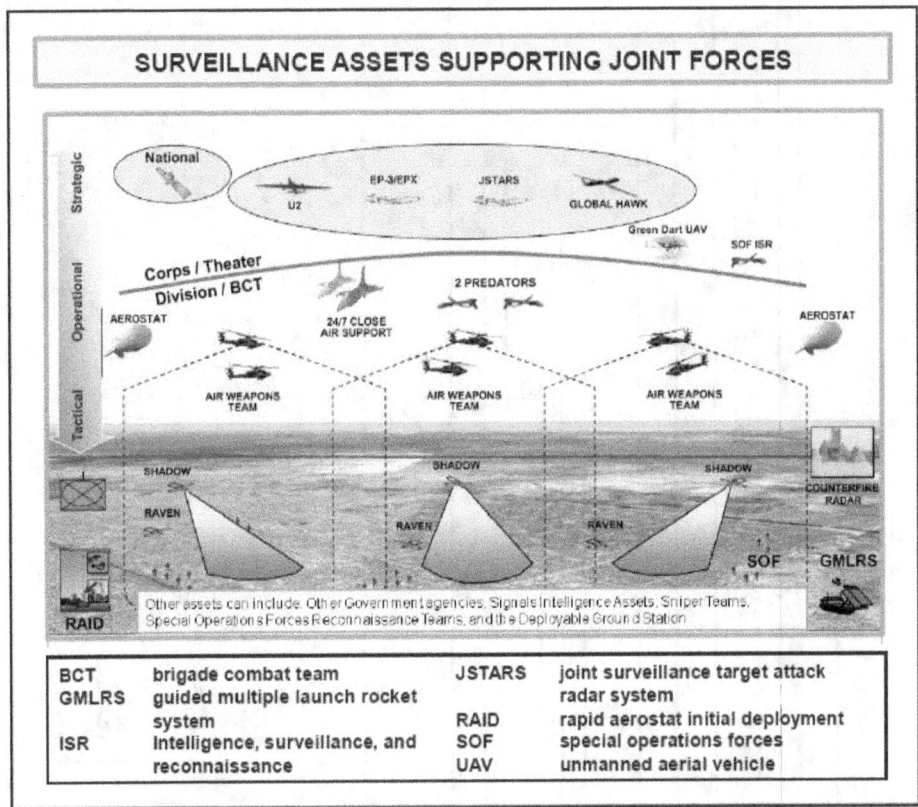

BCT	brigade combat team	JSTARS	joint surveillance target attack radar system
GMLRS	guided multiple launch rocket system	RAID	rapid aerostat initial deployment
ISR	Intelligence, surveillance, and reconnaissance	SOF	special operations forces
		UAV	unmanned aerial vehicle

Figure III-5. Surveillance Assets Supporting Joint Forces

b. ISR management is facilitated through the production of a staff synchronization matrix. The matrix, derived from network templating, enables the staff to visualize the optimal massing of ISR assets against the correct named area of interest at the right time. At a minimum, the matrix (Figure III-6) has rows for each subordinate maneuver unit, those critical vulnerabilities that friendly forces have decided to track, threat indicators of those critical vulnerabilities, the friendly force commander's decision points, focus of enemy fires, asset allocation and assigned NAIs, and collection focus for each intelligence discipline.

For a detailed examination of ISR planning considerations, see JP 2-01, Joint and National Intelligence Support to Military Operations.

SYNCHRONIZATION MATRIX

Time	1200	1300	1400	1500	1600	1700	1800	1900	2000	2100	2200	2300	0000	0100	0200	0300	0400	0500	0600	0700	0800	0900	1000	1100	1200
Threat Indicators	Movement to Border						Traffic Control Point (TCP) Infiltration							Transportation/Storage				Safe house Operations						
Friendly Actions (PHASE)	PHASE I						HASTY TCP						PHASE II					CORDON & SEARCH						
Task Force 1 (TF1)	Border Assistance																								
Task Force 2 (TF2)	Hasty TCP										Hasty TCP														
Task Force 3 (TF3)	Cordon & Search																		Cordon & Search						
Capability																									
Full Motion Video (FMV)			Named Area of Interest (NAI) 001, 002																						
FMV																									
Signal Intelligence		NAI 001, 002												NAI 007, 008											
Human Intelligence				Interview security forces at TCPs – NAI 003, 004, 005, 006										NAI 007, 008											
Human Intelligence					Interview Locals in remote villages – NAI 002, 005																				
Ground Moving									NAI 011																
Target Indicator																									

Battlefield Interrogation Team/Tactical Questioning (BIT/TQ) in direct support of TF3
BIT/TQ in DS of TF3

Priority Intelligence Requirements

What types of improvised explosive device (IED) components/materials are being used to conduct attacks?

Which members of the local security force are being influenced by insurgent networks?

Where are the cross-boundary smuggling points, cache locations, meeting locations, distribution points and IED assembly areas in the area of operations?

Phases of Operation

Phase I – Detect threat activity (movement of lethal aid)

Phase II – Identify tier II targets and capture/kill/influence

IMINT/GMTI Collection Focus (Phase I)
Task: Monitor sparsely populated boundary areas, cross-cue HUMINT

Purpose: Identify (ID) smuggling routes and potential threat activity

Priority: Unusual activity along porous boundary areas

HUMINT Collection Focus (Phase I)
Task: Interview security forces and locals, cross-cue SIGINT and IMINT

Purpose: ID smugglers or associates and areas where smuggling takes place

Priority: Corrupt security forces, insurgents, smuggling locations, routes, and tactics, techniques and procedures

SIGINT Collection Focus (Phase I)
Task: Intercept to cross-cue IMINT

Purpose: Personality detection at district boundary areas

Priority: Cellular, Push to talk (PTT)

IMINT Collection Focus (Phase II)
Task: Over watch

Purpose: Force protection

Priority: Squirters and potential threat posture

HUMINT Collection Focus (Phase II)
Task: Conduct BIT/TQ in support of task force elements

Purpose: Obtain follow-on targetables

Priority: IED emplacement locations, safe houses, cache locations, distribution/assembly areas

SIGINT Collection Focus (Phase III)
Task: Intercept/direction find

Purpose: Personality detection and location

Priority: Cellular/PTT

Figure III-6. Synchronization Matrix

CHAPTER IV
PLANNING THE JOINT OPERATION AND
ATTACK THE NETWORK PLANNING

"In attacking networks, it is vitally important to determine the major objectives: Are they to destroy the network, simply to degrade its capacity to carry out criminal actions, or to detach the network from its support apparatus in the licit world? The objectives can range from making operations more difficult for the network through creating instability in the environment to more direct attacks on the network itself that are aimed at disruption of its activities, dislocation or degradation of its capabilities, or even its compete destruction. While all are legitimate objectives, it is essential that there is clarity about precisely which of them is being chosen."

Phil Williams, Transnational Criminal Networks

1. Planning

a. Networks can pose substantial challenges to stability and democracy in peace and war. They exist in every country in the world and usually exert some influence over the population and the government's ability to freely function. As discussed earlier, JFCs and staffs normally will encounter three types of networks: the threat that must be neutralized; the neutrals who must either be influenced to join the friendly side or maintain their neutrality; and the friendlies that must be supported and encouraged to grow. Regardless of the type of joint operation, the JFC must be prepared to plan for and integrate AtN activities into operations. AtN planning assists in designing the joint operation and ultimately in achieving strategic and military objectives.

b. AtN normally is planned as part of planning and designing the larger joint operation, which helps ensure AtN planners fully understand the OE and the operational approach. Once the OE and joint mission are better understood, planners can perform operational design to include center of gravity analysis and development of an AtN line(s) of effort. During this process, AtN planners likely will identify gaps in analysis that will prompt requesting assistance from internal or external SMEs who can provide expertise and higher level analysis to further AtN planning.

See Appendix F, "Attack the Network Annex to the Operations Plan" for guidance on documenting AtN plans.

2. Designing

a. **COG Analysis**

(1) **Center of Gravity**. A center of gravity (COG) comprises the source of power that provides moral or physical strength, freedom of action, or the will to fight. In a COIN operation, for example, the COG is the population and an adaptive enemy will do everything possible to maintain control over the COG. The essence of operational art lies in being able to produce the right combination of effects in time, space, and purpose relative to a

COG to neutralize, weaken, destroy, or otherwise exploit it in a manner that best helps achieve military objectives and attain the military end state. In theory, this is the most direct path to mission accomplishment. However, COG analysis is continuous and a COG can change during the course of an operation for a variety of reasons.

(2) **Critical Factors**. All COGs have inherent **critical capabilities** - those means that are considered crucial enablers for the enemy's COG to function and essential to the accomplishment of the enemy's assumed objective(s). These critical capabilities permit an enemy's COG to resist the friendly military end state. Critical capabilities can be thought of as collective tasks. In turn, all critical capabilities have essential **critical requirements** - those essential conditions, resources, and means for a critical capability to be fully operational. Critical requirements can be viewed as individual tasks. **Critical vulnerabilities** are those aspects or components of the enemy's critical requirements which are deficient or vulnerable to direct or indirect attack that will create decisive or significant effects disproportionate to the military resources applied. Collectively, these are referred to as **critical factors**. Critical vulnerabilities are the network's exploitable weaknesses. For example, if the critical capability is to provide logistics and one of the critical requirements that we believe to be a weaknesses is to move those supplies, then possible vulnerabilities may include: transfer of supplies from a cache to a vehicle, distribution of supplies to small (local) transport, or meetings to coordinate resupply. The purpose of identifying critical vulnerabilities is to focus ISR, provide intelligence to the commander so that he can make a decision on how to neutralize the threat, and then take action. Each critical capability and critical requirement requires human interaction, management, and support. These individuals are typically trusted agents with leadership abilities. However, unlike the senior leadership who are carefully shielded from detection, these middle managers must operate in the open. Identifying and tracking the activities of these individuals can reveal substantial information about the inner workings of a network.

(3) Center of gravity analysis and analysis of network activities enables analysts to identify locations (physical nodes such as caches, safe houses, etc) where HVIs would be most vulnerable to identification and attack. Initial NAIs are placed over these locations and are covered by ISR assets. Once enough information is gathered to confirm enemy activity is taking place within the NAI, the staff will rename the location as a TAI. Placing these on a doctrinal template helps analysts understand the relationship of when ISR has to "see" the observables or signatures and when the command has to make a decision to make a strike.

For a detailed discussion on center of gravity considerations in planning, see JP 5-0, Joint Operation Planning.

b. **Analytical Methods**. There are a number of analytical methods that can be used to build a detailed knowledge of a network's interpersonal dynamics and to do so within the context of a dynamic OE. While some of these methodologies are designed to focus on specific types of networks (insurgencies, terrorists, etc.), most can be easily modified to apply to any type of network the joint force may encounter. These methodologies include:

(1) **Social Network Analysis.** Social network analysis (SNA) is a tool for understanding the organizational dynamics of an insurgency and how best to attack or exploit it. Rather than assuming that killing or capturing the leader will achieve desired effects upon a network, SNA helps to identify which nodes in the network can be killed, captured or influenced to achieve desired effects. SNA shows how an insurgent's networked organization behaves and how its connectivity affects its behavior, where the influence resides or how it is distributed among members. However, there is a significant caveat when using SNA – the link analysis is unique to the analyst developing the picture of the network. Additionally, in developing a link analysis it is critical to ensure that the there is an understanding of how or why a link was made between two nodes.

(2) **Advanced Network Analysis and Targeting (ANAT).** A specialized, mathematically based tool that provides quantitative, descriptive measures that reflect the characteristics of social interactions between entities.

(3) **Association Matrix Analysis.** An association matrix portrays the existence of an association, known or suspected, between individuals, the "who." Direct connections include face-to-face meetings and telephone conversations. Analysts can use association matrices to identify those personalities and associations needing a more in-depth analysis to determine the degree of relationships, contacts, or knowledge between individuals.

(4) **Activities Matrix Analysis.** Relationships in large data sets are established by similarities between the nodes. People are identified by their participation in independent activities, the "what."

(5) **Coordinates Register Analysis.** The Coordinates Register is a pattern analysis tool and is also known as an incident map. Analysts may use multiple coordinate registers – each focusing on an individual subject or blend of subjects. It focuses on the "where" of an event.

(6) **Pattern Analysis Plot Sheet.** Pattern analysis plot sheets focus on the time and date, the "when", of each serious incident that takes place within the operational area. When used in conjunction with the Coordinates Register and other templates, the plot sheet supplies most of data needed for an event template.

(7) **Time Event Chart Analysis.** Time event charts are chronological records of individual or group activities. They are designed to store and display large amounts of information in a small space. Analysts can use time event charts to help analyze larger scale patterns of such things as activities and relationships.

(8) **Nodal Analysis.** Vulnerable nodes can be identified using social network and dynamic network techniques. **Nodal analysis** focuses on the activities that need to be affected with the aim of determining the most effective way to influence that node. Nodal analysis examines the interaction and interrelationships among multiple target systems to determine the degree and points of interdependence and the linkages of their activities. Nodal analysis takes time. Nodal analysis is also complimented by **individual component analysis** which focuses on activity taking place within a specific node in a limited geographic area. Individual component analysis relies on perishable unit level tactical

reporting and is designed to support local operations. There is also **nodal component analysis** which examines how nodes in a system function in relation to one another and which should lead to the identification of the critical nodes – those nodes whose disruption or destruction immediately degrades the ability of a force to command, control, or effectively conduct operations. Nodal component analysis will often use models to graphically display the system.

(9) Nodal analysis results in the identification of the specific functional nodes that empower that network. Once these nodes are identified, the next step is to develop detailed information on the specific activities that take place within that node – activities that are observable and which can be influenced by lethal and nonlethal means.

c. **AtN LOE**. The CJTF and staff normally will design AtN activities in terms of LOEs. Figure IV-1 provides an example of this approach using four LOEs.

(1) The first LOE, "Information Operations," is part of the broader joint operation/ campaign plan that seeks to shape the OE as a whole.

(2) The second LOE, "Neutralize Threat Network," is also a shaping effort directed against the identified threat network(s) and designed to weaken it to a point that they no longer pose a credible threat.

(3) The third LOE, "Enable Friendly Networks," is the decisive LOE that is designed to strengthen the HN and its supporting institutions (including societal).

(4) The fourth LOE, "Protect the Force," is aimed at protecting the force to preserve combat power and maintain freedom of action.

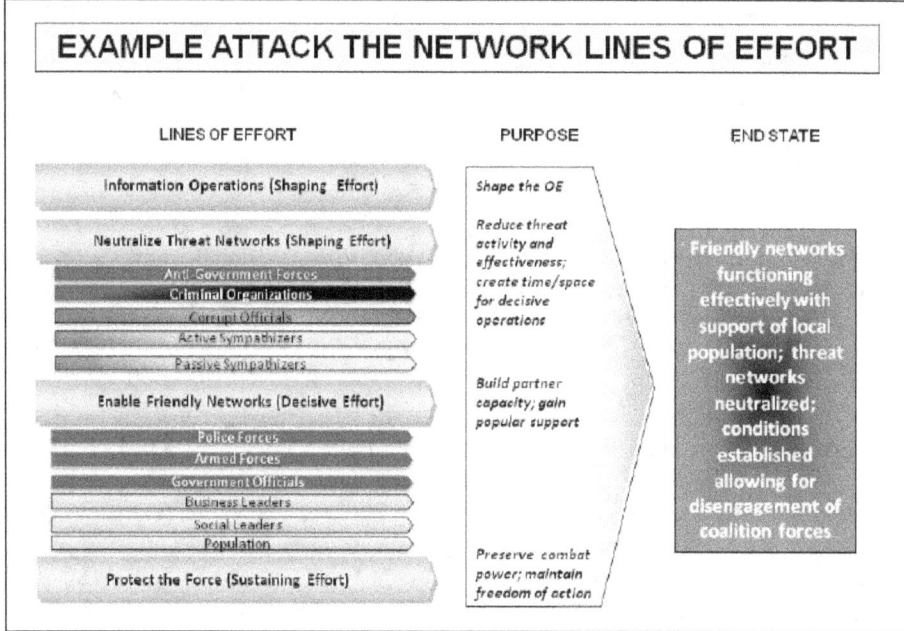

Figure IV-1. Example Attack the Network Lines of Effort

(5) A fifth LOE, Influencing Neutral Networks, part of shaping, may also be added, if required. It is aimed at business and social leaders and members of the general population that may be "sitting on the fence" to support the legitimate government.

    d. **Strategic goal** is to support and enable the friendly networks to function effectively enough to manage the threats posed by other networks.

Intentionally Blank

CHAPTER V
ORGANIZE FOR THE FIGHT

1. Introduction

a. Success in AtN requires integration of all available assets, whether organic or external, into the fight. Units will be required to integrate unique, specialized capabilities into their staffs, leverage other deployed capabilities in theater, and pull reach back support from capabilities based outside of the theater. HN, multinational, and other USG agency capabilities also must be synchronized where possible to achieve unity of effort. Effective joint operations require close coordination, synchronization, and information sharing **across** the staff directorates. The most common technique for promoting this **cross-functional collaboration** is the formation of centers, groups, bureaus, cells, offices, elements, boards, WGs, planning teams, and other enduring or temporary organizations that manage specific processes and accomplish tasks in support of mission accomplishment. These cross-functional staff organizations facilitate planning by the staff, decision-making by the commander, and execution by the HQ. This chapter examines the roles and responsibilities of the JTF staff with attached and assigned AtN enabling organizations. Depending on the size and duration of the operation, there are a number of approaches for organizing the JTF staff to conduct AtN. **Normally, the JTF will create specialized AtN boards, centers and cells within the staff to contribute to the overall battle rhythm and facilitate joint operational planning and execution**. In large scale, long-duration operations, the CJTF may create an AtN task force to manage assigned AtN assets and, in coordination with the JTF staff, plan and conduct AtN. An example of the AtN task force concept is found in the employment of C-IED task forces during OPERATION ENDURING FREEDOM (Task Force Paladin) and OPERATION IRAQI FREEDOM (Task Force Troy).

b. While all elements within the staff are expected to contribute to the AtN effort, the primary responsibility for organizing and leading the effort lies with the J-2, J-3, and IO/ strategic communications section. The successful conduct of AtN depends on the J-2's ability to organize and direct intelligence collection and surveillance efforts that are designed to develop timely, predictive, actionable intelligence on specific operational-level AtN related targets; the J-3's ability to direct forces to act on that information; and the IO/strategic communications section's ability to ensure that the JTF is positively engaging the many audiences in the OE, i.e., population, enemy, multinational participants.

c. **At each level of command, the cell or unit which gets assigned an AtN action needs to be properly resourced with the appropriate skills and specialist enablers**. Although similar tasks and requirements are present at different levels, proper mission analysis needs to be conducted in order to create an appropriate structure to be able to fulfill the assigned tasks and requirements. **The CJTF, as part of the normal JTF battle rhythm, may establish a series of AtN specific boards, cells, and working groups** to assist in the management of the AtN related information flow, to provide direction to attached and supporting specialized AtN assets (including analytical, intelligence collection, law enforcement, human terrain, MISO, etc.), and to develop and continuously refine the CJTF's AtN targeting and countermeasures programs. **National (civil agency),**

joint, and Service assets in the form of specialized AtN analysis teams may be formed and deployed forward to assist organic/assigned AtN teams. Reporting from those units will not only be shared immediately within the JTF (to help refine unit/individual tactics, techniques and procedures (TTP), but also will be forwarded for more detailed evaluation by specialized national capabilities. These evaluations will drive the development of improved active and passive force protection measures, further refine the MISO construct, and develop the information needed to support targeting of the AtN support infrastructure. Success normally relies upon a clear understanding of missions, roles and responsibilities; a clearly established information gathering, analysis, and dissemination architecture that simultaneously links all participants at all echelons; and an aggressive, innovative, proactive mindset that develops the tools and strategies to carry the fight to the enemy.

For a detailed examination of the organization, roles and functions of a JTF staff, see JP 3-33, Joint Task Force Headquarters.

2. Intelligence

a. **Functions and Capabilities**. The J-2's mission is to provide the commander with timely and accurate intelligence to support the CJTF's objectives, per the joint operation/ campaign plan, and to meet the information needs of the staff and component commands for operations and planning. The J-2 has primary responsibility for organizing and directing the operations of the JTF's intelligence assets. The CJTF may establish a JTF-level intelligence element such as a joint intelligence support element (JISE) or a joint intelligence operations center (JIOC), under the direction of the JTF J-2, to manage the JTF's intelligence collection, production, and dissemination. The J-2's AtN related information resources within the operational area will include the JTF's organic intelligence assets (SIGINT, GEOINT, DOMEX, MASINT, and especially HUMINT), HN/multinational sources, unit level reporting, and national assets that have tasked to conduct specialized analysis and exploitation in support of AtN. In organizing for the AtN fight, the J-2 must ensure that the intelligence staff is suitably augmented by AtN specialist personnel drawn from military and civil resources.

For additional information on the responsibilities of the J-2, see JP 3-33, Joint Task Force Headquarters.

> *"A cell is a subordinate organization formed around a specific process, capability, or activity within a designated larger organization of a JFC's HQ. A cell usually is part of both a functional and traditional staff structures."*
>
> **Joint Publication 3-33,** *Joint Task Force Headquarters*

b. **AtN Intelligence Cell**. Because of the specialized collection and analysis requirements for AtN support, the J-2 can create an AtN intelligence cell, within the JISE, to be the AtN focal point for analysis and target development. The AtN intelligence cell produces and disseminates timely, all-source fused intelligence that will serve as a basis for the development and conduct of the JTF's AtN effort. (Note: If the CJTF forms a separate AtN TF, the AtN intelligence cell could be attached to the AtN TF and the JTF J-

2 will then support the TF's AtN intelligence cell facilitating the collection, analysis, and application of all-source intelligence to the AtN fight.

(1) The AtN intelligence cell conducts all source collection planning in support of the JTF's AtN targeting efforts, develops AtN related information requirements (essential elements of information) for nomination as intelligence requirements and PIR, and constantly refines collection planning as the JTF's knowledge of the targeted networks grows. It is responsible for conducting nodal analysis of and developing targeting packages (for component execution) on high value threat networks. These targeting packages form the basis for much of the planning conducted by the JTF's joint targeting coordination board. The cell also develops and disseminates enemy TTP data to facilitate friendly operations and advise friendly forces on risk mitigation. When specialized AtN related ISR assets are deployed for the AtN fight, the AtN intelligence cell assists the J-2 collection manager in planning for the employment of those resources. The AtN intelligence cell also participates in the JTF's request for information (RFI) process, and assists the J-2 collection manager in the validation, prioritizing, and satisfaction, if possible, of AtN related RFIs.

(2) The JISE, as part of the continuous JIPOE process, conducts detailed all source analysis of the networks (enemy, neutral and friendly) in the operational area. Threat network analysis is the responsibility of the AtN intelligence cell within the JISE. The AtN intelligence cell's analytical efforts are integrated with JTF's operations and planning elements and is responsible for helping the CJTF to better understand how the enemy thinks (e.g., how an enemy will conceptualize the situation, what options an enemy will consider, and how an enemy will react to the JTF's actions). The AtN network analysis is included in the JTF's J-2's intelligence products to support overall JTF staff planning and to inform the components.

(3) The specific specialties required to staff the AtN intelligence cell are directly related to the type of threat network under consideration. While threat networks share many fundamental characteristics, effective AtN requires an understanding of the unique details that characterize each network – transnational criminal networks, narco-terrorists, insurgents, human trafficking networks. A typical JTF JISE does not have the skill sets required to conduct detailed network analysis and production. It must be augmented by specialists (for that particular type of network). These specialists are normally drawn from theater and national military, USG civilian agencies (Federal Bureau of Investigation, Department of Treasury, Drug Enforcement Administration, etc), multinational (with appropriate classified access), and even HN security resources. Specialist AtN resources can be deployed forward with the JTF or be available through reachback, or both. Ideally a whole-of-government intelligence specialist package would be deployed forward with the JISE. An example of an augmented JISE cell can be drawn from current C-IED operations where specialists AtN enablers have been assigned to the JISE and include:

(a) **C-IED Operations Integration Center (COIC) Analysts** focus on the networks in the operational area and conduct detailed analysis of their operations. The forward deployed COIC analysts have robust reach-back capabilities to provide additional research, intelligence, and information that can facilitate precise attacks against networks.

(b) **Operations Research/Systems Analyst (ORSA) Analysts** apply a variety of analytical methods to define and refine threat networks and identify optimal AtN strategies.

(c) **Asymmetric Warfare Group Analysts (AWG)** analysts observe, assess, and analyze information regarding the evolving OE and the threat. AWG analysis identifies and develops solutions for capability gaps that exploit enemy vulnerabilities and mitigate friendly vulnerabilities.

3. Operations

a. The J-3 assists the CJTF in directing the attached and supporting forces. The J-3 ensures that sufficient, properly equipped specialized AtN forces are available to support the JTF's mission within the operational area.

b. **J-3 AtN Specialized Staff Sections**

(1) **Operations-Intelligence Fusion Cell.** The JTF J-3 can establish an AtN operations-intelligence fusion cell to coordinate and synchronize all operational and intelligence related AtN activities. The cell produces products for the joint targeting board and supports the planning effort. The cell includes analysts from the J-2, J-3, ORSA, COIC, component liaisons to include special operations forces (SOF), USG agency AtN specialists, etc. It is primarily responsible for determining the best mix of the JTF's lethal and nonlethal resources to be applied against previously designated network high value targets. The cell conducts planning for deliberate (and usually multi-node) AtN that will be conducted by the JTF components. Planning products are provided to the J-3 AtN working group for approval and then forwarded to the J3/J5 planning cell. Targeting recommendations are made to the joint targeting board.

(2) The **AtN working group** is chaired by the J-3 and tasked to work specific issues relating to the development of the AtN portion of the joint operation plan. The AtN working group is described in greater detail in paragraph 4 below.

For additional information on the responsibilities of the J-3, see JP 3-33, Joint Task Force Headquarters.

4. Joint Task Force Specialized Boards, Working Groups, and Cells

a. In order to effectively manage the overall AtN effort, the CJTF may establish a variety of specialized boards, working groups, and cells. These organizations are designed to provide time-sensitive, cross-functional AtN unity of effort within the operational area through the integration and synchronization of the AtN activities of the JTF with enabling theater and national resources. The inclusion of such boards, cells, and working groups within the normal staff structure of a JTF assists the CJTF in organizing and managing constrained resources, design AtN with pooled resources, and clearly delineate staff section responsibilities and eliminate redundancies so that they perform mutually complementary functions with minimum overlap.

*"A **board** is an organized group of individuals within a JFC's HQ, appointed by the commander (or other authority) that meets with the purpose of gaining guidance or decision ... A **functional board's** purpose is to gain functionally specific guidance and decisions from the commander (or designated representative) based on a staff recommendation. These boards often focus on:*

1. Synchronizing a particular function (e.g., IO, targeting, collection, and distribution) across multiple planning initiatives.

2. Allocation of resources between ongoing or future operations.

3. Maintaining continuity of purpose across ongoing operations."

Joint Publication 3-33, *Joint Task Force Headquarters*

b. **AtN Management Board**. The CJTF may decide to establish an AtN management board as a senior steering committee to manage the JTF's AtN efforts. The AtN management board brings senior JTF leadership together with AtN specialists to shape and direct the AtN fight. The AtN management board normally is chaired by the Deputy CJTF. It is designed to allocate resources, including ISR, in support of the overall AtN effort. Membership includes the JTF's primary staff and senior representatives of the component commands. The management board, if established, reviews and decides upon the recommendations developed by the J-3's AtN working group (introduced above). The AtN management board provides flag officer-level updates on the threat network's activities and trends and component (major subordinate commands) concerns relating to AtN efforts in equipment, training, and intelligence. Recommendations produced by the management board include:

(1) AtN specific IO recommendations.

(2) Priorities for asset allocation as they pertain to AtN efforts (e.g., ISR, air platforms).

*"A **Working Group** is an enduring or ad hoc organization within a JFC's HQ formed around a specific function whose purpose is to provide analysis to users. The WG consists of a core functional group and other staff and component representatives."*

Joint Publication 3-33, *Joint Task Force Headquarters*

c. **AtN Working Group**. This working group can be chaired by the deputy CJTF, but will usually be managed by the J-3 with a representative from the chief of staff as the deputy. It consists of representatives from the J-2 (plans, collection management, and operations), J-3 (plans and operations), supporting specialized enablers (COIC, LEP, and JCAST), component liaisons, and other members as required (Figure V-1). It is tasked to work specific issues related to the AtN plan. These issues can include anything from developing major refinements to the AtN plan to developing the command response to major developments in the enemy's activities (Figure V-2). While the AtN working group usually focuses on a specific AtN related issue of significant importance to the JTF, it can be used to establish and manage a multinational force's overall AtN initiatives.

(1) The AtN WG primarily:

(a) Supports the efforts of the J-5's joint planning group in developing a joint operation plan that is responsive to attaining the overall desired effects and operational objectives.

(b) Provides specific recommendations for lethal and nonlethal targeting of critical network nodes (high value individuals (HVIs), high payoff targets) to the J-3's joint targeting coordination board and time sensitive targeting cells.

(c) Identifies potential targets and exploitable vulnerabilities to the J-3's IO cell.

(d) Works with the J-2 in developing AtN targets for collection, exploitation and analysis.

(e) Develops and provides intelligence information requirements for action by the J-2's joint document exploitation center, joint interrogation and debriefing centers, and the joint captured material exploitation center.

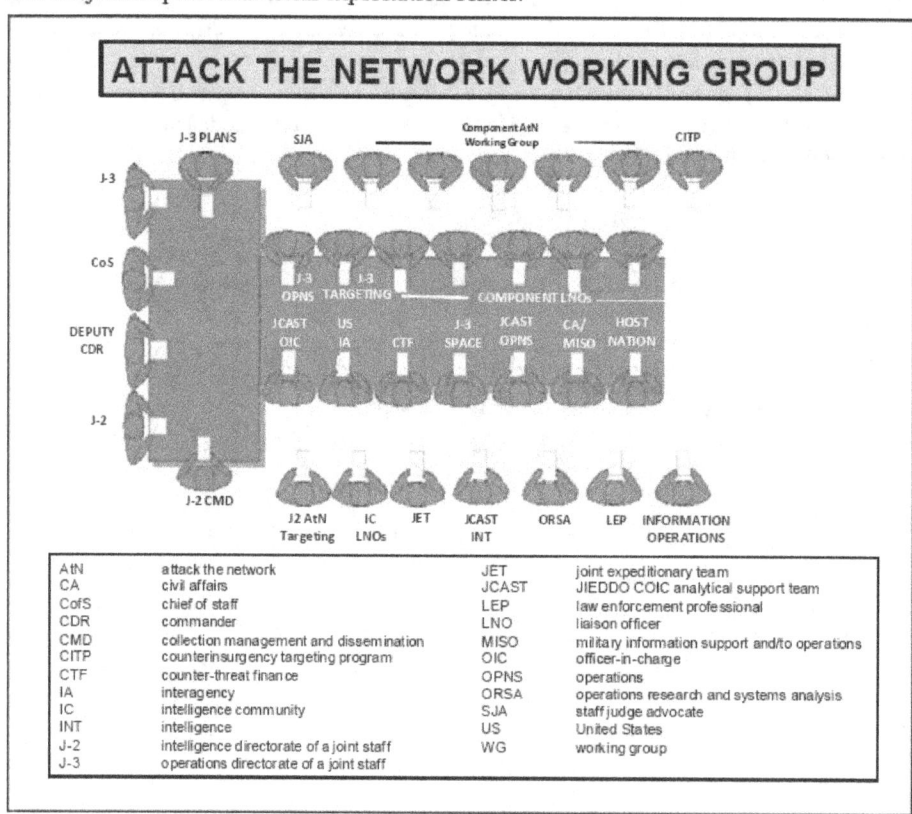

Figure V-1. Attack the Network Working Group

(f) Provides guidance and specific recommendations on the development of AtN data collection standards and an AtN information dissemination plan with the J-6 and the components.

(g) Provides the CJTF and staff with an assessment of on-going AtN activities and recommends adjustments, if required. This information will normally be provided to the JTF's assessment cell, if one is established.

(2) The AtN working group can have up to four cells as follows:

(a) **Plans and Policy Cell**. This cell is responsible for developing the AtN-related portions of the joint operation plan and for ensuring that the AtN effort is closely tied to attaining the military objectives and end state. The cell's tasks include:

1. Establishing policies on AtN activity event reporting to include timelines, AtN data collection standards, and dissemination of information in accordance with the CJTF's policy guidance.

2. Establishing policies to update and disseminate AtN TTP force wide on a regular basis in cooperation with the training cell.

3. Employ specialized mobile training teams to routinely conduct assistance visits to subordinate units providing the latest information on AtN related TTP and appropriate countermeasures.

(b) **Assessment Cell**. This cell is responsible for reviewing the effectiveness of friendly force AtN activities, recommending adjustments to ongoing operations and assisting in the development of future AtN plans.

(c) **Training Cell**. This cell is responsible for reviewing friendly force AtN training programs and TTP, identifying potential shortfalls, and recommending near-term (that can be addressed by the force's organic training capabilities, i.e., unit level TTP or by mobile training teams) and long-term (for Service or joint predeployment training) solutions. Near-term recommendations are forwarded through the JTF J-3 for implementation within the command.

(d) **Targeting Cell**. The AtN working group plays a critical role in developing and recommending AtN related targets for attack to achieve the desired lethal and nonlethal effects. AtN target development is closely coordinated with the J-2 and is closely tied to the J-2 overall analytical and collection management efforts. The AtN working group develops critical vulnerability candidates in each function area within the overall threat network. Actionable targets and targets for development are matched to these critical vulnerabilities. Targets for development steer requirements for intelligence. Actionable targets that, if serviced together, will disable a critical vulnerability, are prioritized in a list of recommended targets with recommended means of engagement (lethal and nonlethal). This list is forwarded for consideration and action by the JTF's joint targeting coordination board.

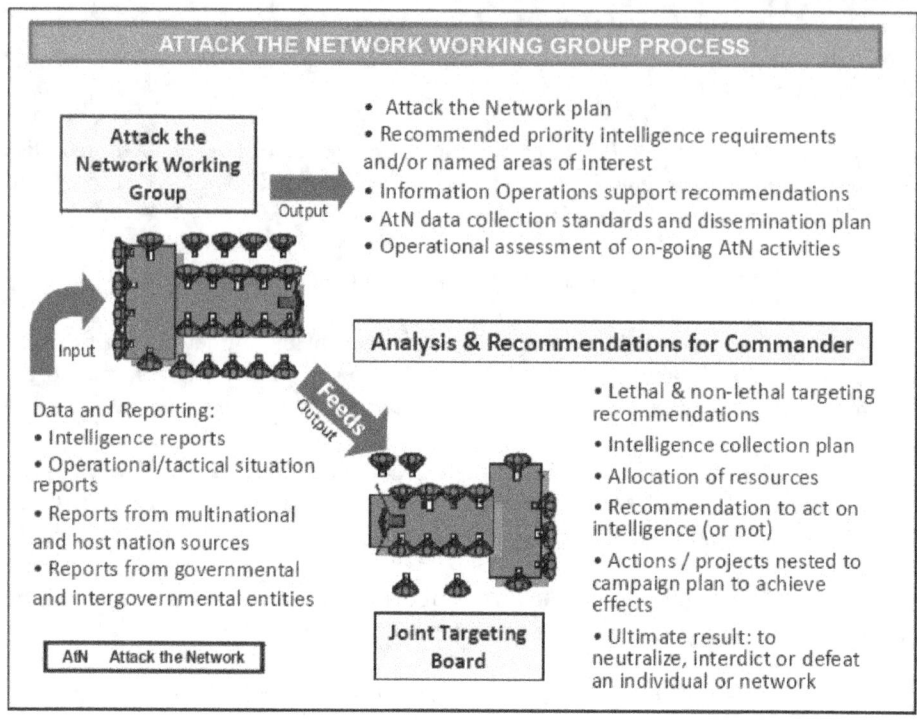

Figure V-2. Attack the Network Working Group Process

d. **Lethal Working Group.** Typically chaired by the unit deputy commander or executive officer and under the staff J-/G-/S-3 operations, the lethal working group develops comprehensive courses of action for all targets utilizing a combined arms approach (air, ground, maritime) for the specified time period. It basically identifies the specific assets or systems (enablers) that will be applied to attack and destroy those targets that the commander has designated for attack. Membership includes representatives from the staff principles and their planning elements, fire support officer, air liaison, staff judge advocate, provost marshal, public affairs, chaplain, component/ subordinate unit liaisons, interagency liaisons, special operations liaisons, and the human environment team.

e. **Nonlethal Working Group.** Organized and directed in the same way as the lethal working group, the nonlethal working group focuses on developing appropriate nonlethal responses for those targets the commander desires to influence rather than destroy. The working group develops potential themes, messages, and products to support planned operations to include use of media and psychological operations. Nonlethal options require imagination, patience, and a continuous PMESII based assessment; the effects can not be immediately determined but offer a more lasting solution than a "wack-a-mole" approach. Specific taskings to enablers are developed – for example, "the human environment (HTT) in the areas around NAI 3108, Median Jabal and Medina Wasl, to identify and understand the drivers of instability that can be leveraged to separate the population from the insurgents." Nonlethal options include:

to finance projects that will employ local workers. Both are designed to turn people from high risk activities supporting the enemy to more legitimate forms of employment.

See also the USJFCOM publication, "Commander's Handbook on Integrated Financial Operations," for a detailed discussion on financial initiatives.

(2) **Key Leader Engagements.** A multi-echelon effort that focuses on how HN security forces and government leaders are improving and what can we do to help connect the population with their governmental leaders and security forces. Funding projects helps to quickly connect the two together and stimulate employment.

(3) **Information Operations.** Military information support operations (MISO), public affairs (PA), and civil affairs (CA) personnel are responsible for designing and assisting in the implementation of a media activities to exploit the effects of friendly operations and facilitate the attainment of the military objectives regarding creation of a secure environment for the populace. HN security forces, local leadership, and the local population are the primary focus for these efforts; secondary efforts include using MISO personnel to counter enemy propaganda. The human environment team is also utilized to develop detailed information on local social networks.

f. **Targeting Working Group.** This working group is a critical step in the targeting process because it brings all the staff working groups and unit planning efforts together and synchronizes and resources operations for execution during the next cycle. It is typically chaired by the deputy commander and organized by the J-/G-/S-3, the working members include representatives from the principle staff – operations, intelligence, engineer; public affairs, staff judge advocate, subordinate unit liaisons, HN, multinationals, interagency representatives, and others as required. Based on an updated enemy situation, staff running estimates recommended talking points and MISO products and the courses of action that were developed during each working group, the working group resources and synchronizes the command's operations for the next targeting cycle. There are multiple techniques to war gaming but at a minimum teams need to have tools that allow them to allocate assets across time and identify additions or changes required based on estimated enemy actions. The outcome of this working group is fully resourced and synchronized courses of action that together make up the command's overall targeting CONOPS.

g. **C-IED Working Group.** The J-/G-/S-3 operations can chair a C-IED working group; consisting of representatives from the J-/G-/S-2, J/G-S-2 collection management, J-/G-/S-2 plans, J-/G-/S- staff engineer, J-/G-/S-3 plans, J-/G-/S-3 operations, explosive ordnance disposal (EOD) battalion, and other members, as required; tasked to work specific issues related to the C-IED plan. (Note: When the CJTF establishes a C-IED TF, the responsibilities of the JTF J-3's C-IED working group will normally transfer to the C-IED TF.) The working group develops C-IED related courses of action for inputs to the command's targeting board. It focuses on the C-IED portion of the enemy's overall activities and nominates specific C-IED related targets for engagement in order to produce lethal or nonlethal effects.

See JP 3-15.1, *Counter-Improvised Explosive Device Operations*, for a detailed discussion on C-IED working groups.

h. **ISR Working Group**. Based on the CJTF's guidance and the targets developed by the other working groups, the ISR WG develops a comprehensive ISR coverage plan for the targeted time period. This is a multi-component, multi-echelon effort synchronizing the JTF's intelligence collection capabilities to include those of USG agencies, multinational forces and agencies, and the HN. Where gaps in coverage exist, the ISR working group will prepare requests for support to higher and supporting headquarters. The ISR working group must also plan for appropriate asset allocation within the JTF to support force wide operations.

i. **Component AtN Working Groups**. AtN working groups may also be established by the component commanders. These working groups are responsible for focusing AtN efforts within their respective areas of operation. Component level working groups are designed to identify AtN related issues that require JTF level action/intervention. AtN level issues are presented to the J-3 AtN working group via the representatives of the component working groups.

5. Coordinating with Supporting Theater and National Level Organizations

a. In organizing the AtN effort, the JTF staff likely will require augmentation with "specialized enablers" (i.e., experts on the particular network the JTF is confronting). These enablers, ranging from individual SMEs to entire units, will be drawn from theater and USG agencies. These enablers can participate in a wide variety of activities designed to degrade the threat network's infrastructure including managing HVI targeting. Identifying the right mix of USG assets to support AtN requires the JTF conduct an initial analysis to define the network; conduct an internal evaluation of the JTF's personnel's skill sets for the planning and conduct of AtN activities; and, identify any shortfalls in technical (usually intelligence collection and analysis) capabilities required to support AtN. The GCC's joint interagency coordination group (JIACG) can assist the CJTF and staff with an increased capability to coordinate with civil USG agencies and departments. The JIACG is an interagency staff group that establishes regular, timely, and collaborative working relationships between civilian and military operational planners. In C-IED operations, for example, external AtN enablers include representatives from the COIC, the C-IED Targeting Program CITP) (now called the COIN Targeting Program), Federal Bureau of Investigation (FBI), Department of Justice (Alcohol, Tobacco and Firearms) while specialized military augmentation include weapons intelligence teams and EOD units. Depending upon how the CJTF has designed the overall AtN support to the operation, these specialized enablers can be deployed throughout the command from the JTF headquarters to battalion to support AtN-related activities. Two combatant command level programs that support current C-IED operations illustrate how a whole-of-government approach to ATN is operationalized:

(1) **High-Value Individual Targeting Program**. This combatant command program is a joint, interagency task force (TF) that plans, manages, and conducts the targeting of

HVIs who are in or transiting the operational area in order to capture key individuals who are significantly influencing enemy operations, and directing and/or funding transnational terrorists and local members of the network. The TF actually is manned by a variety of specialists from the JTF and from supporting interagency partners. Interagency participants could include an on-site team with representation from the Department of Defense (DOD) investigations, legal, the Department of Homeland Security, FBI, and the Department of the Treasury. Interagency intelligence reach-back for analytical support would also be provided. Liaison officers from the major participants in the JTF would be present to assist in organizing forces to take action against identified targets.

(2) **Threat Finance Exploitation Unit**. The JTF threat finance exploitation (TFE) unit works with DOD and non-DOD intelligence, law enforcement, and regulatory agencies that are responsible for taking action against enemy (usually terrorist and insurgent) financial networks. The unit is an integral part of the overall national program to detect, collect, and process information on, and target, disrupt, or destroy the enemy's financial systems and networks. In C-IED operations, the TFE effort denies the enemy the uninterrupted financial resources needed to obtain IED related supplies and support their personnel (bomb makers, transporters, and emplacers). At the JTF level, threat finance information derived from raids, cache exploitation, and interrogations is analyzed and passed through intelligence channels to the TFE unit for target development and further exploitation in coordination with national resources. Appropriate targeting recommendations are then passed back to the JTF for action using lethal and nonlethal means.

See also the USJFCOM publication, "Commanders Handbook for Counter Threat Finance," for a detailed discussion of counter threat finance planning considerations and operations.

6. Interagency Coordination

"Collaborative warfare required collaborative organizations. It meant in practice going beyond "jointness" to intense give and take (or mutual adjustment) between otherwise disparate military and nonmilitary organizational elements. On the interagency high-value target teams, the collaboration was between the SOF Task Force and diverse intelligence organizations. On the conventional force command staffs, the collaboration was between conventional forces, SOF, and other departments and agencies and Iraqi government entities. When the high-value target teams and integrated conventional force commands collaborated tactically, they produced quick and powerful results. When Petraeus and Crocker used collaborative warfare more broadly in pursuit of a consistent counterinsurgency strategy, the situation in Iraq turned around dramatically. Collaborative organizations are not only powerful but also cost effective. In comparison with new weapons or reconstruction funding, interagency teams cost next to nothing and can be used almost anywhere. However, collaboration is a difficult force to harness and institutionalize. It is not just a function of good leadership, as is often assumed. On the contrary, and as one interagency veteran we interviewed said, organizations that want a

reliable record of success do not rely on personalities to generate unity of effort."

**Christopher J. Lamb,
"Secret Weapon: High-value Target
Teams as an Organizational Innovation"
March 2011**

a. **Interagency Teams and Collaboration**. The experience of the past ten years has clearly established the advantage of interagency teams (e.g., combining military with civil operations and intelligence specialists). When configured as all-source fusion cells, these teams expand the conventional force's ability to leverage external resources to collect, analyze, and disseminate information on threat networks. For this type of collaborative effort to work, three elements must be present:

(1) The first is network based targeting (i.e., F3EAD) using all-source intelligence to provide situational awareness of the local environment, its social networks, key decision makers, and their motivations. In COIN operations, this requires a detailed knowledge of the human terrain (both enemy clandestine cells and the local population), which can only be achieved by collaboration and information exchange among all the participants (military, interagency, and HN).

(2) The second requires the fusion of all-source intelligence with operations and employing persistent surveillance with improved discrimination and timely decision making. This fusion provides operators with improved situational awareness and facilitates a commander's ability to determine the time and place to apply force. In COIN operations, this fusion also enables operators to know the value of a source and whether they should continue to develop that source or comprise it.

(3) The third is the coordination and synchronization of complimentary LOEs at all echelons of command to promote synergy. In Iraq, those LOEs were COIN and counterterrorism. It resulted in high-value target teams putting terrorist and insurgent cells on the defensive and conventional force commanders partnering with civil agencies and SOF to guide the activities of those teams with a broader awareness of their second- and third-order effects.

b. **Attack the Network Collaboration Center**. AtN activities will prompt significant interaction among USG and foreign governmental agencies (law enforcement, intelligence, etc.) and HN security forces. In order to leverage the capabilities that these entities bring to the operation, CJTF can establish an AtN collaboration center. Based on the stability operations model employed in Afghanistan, the center would focus on operational level AtN information sharing, timely AtN assessments, lethal and nonlethal AtN target development, and support to operational and tactical AtN planning. Manned by military and civil SMEs, it would help to define the OE and provide detailed insights into the threat network's organization and operations. While the exact configuration of the center would be situation dependent, it could consist of:

(1) **Operational Environment Cell**. This cell consists of PMESII SMEs on the region and on the threat network. It seeks to define how the threat network operates within the region's social/political/economic infrastructure and identify the exploitable vulnerabilities that can be subject to targeting by military and civil capabilities. It acts as an information clearing house and provides in-depth analysis relying on reach back to national intelligence resources. It maintains the JTF's agility by providing continuous feedback, assessment, and rapid recognition of changing environmental conditions.

(2) **Fusion Cell**. Basically a targeting cell, the fusion cell consists of operations personnel, intelligence analysts and collectors, and liaisons from JTF members and allied partners. It incorporates information derived from the OE cell with tactical reporting to develop the AtN focused portion of the JTF's overall intelligence collection plan – determining "how" a threat individual or activity is to be detected or found; and, develops and recommends specific AtN targets ("who" should be targeted, not "what" should be targeted) for lethal and nonlethal engagement. The goal is to shape behavior and the environment.

(3) **Exploitation Cell**. The cell consists of two components. The **forensics exploitation team** exploits recovered or captured material – usually with the cooperation of the HN which has jurisdictional primacy – using deployed or reachback forensic laboratories and featuring document exploitation and biometrics. The **law enforcement cell** features law enforcement professionals, who assist local authorities in the preparation and preservation of evidence for administrative or criminal prosecution and other "Rule of Law" initiatives.

Intentionally Blank

CHAPTER VI
ENGAGE THE NETWORK

"It takes a network to defeat a network. But fashioning ourselves to counter our enemy's network was easier said than done, especially because it took time to learn what, exactly, made a network different. As we studied, experimented, and adjusted, it became apparent that an effective network involves much more than relaying data. A true network starts with robust communications connectivity, but also leverages physical and cultural proximity, shared purpose, established decision-making processes, personal relationships, and trust. Ultimately, a network is defined by how well it allows its members to see, decide, and effectively act. But transforming a traditional military structure into a truly flexible, empowered network is a difficult process."

General (Retired) Stanley McChrystal,
Foreign Policy,
March/April 2011

1. Introduction

a. There are few major differences between attacking a conventional force and attacking a threat network. The emphasis for AtN is on the employment of specialized intelligence resources and analysis to identify and define the network, and the implementation and synchronization of multi-echelon targeting mechanisms against the network. Further, depending on the target set, **small tactical units usually will be tasked with the primary responsibility for execution; while higher echelons have the primary responsibility for planning, coordinating and allocating supporting resources.**

b. Successfully exploiting a threat network is very difficult; however, certain critical vulnerabilities may be identified and attacked. Networks operate as integrated entities – the whole is greater than the sum of its parts. Thus targeting the vulnerable critical capabilities and requirements such as those associated with an IED support network also affect the rest of the threat network's infrastructure. However, since networks are by their nature resilient and reconstitute, the targeting effort must be continuous and multi-nodal. Actions to attack critical vulnerabilities must be synchronized and integrated with the overall joint operation/campaign against the enemy. Joint force targeting efforts must employ a comprehensive approach, leveraging military force and civil agency lethal and nonlethal capabilities that keep continuous pressure on multiple nodes and links of the network's structure. There are a few instances when specific critical capabilities and requirements may be separated from the enemy's overall operational patterns and subject to attack. When conducting C-IED operations, for example, these include bomb making facilities and the bomb makers, and the acquisition of specialized components. By targeting these specific capabilities, the joint force may temporarily disrupt IED attacks at the tactical level, but the only effective way to counter an enemy's IED employment is to effectively neutralize the threat network's overall ability to operate.

c. Threat network engagement often focuses on HVIs, who are the heart of most networks and without whose presence the network can collapse. Engagement activities, however, must avoid the "wack-a-mole" approach that seeks to kill or capture as many of the threat network members as possible. Alternatively, threat network engagements should be intelligence-driven and based on careful analysis that identifies the critical vulnerabilities that should be targeted to produce the desired effect on the network.

2. Networked Threats and the Levels of War

a. Engaging networked threats starts with the comprehensive application of the instruments of national power (diplomatic, military, information, economic) at all (strategic, operational, and tactical) levels of war. The AtN activities conducted at each level of war must be synchronized and coordinated to ensure that the efforts are complimentary with regard to friendly plans and operations and cumulative with regard to the targeted threat network.

b. At the strategic level, AtN is focused on global networked threats. AtN activities are normally a subset of a broader stability operation which includes positively shaping the OE and developing and providing the partnerships, information, and resources required for strategic success. Success at this level normally depends heavily on influencing a range of audiences including local populations, threat network members and supporters, allies, and the US public. Strategic actions also can be specific actions designed to gain intelligence, conduct analysis and targeting, and neutralize or eliminate nodes that are far enough outside the operational area as to be vulnerable only to USG agency or partner

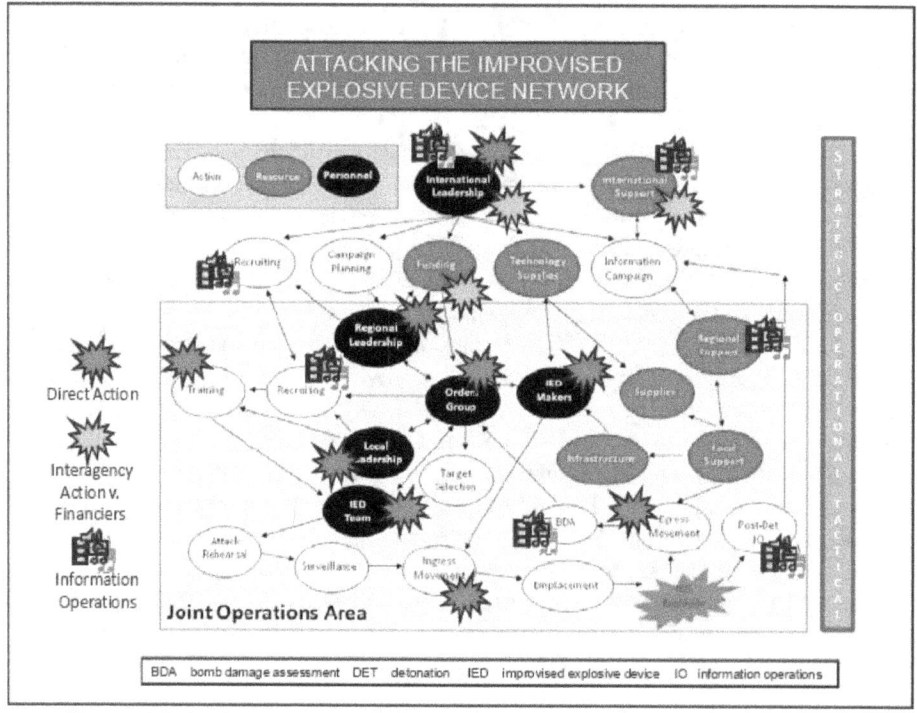

Figure VI-1. Attacking the Improvised Explosive Device Network

nation actions. Figure VI-1 is an example of a multi-level approach to attacking various critical nodes in an insurgent based network employing IEDs by leveraging the multi-agency capabilities at each level of war through a mix of actions designed to achieve the desired lethal and nonlethal effects.

    c. At the operational level, commanders focus on the threat networks operating in the assigned operational area. Through the use of specialized analytical tools, commanders will be able to refine their understanding of the OE and focus resources on key nodes in the network's infrastructure. For example, geospatial intelligence can be used to identify threat network nodes such as safe houses, bomb building locations, and cache sites. Operational level organizations normally develop detailed plans for attacking critical network nodes and coordinate with tactical units for actual execution. Operational commanders usually will supplement the tactical echelons with specialized AtN enablers – intelligence collection and analysis - to facilitate their operations. When operating in sector, units employ their intelligence capabilities and employ specialized network enablers to develop an extended intelligence picture. They coordinate and inform lower echelons of the effects desired, ensure unified actions are taken to favorably shape the OE, and employ IO to influence the friendly, neutral, and threat network members.

ACTIVITIES	TACTICALLY FOCUSED	OPERATIONALLY FOCUSED
Community Outreach	Execute	Facilitate
Civil Military Operations	Support, Execute	Facilitate, Execute
Information Operations	Support, Execute	Facilitate, Execute
Biometrics Enrollment	Execute	Facilitate, Support
Security Enhancement	Facilitate, Execute	Facilitate, Support
Interdiction of Network Infrastructure	Execute	Facilitate, Support
Action Against Corrupt Local Officials	Facilitate, Execute	Facilitate, Support
Interdiction of Regional and International Facilitators	Execute	Facilitate
Kill or Capture	Facilitate, Execute, Support	Facilitate

Figure VI-2. Attack the Network Related Activities

d. At the tactical level, the focus is on executing AtN. Accurate, timely and relevant intelligence will drive this effort and tactical units exercise refined procedures to conduct analysis, template, and target networks. In a COIN operation, for example, friendly operations include efforts to secure the population, strengthen HN security forces, and counter the enemy's ideology and propaganda. See Appendix G, "A Comprehensive Approach to Counterinsurgency." These efforts contribute to the overall AtN effort by serving to isolate the threat network from its supporters, suppliers and sympathizers. Tactical units also will conduct precise kill/capture operations, often based on time-sensitive targeting. Figure VI-2 is an example of some of the types of AtN related activities that can be conducted by a JTF and the tactical and operational level roles in the conduct of those operations.

3. Targeting the Network

a. Friendly, neutral, and threat networks must be methodically targeted to achieve desired effects consistent with the commander's intent and the joint operation/campaign objectives. The CJTF and staff need to establish an integrated process to identify targets, determine the desired effects on those targets, predict second and third order effects, and execute nonlethal and lethal operations to achieve those effects.

b. The CJTF establishes priorities and synchronizes the efforts of subordinate organizations through an iterative planning process. Within the framework of the joint operation/campaign plan, the JTF components and units uses a targeting process which applies multiple assets on multiple levels to develop and prosecute targets. The joint targeting cycle provides the mechanism which translates the commander's guidance and targeting objectives into actions to engage targets through both lethal and nonlethal means. A comprehensive targeting program requires participation from the entire staff and specialized enablers from external civil organizations and military forces. At a minimum, an operations-intelligence time sensitive targeting cell will be established to develop actionable intelligence to target threats in real-time and a longer term planning cell will address development of AtN targets.

c. In real terms, targeting of threat network critical vulnerabilities is driven by the situation, the accuracy of intelligence, and the ability of the joint force to quickly execute various targeting options to achieve the desired lethal and nonlethal effects. In COIN and C-IED operations, individuals who perform tasks that are vulnerable to detection/ exploitation and impact more than one critical requirement are a higher priority for targeting. However, while a paymaster is a critical target the day before payday, that individual is less valuable a week after payday as you move up the financial chain seeking the funding source before the next payday. Timing is everything when attacking a network and, in an irregular warfare environment, the opportunities for attacking identified critical vulnerabilities are limited.

d. **Targeting Types**. There are basically two types of AtN targets: those that must be serviced immediately, such as HVIs; and longer term network infrastructure targets (caches, supply routes, safe houses) that are normally left in place for a period to exploit them. Resources to service/exploit these targets are allocated in accordance with the CJTF's priorities – which are constantly reviewed and updated through the command's targeting coordination mechanisms. This allocation is validated through a daily asset synchronization meeting

(1) **Dynamic Targeting**. A **time-sensitive targeting cell** consisting of operations and intelligence personnel with direct access to lethal means and the authority to act on pre-approved targets is an essential part of any AtN effort. Using a dynamic targeting process, the cell services targets that have been identified too late or not selected in time to be included in deliberate targeting and that meet criteria specific to achieving the stated objectives.

> *"In November of 2009, the targeting team was tasked with standing up and running a group to focus on developing these identified opportunities into targetable events for the combined, joint task force (CJTF) commander, and the Regional Command – East (RC-E) Fusion Center was born. The fusion center contained personnel from multiple staff functions from within the CJTF, but also included inter-agency partners, special operations personnel and host nation intelligence personnel. As the team developed into a cohesive group, it was given the specific responsibilities of threat network targeting; the development of measures of effectiveness and measures of performance; and negative influence targeting, which focused on the nonlethal enablers that supported and reinforced threats facing coalition force efforts and Afghan stability. The overall success of the RC-E Fusion Center was the creative and asymmetrical way in which they not only viewed the problem set, but the recommended offensive and defensive actions and responses to enemy action for the CJTF commander to consider. The lasting effect of this effort is the creativity injected back into the targeting elements of the staff and the infusion of all staff functions and how everyday activities can have significant impacts on the area of operation."*
>
> **Fires Red Book**
> **November-December 2010**

(2) **Deliberate Targeting**. Organizing the participants in the targeting process can be accomplished through the standard boards, working groups, and cells process. One approach is to establish a **joint fires cell** to provide mission analysis planning, execution oversight, coordination, and critical liaison duties that reach from the strategic and operational levels to the tactical level. A joint fires cell is given responsibility for refining targeting conducted by the intelligence cell, and coordinating the daily management of the close air support allocation and apportionment for the command's area of operation. The cell also provides field grade and company grade officers to multinational, interagency (as required), and HN partners. These officers performed duties ranging from fire support officers to targeting officers. The joint fires cell is tasked to look at an extended timeline for threats and the overall working of threat networks. With this type of deliberate investigation into threat networks the cell can identify catalysts to the threat network's operations and sustainment that had not traditionally been targeted on a large scale. With a constant flow of intelligence about individual actions and movements, the cell will examine what facilitated any number of events, such as terrorist, criminal, narcotics activities, failed public services and governmental corruption. It will also focus on how

these events ultimately impacted not only the JTF's operations in support of the overall joint operation/campaign plan, but also international development and aid efforts and the local government and population. This type of analysis will usually reveal a web of interconnected relationships and associations of which only a small percentage can be affected by lethal targeting and actions. When augmented with appropriate USG agency, special operations, and HN intelligence analysts, the joint fires cell (often called a "**fusion center**") can plan to exploit these relationships and associations using nonlethal means and seek to reduce their contribution to the overall effectiveness of the enemy's network. At the JTF, the joint fires cell (or its equivalent) develops AtN related targets to nominate to the joint targeting coordination board for approval and subsequent execution on an on-call or deliberate basis.

e. **Targeting Methodologies.** The joint targeting cycle provides a framework to describe the steps that must be satisfied to successfully target threat network nodes or links. **Currently, there are three primary targeting methodologies within phase five (mission planning and execution) of the joint targeting cycle as illustrated in Figure VI-3.** Depending on the situation, multiple methodologies may be required to create the desired effect.

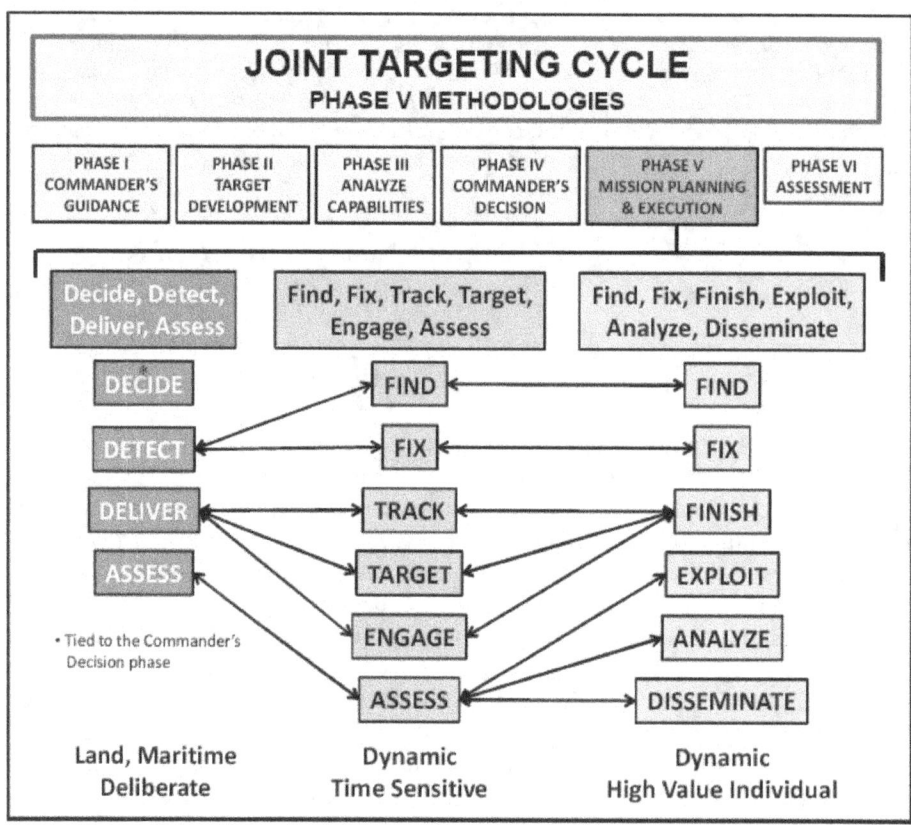

Figure VI-3. Joint Targeting Cycle: Phase V Methodologies

(1) Decide, detect, deliver, and assess (D3A) is a deliberate and dynamic targeting method. The find, fix, track, target, engage, assess (F2T2EA) and F3EAD methodologies

support dynamic targeting. All of these methodologies, including F2T2EA, supports the joint targeting cycle execution phase and facilitate the servicing of time sensitive targets (TSTs).

(2) The F3EAD model was developed for personality-based targeting and has been widely adopted as the principal targeting process for AtN. Successful employment of the D3A and F3EAD methodologies requires the assignment of persistent surveillance assets. Figure VI-3 depicts the relationship of these three targeting methodologies.

See the USJFCOM publication "Joint Fires and Targeting Handbook," *for a detailed discussion of the joint targeting process.*

4. Find-Fix-Finish-Exploit-Analyze-Disseminate Methodology

"The (friendly) network needed to expand to include everyone relevant who was operating within the battlespace. Incomplete or unconnected networks can give the illusion of effectiveness, but are like finely crafted gears whose movement drives no other gears. This insight allowed us to move closer to building a true network by connecting everyone who had a role — no matter how small, geographically dispersed, or organizationally diverse they might have been — in a successful counterterrorism operation. We called it, in our shorthand, F3EA: find, fix, finish, exploit, and analyze. The idea was to combine analysts who found the enemy (through intelligence, surveillance, and reconnaissance); drone operators who fixed the target; combat teams who finished the target by capturing or killing him; specialists who exploited the intelligence the raid yielded, such as cell phones, maps, and detainees; and the intelligence analysts who turned this raw information into usable knowledge. By doing this, we speeded up the cycle for a counterterrorism operation, gleaning valuable insights in hours, not days."

General (Retired) Stanley McChrystal,
Foreign Policy,
March/April 2011

a. The remaining portion of this handbook uses the F3EAD targeting model and presents additional information on network targeting based upon that methodology. The F3EAD cycle (Figure VI-4) provides the overarching structure for engaging the threat network. F3EAD facilitates the targeting of individuals in an asymmetric environment when timing is crucial. F3EAD facilitates synergy between operations and intelligence as it refines the targeting process. It is a continuous cycle in which intelligence and operations feed and support each other.

b. F3EAD assists in:

(1) Refining the threat network's ideology, methodology, and capabilities, and helps templates its inner workings—personnel, organization, and activities.

(2) Identifying the links between enemy critical capabilities and requirements, and observable indicators of enemy action.

(3) Focusing and prioritizing dedicated ISR assets.

(4) Providing the resulting intelligence and products to elements capable of rapidly conducting multiple, near-simultaneous attacks against the critical vulnerabilities.

(5) Provides an ability to "see" the OE, and array and synchronize forces and capabilities.

c. The F3EAD process is optimized to facilitate targeting of HVIs – Tier I (enemy top level leadership) and Tier II (enemy intermediaries who interact with the leaders and establish links the links with facilitators within the population). Tier III individuals (the low skilled foot soldiers who are part of the general threat network population) may be easy to reach and provide an immediate result but are a distraction to AtN success because they are easy to replace and their elimination is only a temporary inconvenience to the enemy. Targeting Tier III individuals also runs the risk of alienating the individual's family members in a wider tribal context. Tier I targets require dedicated ISR assets routinely available only at the JTF and higher headquarters. Using regional fusion cells (for operations – intelligence integration) to synchronize the employment of SOF with maneuver units can provide access to enablers they cannot traditionally leverage against Tier I and II targets in their operational area.

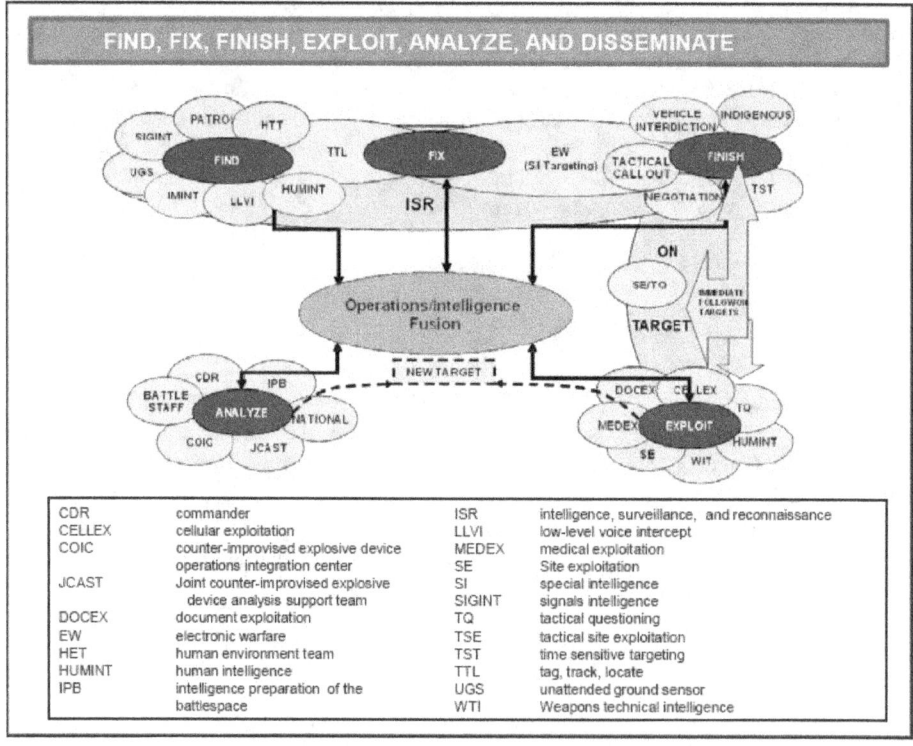

Figure VI-4. Find, Fix, Finish, Exploit, Analyze, and Disseminate

d. **F3EAD Elements**. In the F3EAD process, friendly forces **find** which network needs to be the focus of effort. In many environments, there are a number of networks operating simultaneously, some of which are hostile to friendly forces and the HN (insurgents and terrorists), others which represent a general threat to stability (criminal, narcotics, etc.). Analysts then **find** the network's critical vulnerabilities. Friendly forces then **fix** the targets to an area, then to specific locations in real time. This enables friendly forces to **finish** the target through decisive action. Throughout the F3EAD cycle, analyze-exploit-disseminate is the main effort. Friendly forces analyze networks across the operational area to ensure they address the most significant threats as the highest priority, and analyze threat network inner workings to ensure they attack the most lucrative targets within the network. Results of friendly force actions are exploited through numerous means including tactical questioning of suspects, document and media exploitation, medical exploitation, and political and media releases. Information and intelligence derived from friendly exploitation is disseminated vertically and horizontally throughout the joint force and its' supporting civil participants. Information derived from this exploitation effort is used to plan and direct further operations against the network.

(1) **F3EAD – Find**. During this step, the intelligence team is building on the initial macro analysis of the threat network and preparing a JIPOE study which develops a picture of the network's support infrastructure, to include identifying nodes and working relationships, i.e., linkages between nodes. During the final step, all available intelligence sources and resources (including available HN, USG agency, and multinational partners) are utilized but efforts are often heavily weighted to the tactical level, e.g., HUMINT oriented collection capabilities. In many operational areas, a number of networks will be operating and it will be necessary to identify the networks that pose the greatest threat to the success of the friendly operation. As friendly "Find" activities meet with success, the threat network members will change their operating modes – stop using cells phones, moving their leadership to safe havens, etc. On one hand, inducing paranoia will keep them off balance and severely restrict their ability to function; on the other, it will make them harder to find and even cause decentralization of their internal C2 structure so that friendly forces may be dealing with a greater number of groups. **Under no circumstances should friendly force intelligence personnel reveal successful "find" techniques outside of intelligence channels; operations personnel and leadership only need the information, not how it was collected**.

(2) **F3EAD – Fix**. During this step, intelligence analysts continue to develop and refine the analysis of the network with sufficient detail to produce actionable intelligence and targeting plans. As analysis identifies the network's working nodes, the J-2 prioritizes the collection effort and works with the J-3 to determine an appropriate response. Some nodes require immediate response/attack; while others require further refinement as they lead to more critical nodes. The CJTF's guidance will normally provide the criteria for this decision. Practicing "tactical patience" or delaying an attack involves risk and operational risks must be balanced against the opportunities for further intelligence gains. Exploiting potential network targets is also resource intensive and cannot be conducted indefinitely. For example tactically tracking network operatives back to their safe house or cache and from there to other links in the network must have a cutoff at some point for action to be taken.

(a) **Targeting is a part of the Fix step** and is conducted once analysis and templating have been completed and refined by additional intelligence collection (Figure

VI-5). There are a variety of mechanisms that can be employed to facilitate the targeting of threat networks. These include the traditional targeting working group process and quick response dynamic targeting cells that usually focus on specific type of targets (HVIs, caches, or emplacers) which vary depending on the echelon conducting the planning. The results of analysis and templating are assessed to ensure that AtN efforts are aimed at the right network members and functions using the means most like to achieve the desired lethal and nonlethal effects. When possible, targeting will result in multiple, near-simultaneous operations aimed at several network targets.

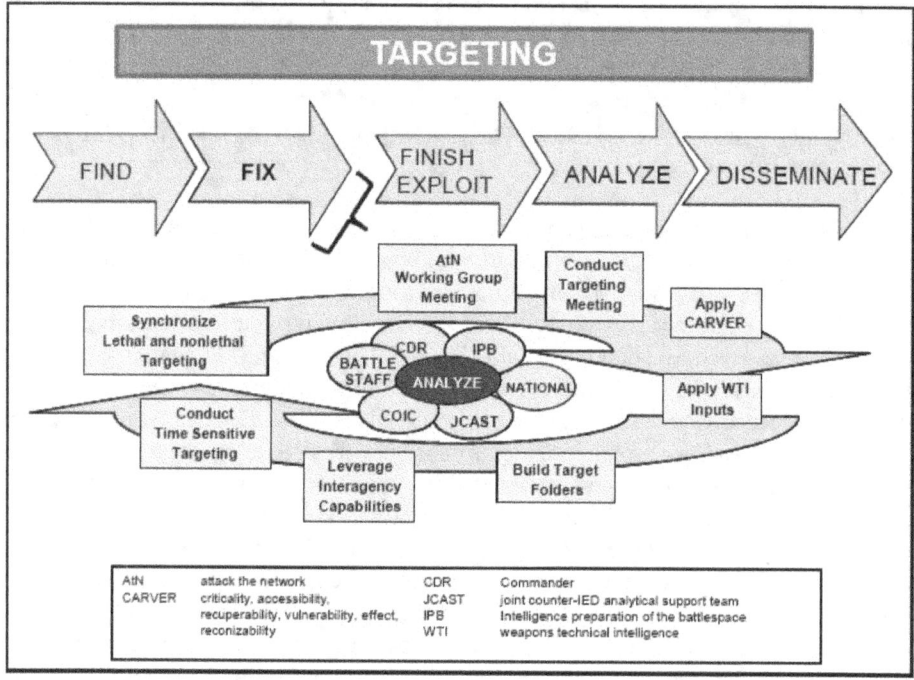

Figure VI-5. Targeting

(b) One useful tool for developing evaluating potential targets is a **CARVER** matrix which assesses and compares networks or specific nodes within a network to one another. CARVER poses six questions to answer:

1. **Criticality**: What is the importance of the node or network?

2. **Accessibility**: What assets can reach the target?

3. **Recuperability**: How long will it take the enemy to replace the target?

4. **Vulnerability**: What is the relative security of the target?

5. **Effect**: What are the second and third order effects on the network?

6. **Recognizability**: How easily can friendly forces positively identify the target?

(3) **F3EAD – Finish**. J-3 directs the conduct of network wide engagements; however, the CJTF likely will direct the engagement of an HVI. The CJTF's engagement guidance will determine what specific options will be employed during this step. When executing the preferable option, it is important to employ a multi-echelon approach to disrupt as much of the network as possible and then exploit the results with previously planned collection assets. Where network wide engagements are not possible, targets of opportunity that may otherwise escape should be engaged. During Finish, intelligence enablers maintain near-real time surveillance of the target(s), and near-real time situational awareness during and after the initiation of the operation (Figure VI-6). HUMINT and UAS resources provide the most responsive information during Finish.

(4) **F3EAD - Exploit**. Every target should be exploited for information. Results from the exploitation are documented and provided to operational level analysts for further dissemination and refinement, and future targeting actions. Exploitation can include examination of documents, cell phones, computer hardware, tactical questioning or interrogations of detainees, and biometric information from a variety of sources (Figure VI-6). While individual pieces may not seem significant; over time, as information accumulates and is correlated, these actions can reveal significant additional detail about the network's nodes and individual participants. An exploitation team should be employed as soon as the site is secured to find documents, cell phones, computers, media, and bomb components – anything that can have value and facilitate immediate engagement of follow-on targets. Even pocket litter may reveal where the individual has been or with whom they have been communicating. Exploitation is a continuous process. As the network is dissected, information sources are developed and targets are identified and attacked. The results of the multiple AtN efforts are gathered and subject to multi-disciplinary analysis and evaluation. In most cases, speedy multi-discipline analysis will usually produce additional leads that further reveal the network's inner workings and further refine the development of actionable intelligence.

(**Note: Finish and Exploit occur almost simultaneously**. The immediate exploitation of a target is essential to developing new, usually perishable, targets and maintaining the momentum of the overall operation.)

(5) **F3EAD - Analyze**

(a) Exploitation and analysis are the main focus of the F3EAD process. Effective exploitation requires a detailed understanding of the network and how its components (individual and material) interact. Since networks involve overlapping relationships (individual and logistical), the degree to which these overlap and the structure of these relationships can become exploitable vulnerabilities. The higher the overlap, the greater the vulnerability, since a successful exploitation of one node affects many others.

(b) As targets are exploited or as information is received from ongoing collection activities, the intelligence picture of the network is further refined and the foundation is laid for the next set of actions against the network. This is a continuous process that results in a return to the first step – refining the JIPOE analysis. During Analysis (Figure VI-7) of the threat network, the joint force should acquire detailed knowledge of the interpersonal dynamics among network members, while maintaining situational awareness of the changing OE. The outcome of F3EAD Analysis is the capability to identify those network members and activities that are most vulnerable, i.e., actionable intelligence. Analysis end products should also support those friendly actions that are most likely to yield the desired effects upon the threat network.

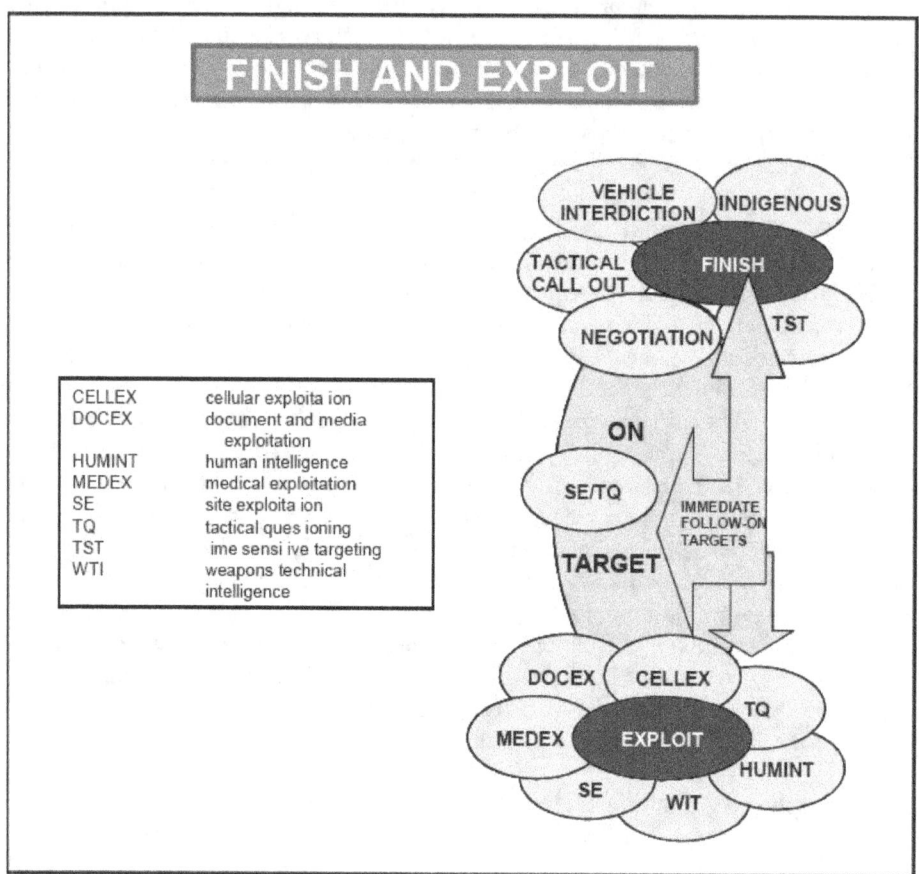

Figure VI-6. Finish and Exploit

(c) The second part of the F3EAD - Analyze step involves templating network activities on the ground so that ISR assets can be focused at the right time and place. The key output in templating is the modified intelligence synchronization matrix, which is intended to synchronize intelligence asset collection with the AtN activities of maneuver units. Templating actions will also assist efforts in identifying when friendly forces should initiate AtN. **As an analytical function, templating occurs early (and is conducted continuously) throughout the F3EAD process.** Initially it uses the minimal amount of information that is developed on a network's activities to develop a logical template to focus intelligence collection to further develop the network. The template is a starting point that is subject to updating on a regular basis. The intent of network templating is to detail the process of the threat's critical capabilities so that analysts and action officers can understand critical requirements and critical vulnerabilities at the lowest level possible. It is the first step in synchronizing the information gathering that leads to decision making in the JTF's fight. It begins with identifying the major activities of the network and laying them out on the ground. Then templating seeks to identify and list the enemy's observable indicators – those enemy activities that we can see and measure. The last step is in identifying those areas where friendly collection capabilities can detect enemy activity or individuals and have the greatest negative impact on the enemy if interdicted – their critical vulnerabilities – which are designated as NAIs. Combining analysis of critical requirements, observable indicators, and critical vulnerabilities is the basis for the development of the intelligence collection plan.

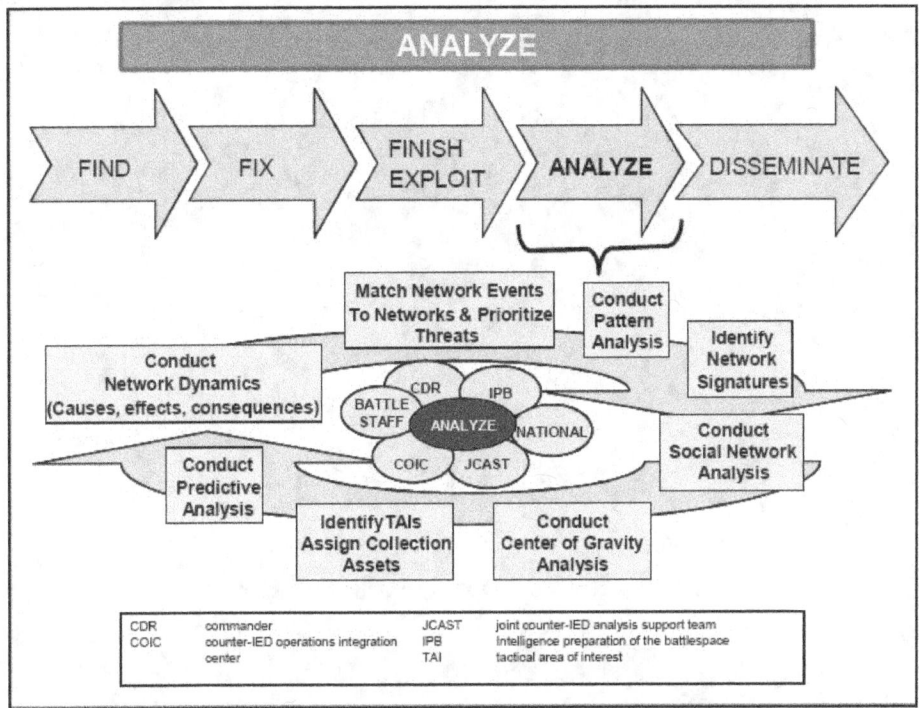

Figure VI-7. Analyze

(6) **F3EAD – Disseminate**. Dissemination is a continuous process. The success or failure of an AtN strategy is directly dependent on the command's ability to "push/pull" information among from all the participants in a timely manner. This requires a robust communications architecture that connects all the participants in the AtN process, data storage and processing hardware and software and well thought out procedures establishing reporting responsibilities and formats. Participants must establish and routinely update their information requirements. The exact communications architecture will be determined by the CJTF but should be flexible enough to include a multinational, partner nation capability. The J-2 ensures that the commanders and staffs receive time sensitive information and intelligence products in a format that best supports the commander's decision making.

Intentionally Blank

CHAPTER VII
ASSESS

"The (friendly) network expanded to include more groups, including unconventional actors. It valued competency above all else — including rank. It sought a clear and evolving definition of the problem and constantly self-analyzed, revisiting its structure, aims, and processes, as well as those of the enemy. Most importantly, the network continually grew the capacity to inform itself."

General (Retired) Stanley McChrystal,
Foreign Policy,
March/April 2011

1. Introduction

a. Commanders and staffs at all echelons need to be able to measure the effectiveness of their operations in order to refine subsequent operations. MOE and MOP need to be determined and resources allocated to collect data against indicators of effectiveness.

b. Assessment is continuously monitoring and evaluating the current situation and the progress of an operation. In AtN, commanders and staffs must continuously assess the impacts their operations have on the network, the population, and the threat. They must look "three moves ahead" to consider the second and third order effects their actions may have on their envisioned outcomes and how those actions will impact both the threat and friendly networks, and the population.

c. Continuous comprehensive holistic assessment is critical to the success of an operation. Apparent initial success can lead to disastrous consequences without a well organized assessment plan. The threat network adapts and these adaptations must be taken into account when executing the AtN plan.

2. Assessment

a. **Assessment is a process that measures progress** of the joint force toward mission accomplishment. Commanders continuously assess the OE and the progress of operations, compare them to their initial vision and intent, and adjust operations based on their assessment. Staffs monitor key factors that can influence operations and provide the commander with timely information needed for decisions. Successful commanders devise ways to continually update their understanding of the OE and assess their progress toward achieving assigned objectives without mistaking activity for progress.

b. Assessment begins during mission analysis when the commander and staff consider what to measure and how to measure it **to determine progress toward accomplishing tasks, creating effects, or achieving objectives**. During planning and preparing for an operation, for example, the staff assesses the JTF's ability to execute the plan based on available resources and changing conditions in the OE. As the operational approach emerges during design, the CJTF and staff begin to devise indicators of progress that will be incorporated in the plan or order and used during execution. Certain assessment indicators act as triggers during the operation to help the CJTF determine the necessity to revise the original design.

c. During execution, assessment continually monitors progress toward accomplishing tasks, creating effects, and achieving objectives. Assessment actions and measures help commanders adjust operations and resources as required, determine when to execute branches and sequels, and make other critical decisions to ensure current and future operations remain aligned with the mission and military end state. Normally, the JTF J-3, assisted by the J-2, is responsible for coordinating assessment activities. The chief of staff facilitates the assessment process and ensures it is incorporated into the headquarters' battle rhythm. Various elements of the CJTF's staff use assessment results to adjust both current operations and future planning.

d. Actions by friendly forces, the HN and population, adversary, and neutral diplomatic, informational, and economic entities in the OE can affect military actions and objectives. When relevant to the mission, the CJTF must determine how to assess results of these actions. This typically requires collaboration with other USG agencies and multinational partners—preferably within a common, accepted process—in the interest of unified action. Many of these organizations may be outside the CJTF's authority. Accordingly, the CJTF should grant some joint force organizations authority for direct coordination with key outside organizations — such as USG elements from the Departments of State or Homeland Security, national intelligence agencies, intelligence sources in other nations, and supporting combatant commands—to the extent necessary to ensure timely and accurate assessments.

3. Measures of Effectiveness and Measures of Performance

a. Assessment entails three distinct tasks: continuously **monitoring** the situation and the progress of the operations; **evaluating** the operation against established criteria to determine progress relative to the mission, objectives, and end states; and reframing if necessary. Criteria can be expressed as MOEs and MOPs. **A *MOE* is a criterion used to assess changes in system behavior, capability, or OE that is tied to measuring the attainment of an end state, an objective, or the creation of an effect. It measures the relevance of actions being performed. A *MOP* is a criterion used to assess friendly actions that is tied to measuring task accomplishment.**

b. Many aspects of operations are quantifiable. Examples include movement rates, fuel consumption, and weapons effects. While not easy, assessing physical aspects of joint operations can be straightforward. However, the dynamic interaction among friendly forces, adaptable networks, and the relevant population make assessing many aspects of AtN difficult. For example, assessing the results of planned actions to change a group of people to support their central government is very challenging. As planners assess complex human behaviors like this, they draw on multiple sources across the OE, including both analytical and subjective measures which support a more informed assessment.

c. In AtN, metrics such as BDA can be easily determined; however, the effects of that operation on the attitudes of local villagers, leadership, and other members of the threat network are much harder to quantify. Assessment must always look at the operation's effectiveness in terms of supporting friendly networks; influencing neutral networks; and, neutralizing threat networks.

Intentionally Blank

APPENDIX A
INFORMATION OPERATIONS

"...there were other combatants circling the battlefield. Mirroring our movements, competing with us, were insurgent leaders. Connected to, and often directly dispatched by, the Taliban's leadership in Pakistan, they moved through the same areas of Afghanistan. They made shows of public support for Taliban shadow governors, motivated tattered ranks, recruited new troops, distributed funds, reviewed tactics, and updated strategy. And when the sky above became too thick with our drones, their leaders used cell phones and the Internet to issue orders and rally their fighters. They aimed to keep dispersed insurgent cells motivated, strategically wired, and continually informed, all without a rigid — or targetable — chain of command.

While a deeply flawed insurgent force in many ways, the Taliban is a uniquely 21st-century threat. Enjoying the traditional insurgent advantage of living amid a population closely tied to them by history and culture, they also leverage sophisticated technology that connects remote valleys and severe mountains instantaneously — and allows them to project their message worldwide, unhindered by time or filters."

GENERAL (Retired) Stanley McChrystal,
Foreign Policy,
March/April 2011

1. Introduction

Winning the battle of the narrative and securing the support of the population is essential to the success of any stability operation and is an integral part of AtN planning and execution. The enemy will often have a well orchestrated propaganda campaign to support their operations and counter friendly efforts. Modern technology provides our enemies with the capability to pass on information, coordinate, exchange ideas, and synchronize their actions instantaneously. When employing IO in support of AtN, commanders and staffs must integrate a wide variety of capabilities (electronic warfare (EW), computer network operations (CNO), military deception (MILDEC), MISO, and operations security (OPSEC)) into the overall campaign plan to achieve desired and measurable effects on the enemy's leadership, personnel, information, information systems, and other audiences. When combined with other enablers, IO contributes to shaping the OE by accomplishing the following:

    a. **Destroy,** i.e., damaging a system or entity so badly that it cannot perform any function or be restored to a usable condition without being entirely rebuilt.

    b. **Disrupt,** i.e., breaking or interrupting the flow of information.

    c. **Degrade,** i.e., reducing the effectiveness or efficiency of enemy C2 or communications systems, and information collection efforts or means. IO can also degrade the morale of a unit, reduce the target's worth or value, or reduce the quality of enemy decisions and actions.

d. **Deny**, i.e., preventing the enemy from accessing and using critical information, systems, and services.

e. **Deceive**, i.e., causing a person to believe what is not true. MILDEC seeks to mislead enemy decision makers by manipulating their perception of reality.

f. **Exploit**, i.e., gaining access to enemy C2 systems to collect information or to plant false or misleading information.

g. **Influence**, i.e., causing others to behave in a manner favorable to US forces.

h. **Protect**, i.e., taking action to guard against espionage or capture of sensitive equipment and information.

i. **Detect**, i.e., discovering or discerning the existence, presence, or fact of an intrusion into information systems.

j. **Restore**, i.e., bringing information and information systems back to their original state.

k. **Respond**, i.e., reacting quickly to an enemy's or others' IO attack or intrusion.

2. Information Operations Integration into the F3EAD Cycle

a. There are specific IO related actions that take place during each step of the F3EAD cycle. These actions are designed to ensure that IO actively contributes to the operation and is positioned to exploit success or mitigate potential damage. In stability operations, IO must not only be tailored to very specific targets but also have sufficient flexibility and agility to rapidly adjust to environmental changes brought about by friendly actions.

b. IO supports the F3EAD process as follows:

(1) **Find**. This step includes defining the network, atmospherics, and target audiences (enemy, populace, etc.). IO activities will be adapted to the target audience. Information derived from all source intelligence using traditional (HUMINT, SIGINT, etc.), non-traditional sources (law enforcement professionals, civil affairs, human environment teams), and previous reporting (patrols, key leader engagements) will be used to define the network. During this step the command's cultural advisor and IO planner will assist the analysis effort.

(2) **Fix**. During this step, specific IO objectives and tasks are developed for the identified target sets; and, appropriate IO capabilities are identified to achieve the desired effects based on previously identified vulnerabilities. IO planners will identify the most efficient vehicles (KLE, radio/TV broadcasts, handouts, etc) for immediate information

release and exploitation and/or mitigation, as required. Talking points for contacts with the populace and leadership will also be prepared.

(3) **Finish**. During this step, IO capabilities (electronic warfare, MISO, computer network operations) execute tasks in support of the plan's objectives in order to shape the environment. Some of the essential considerations in this step include:

(a) Identify and be prepared to mitigate the enemy's capabilities on target by disrupting or deny them the use of their messaging capabilities.

(b) Record the scene – a video record is a powerful tool for mitigating enemy propaganda.

(c) Be prepared to conduct mitigation utilizing Commander's Emergency Response Program funds in case of physical damage, talking points and press releases to provide the facts and counter enemy propaganda.

(4) **Exploit**. During this step, the IO team seeks to ensure that the desired effects are achieved and to develop the situation to identify additional opportunities for exploitation. The unit will conduct KLEs and utilize all available assets to achieve the required objectives including HN assets, public affairs, civil affairs, and MISO teams. Based on on-site collection, the IO team will adjust the IO effort accordingly to reduce the enemy's freedom of action and the effects of enemy propaganda. Note: while IO resources can influence a broad range of activities, in a stability operation, where you are attempting to separate the enemy from the populace, the majority of the IO efforts will be at the tactical level by small teams and units interacting with the local population.

(5) **Analyze**. Assessment is an on-going process. The IO team must develop MOE and MOP that are tailored to the local, national and regional political and social environments. Whatever IO plan is developed must be capable of making quick adjustments to a rapidly changing situation on the ground. The enemy must be constantly monitored to see what spin they are putting on events and appropriate responses must be crafted and implemented. The IO team must also assess the performance of the friendly force's IO resources in achieving the desired effects and adjust accordingly. The question should always be: "How can we improve our performance?"

(6) **Disseminate**. Based on the assessment, the IO team should continue to engage the populace, reengage key leaders, and identify future engagement opportunities. The IO team should also use the results of the assessment to adjust the command's IO objectives and tasks. IO engagement is a continuous process that maintains pressure on the enemy and either denies them the opportunity to negatively influence the operational and tactical environment, or mitigates the effect of enemy propaganda.

Intentionally Blank

APPENDIX B
ATTACK THE NETWORK FRAMEWORK

This Appendix focuses on understanding threat networks, organizing friendly resources for the fight, and threat network engagement by lethal and nonlethal means. The "AtN Framework" illustrated in Figure B-1 provides the basic methodology and steps for planning, executing, and assessing AtN activities in the context of joint operation/ campaign planning. Figures B-2 through B-11 expand on the Figure B-1 tasks common to any joint operation (shown in purple) and the focused tasks (shown in green) to provide a quick reference for planners and operators on AtN tasks. They assist in identifying the wide variety of resources and enablers that are available to AtN planners and operators at all echelons and how those assets fit into the overall joint operation/campaign planning process.

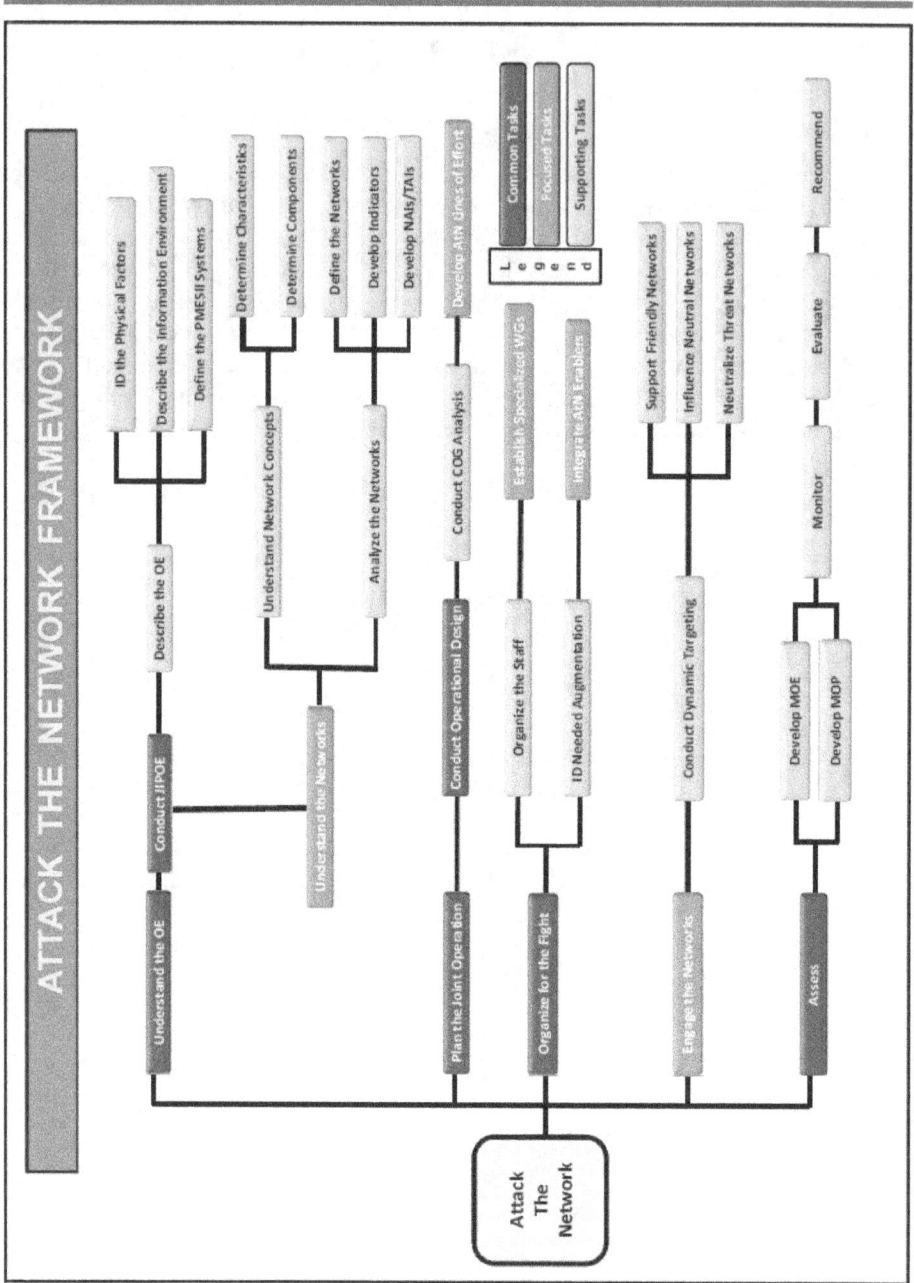

Figure B-1. Attack the Network Framework

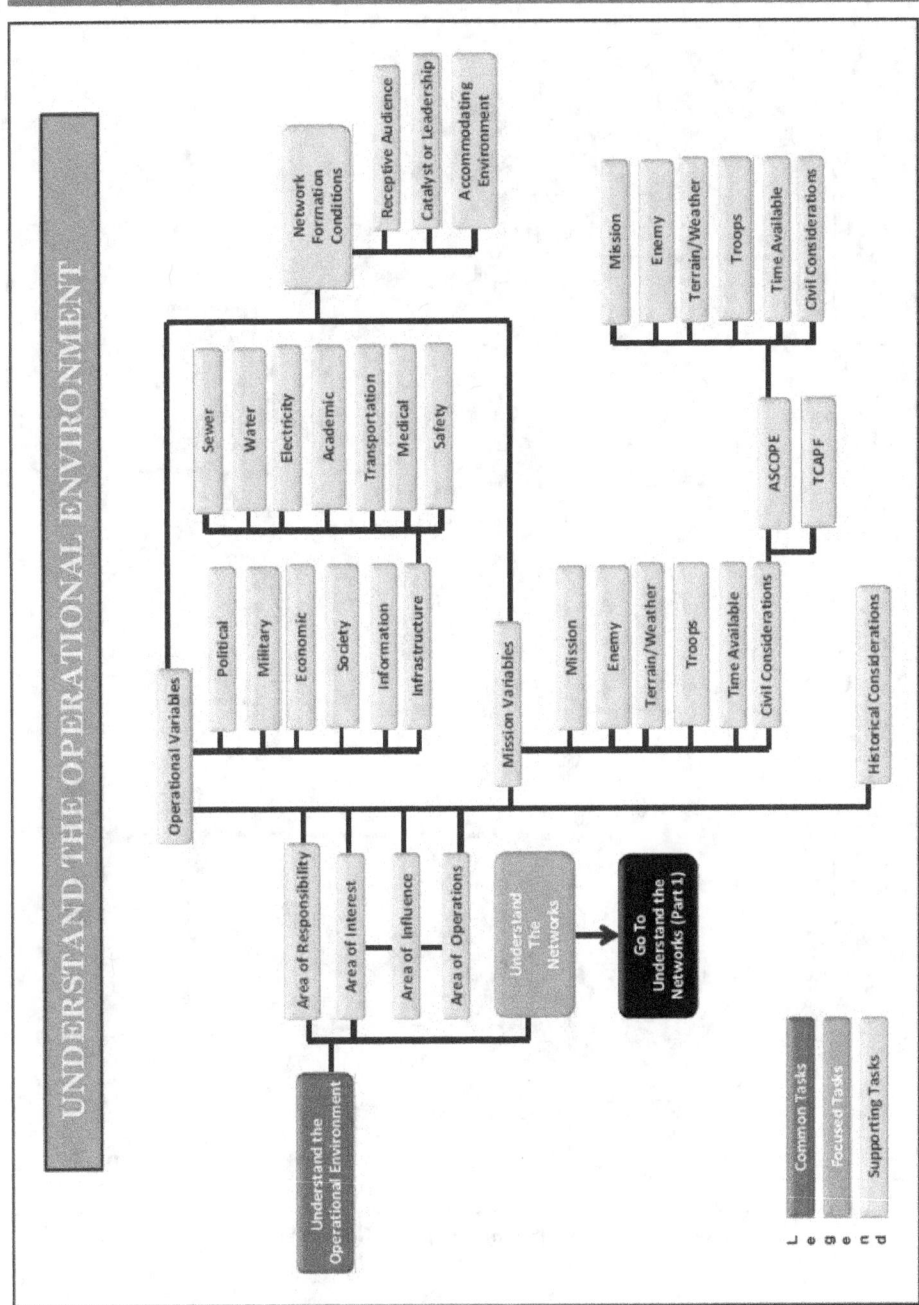

Figure B-2. Understand the Operational Environment

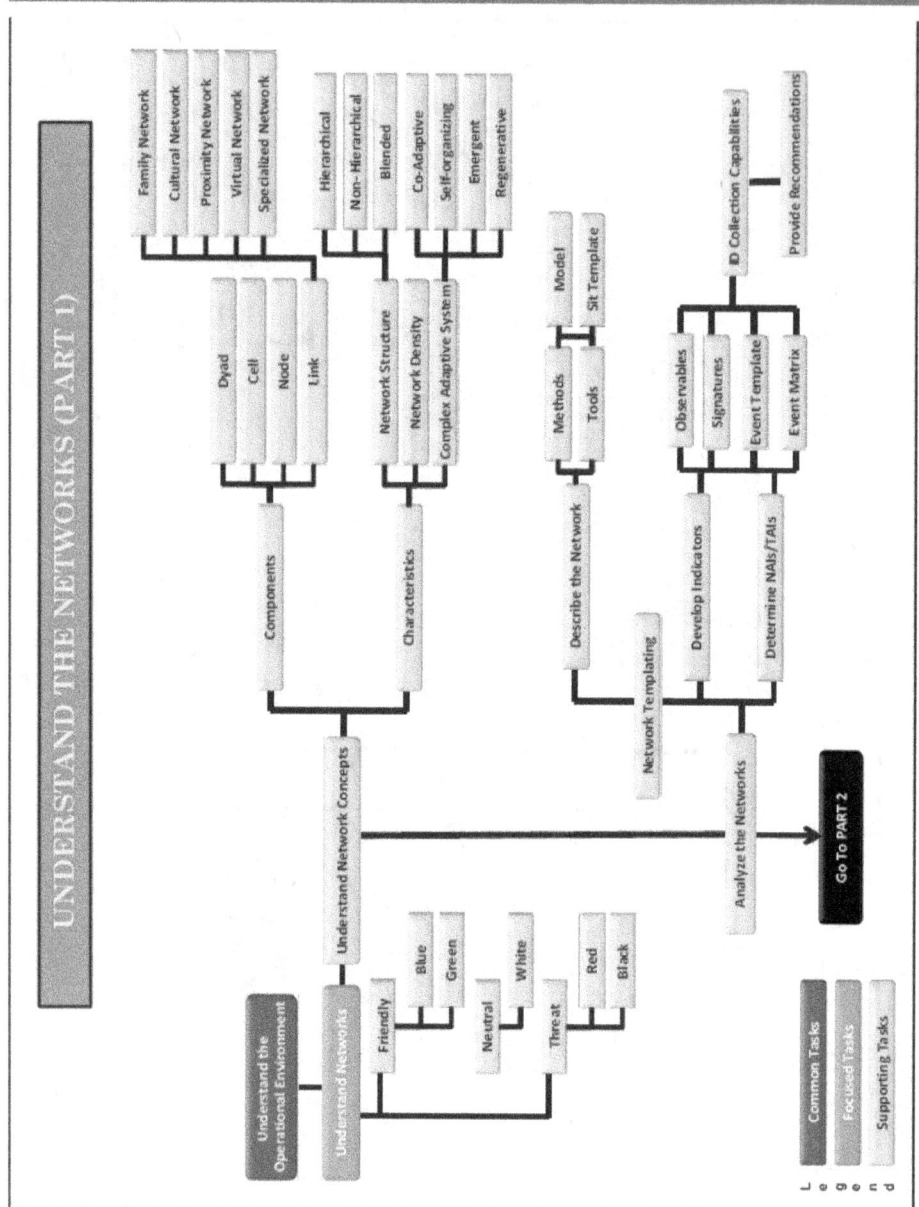

Figure B-3. Understanding the Network (Part 1)

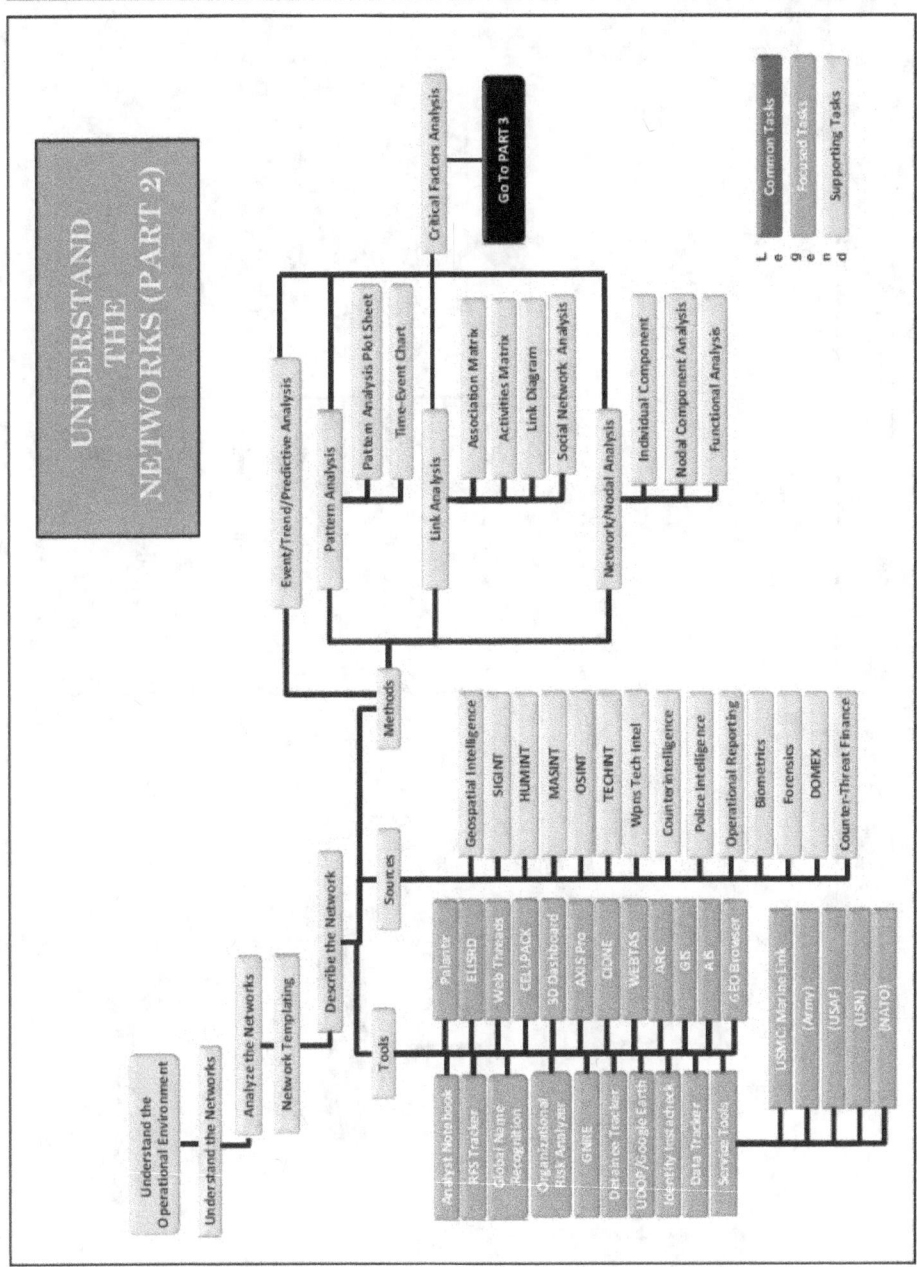

Figure B-4. Understanding the Networks (Part 2)

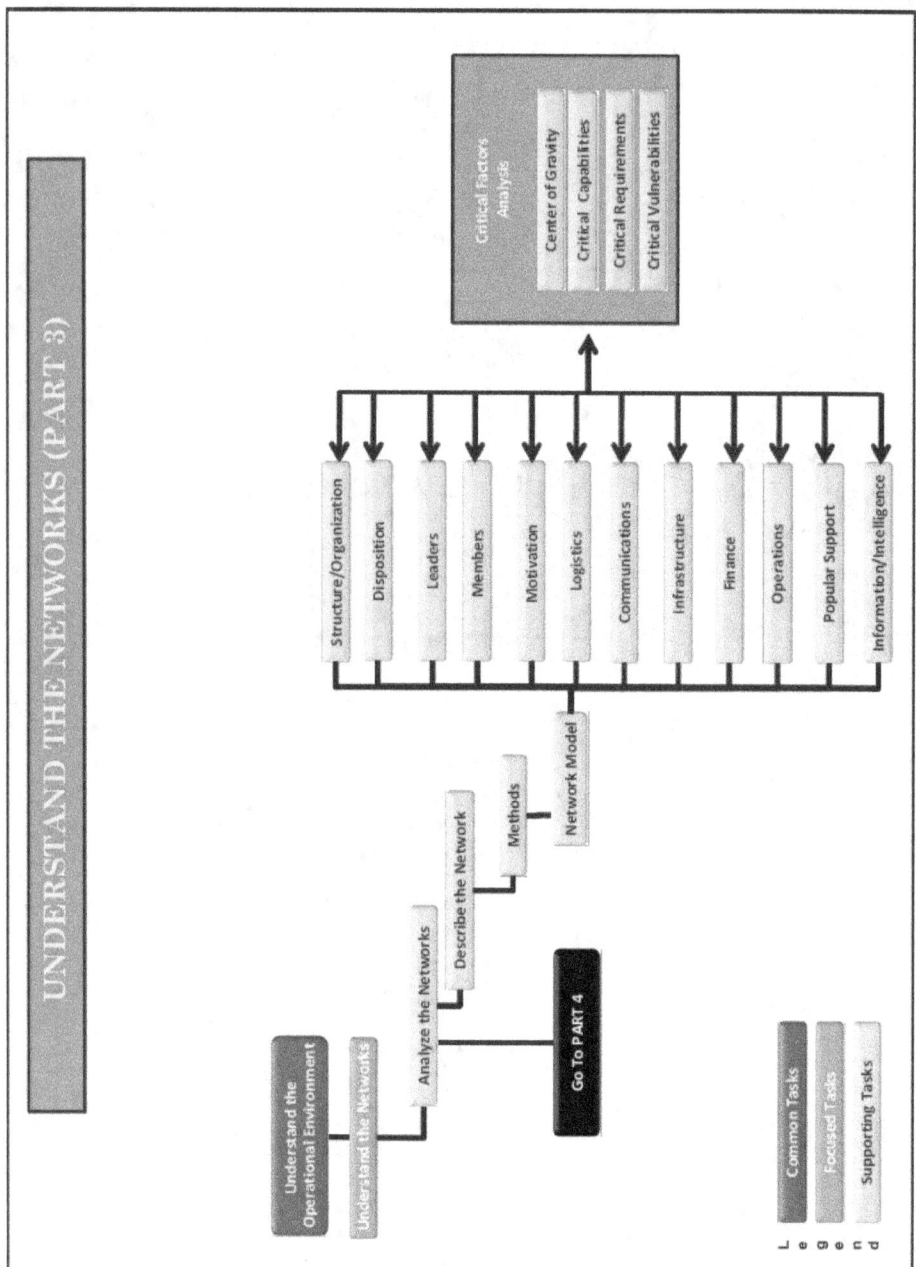

Figure B-5. Understanding the Networks (Part 3)

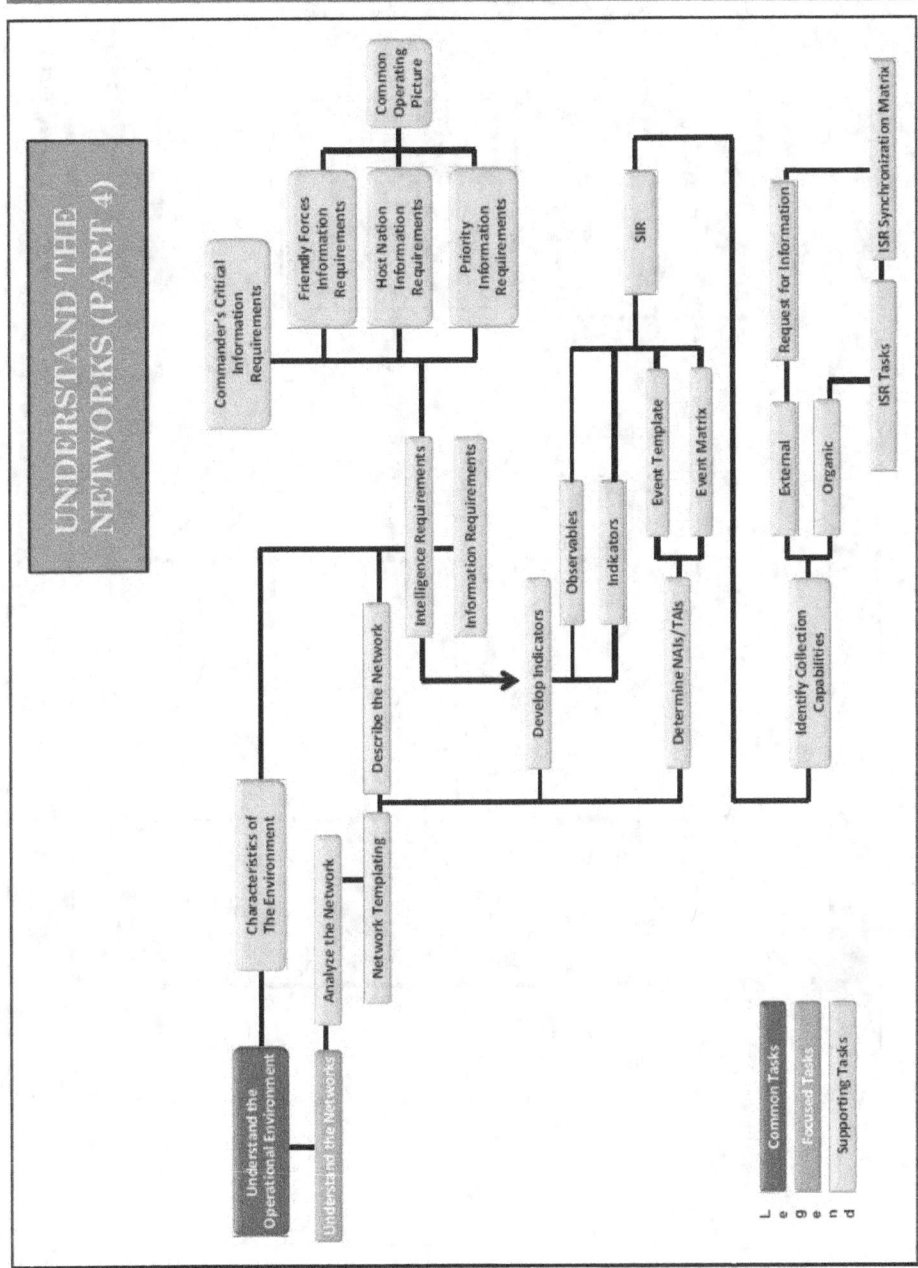

Figure B-6. Understanding the Networks (Part 4)

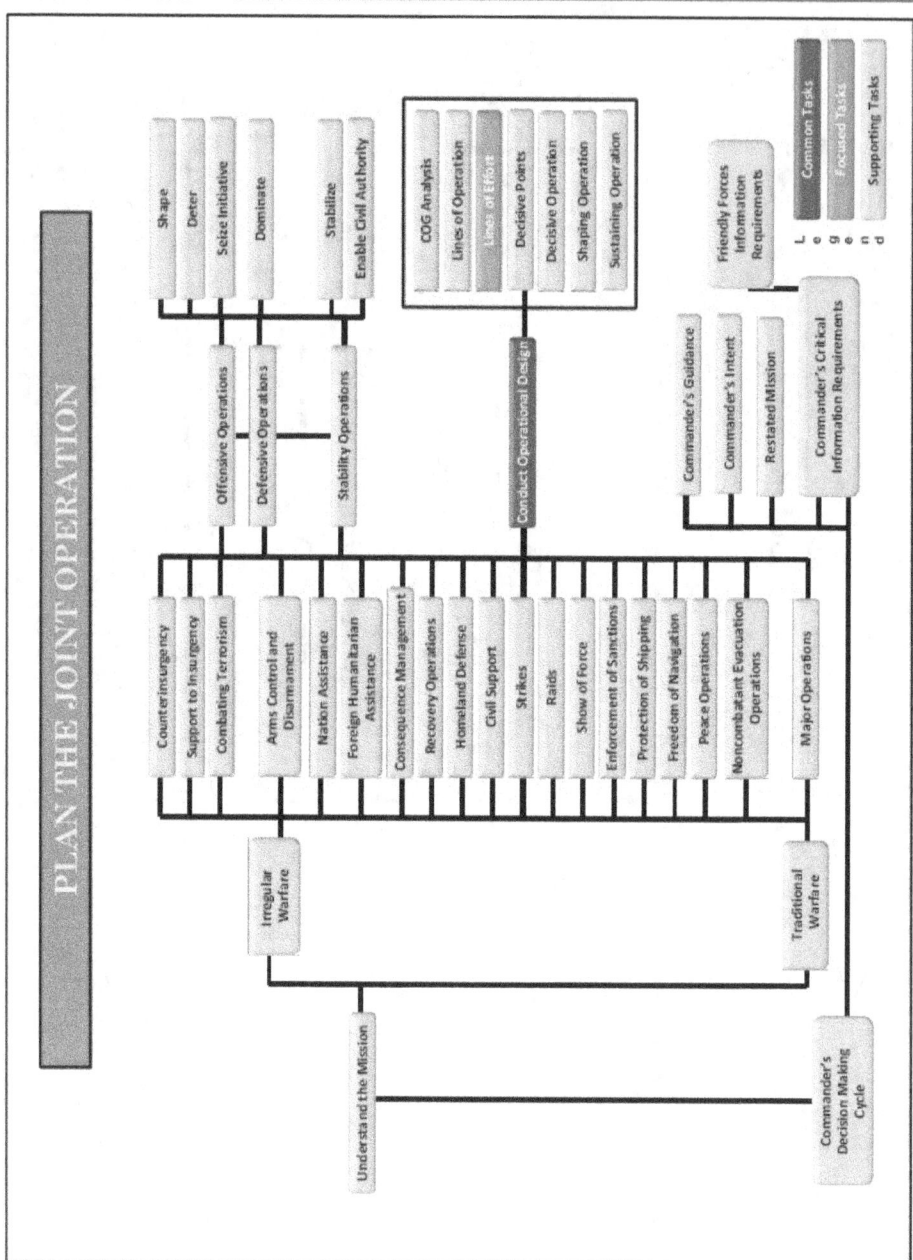

Figure B-7. Plan the Joint Operation

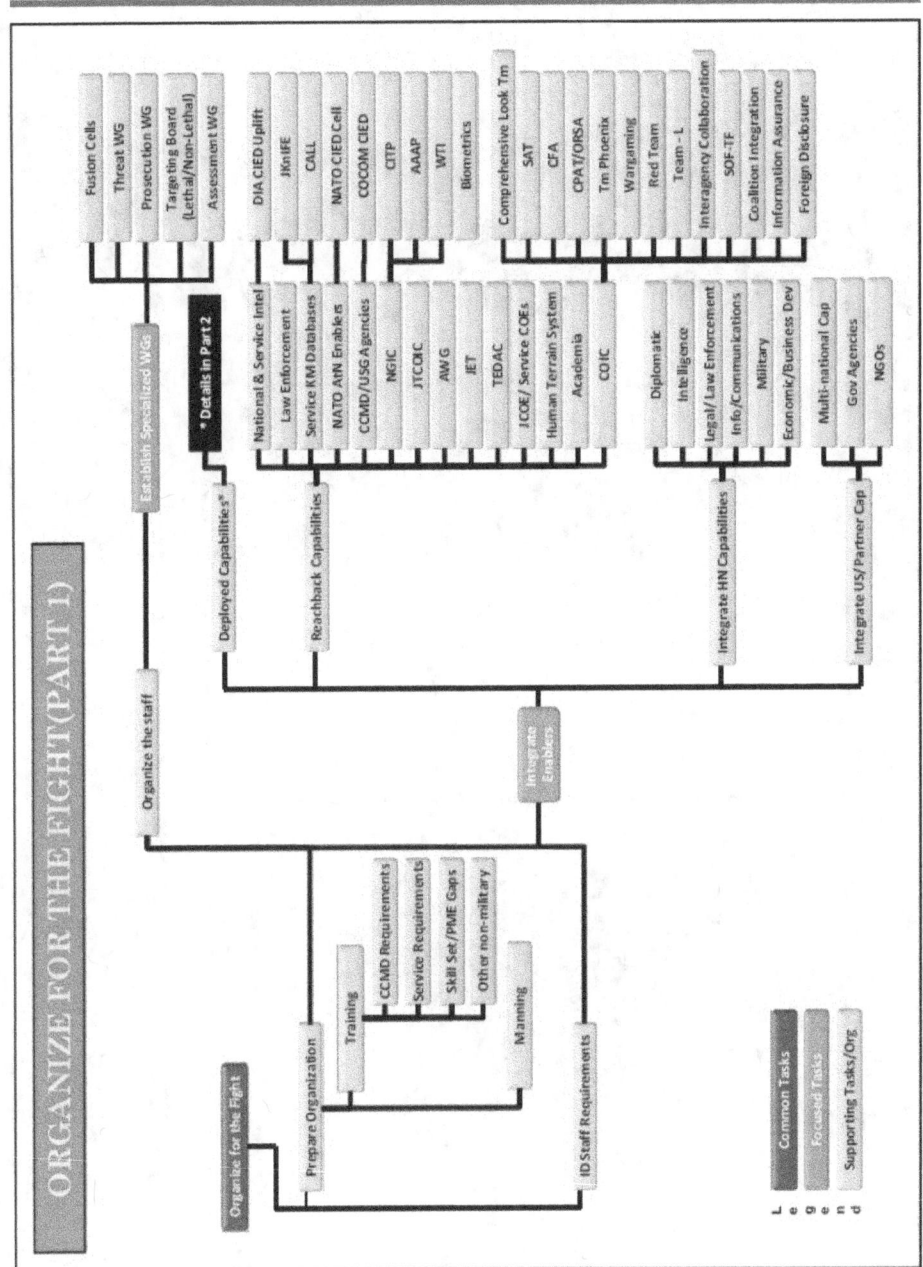

Figure B-8. Organize for the Fight (Part 1)

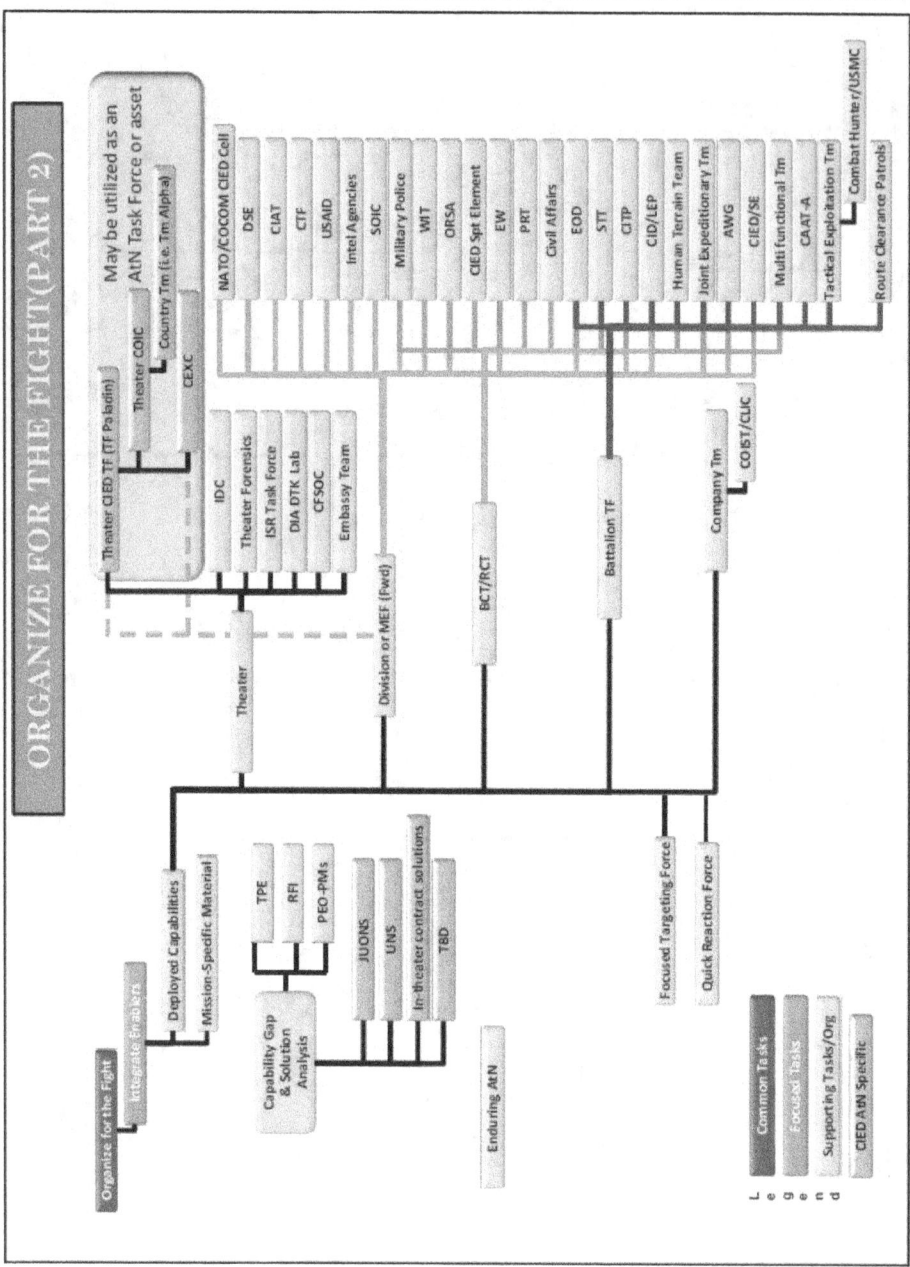

Figure B-9. Organize for the Fight (Part 2)

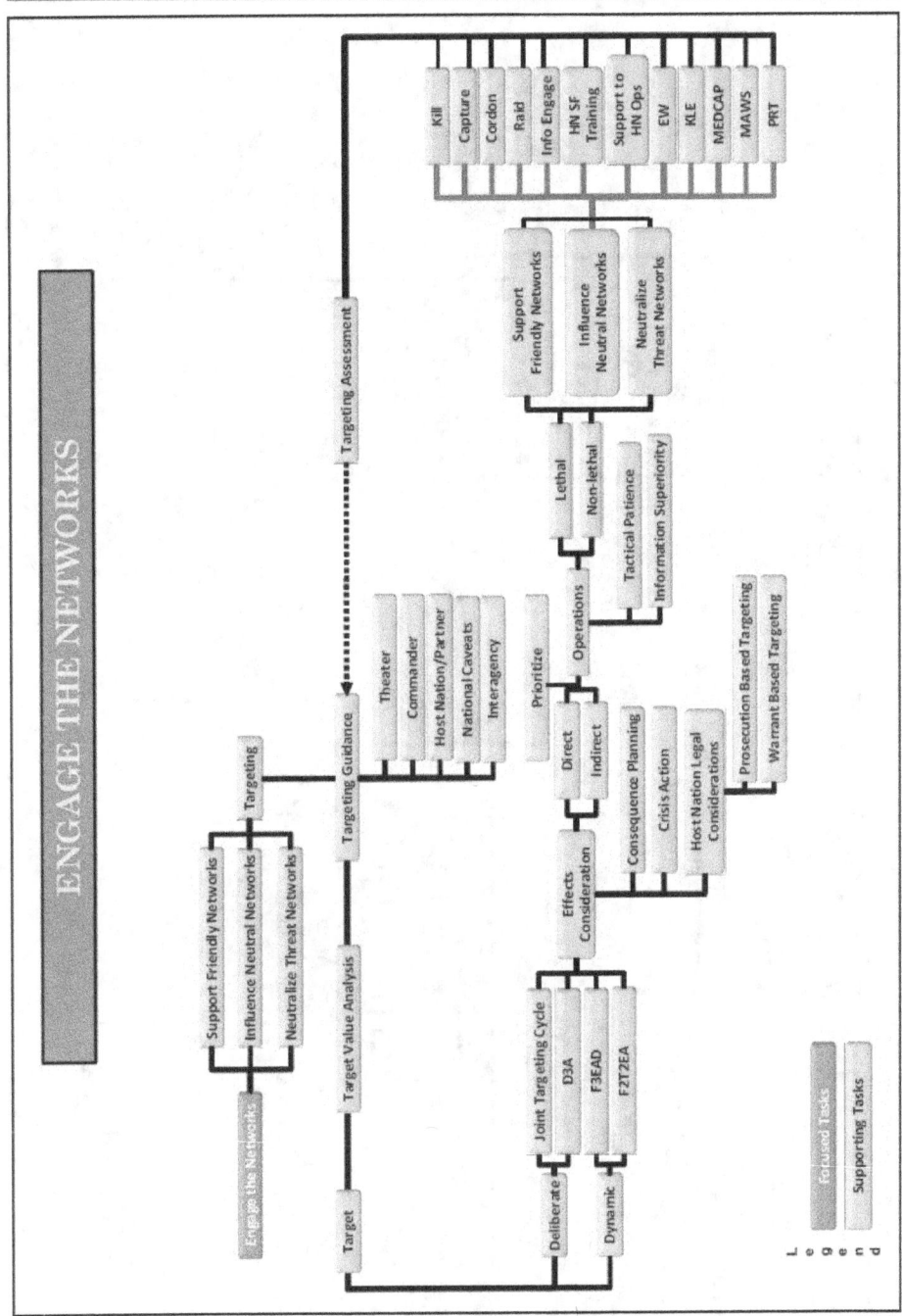

Figure B-10. Engage the Networks

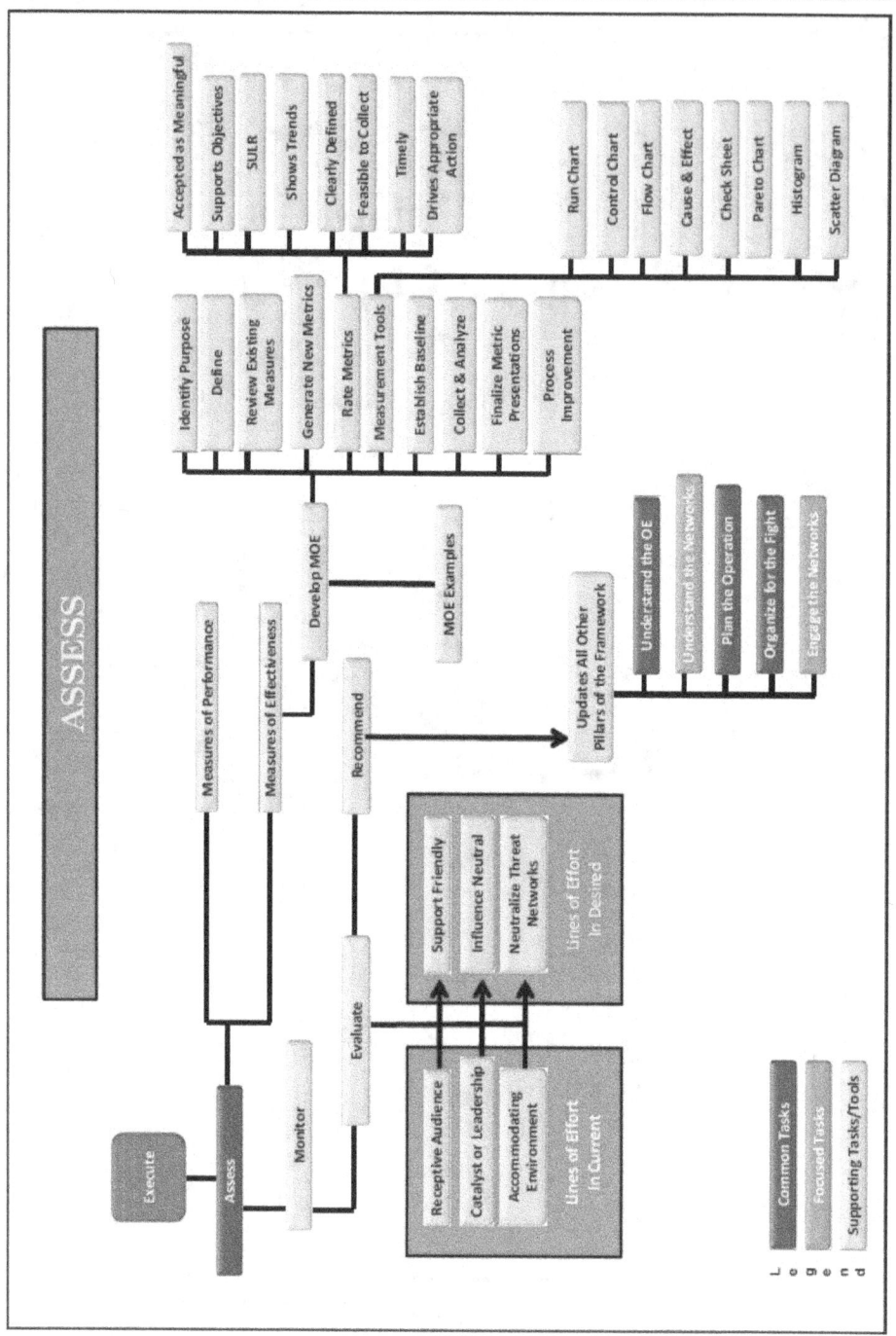

Figure B-11. Assess

APPENDIX C
TRANSNATIONAL CRIMINAL GANGS

"Whereas in decades past, criminal organizations were largely domestic or regional in scope, and due to their centralized nature the arrest of a single key member was sometimes enough to dismantle them, today's global criminal syndicates operate transnationally and are comprised of loose networks that cooperate intermittently but maintain their independence. And unlike their predecessors, they employ sophisticated technology and financial savvy."

GEN James Jones
October 2010

"Criminal organizations and networks based in North America, Western Europe, China, Colombia, Israel, Japan, Mexico, Nigeria, and Russia will expand the scale and scope of their activities. They will form loose alliances with one another, with smaller criminal entrepreneurs, and with insurgent movements for specific operations. They will corrupt leaders of unstable, economically fragile, or failing states, insinuate themselves into troubled banks and businesses, and cooperate with insurgent political movements to control substantial geographic areas."

National Intelligence Council,
Global Trends 2015

1. Introduction

a. Transnational organized criminal activity is considered as one of the major threats to human security, impeding the social, economic, political and cultural development of societies worldwide. By the late 1990s, international law enforcement criminal analysts began to recognize that criminal organizations were rapidly losing their hierarchical structural in favor of loose, temporary networks (embracing local, just-in-time, *ad hoc* networking principles) that linked criminals with each other and with those in positions of political and economic power. Today, transnational organized crime is estimated to be over a $2 trillion industry that spans five continents. Network structures offer criminals a number of advantages as discussed below.

b. Criminal networks operate clandestinely. One of the most significant points about networks, however, is that they are not immediately and obviously visible. Criminal networks can hide behind various licit activities, can operate with a lower degree of formality than other types of organization, and can maintain a profile that does not bring them to the attention of law enforcement.

c. Criminal networks are inherently dispersed without readily obvious centers of gravity. With a minimal physical infrastructure, criminal networks can easily migrate to areas of lower risk when pressure from law enforcement increases.

d.   Criminal networks can exploit differences in national laws and regulations making it difficult for any one nation's law enforcement agencies to effectively interdict them.

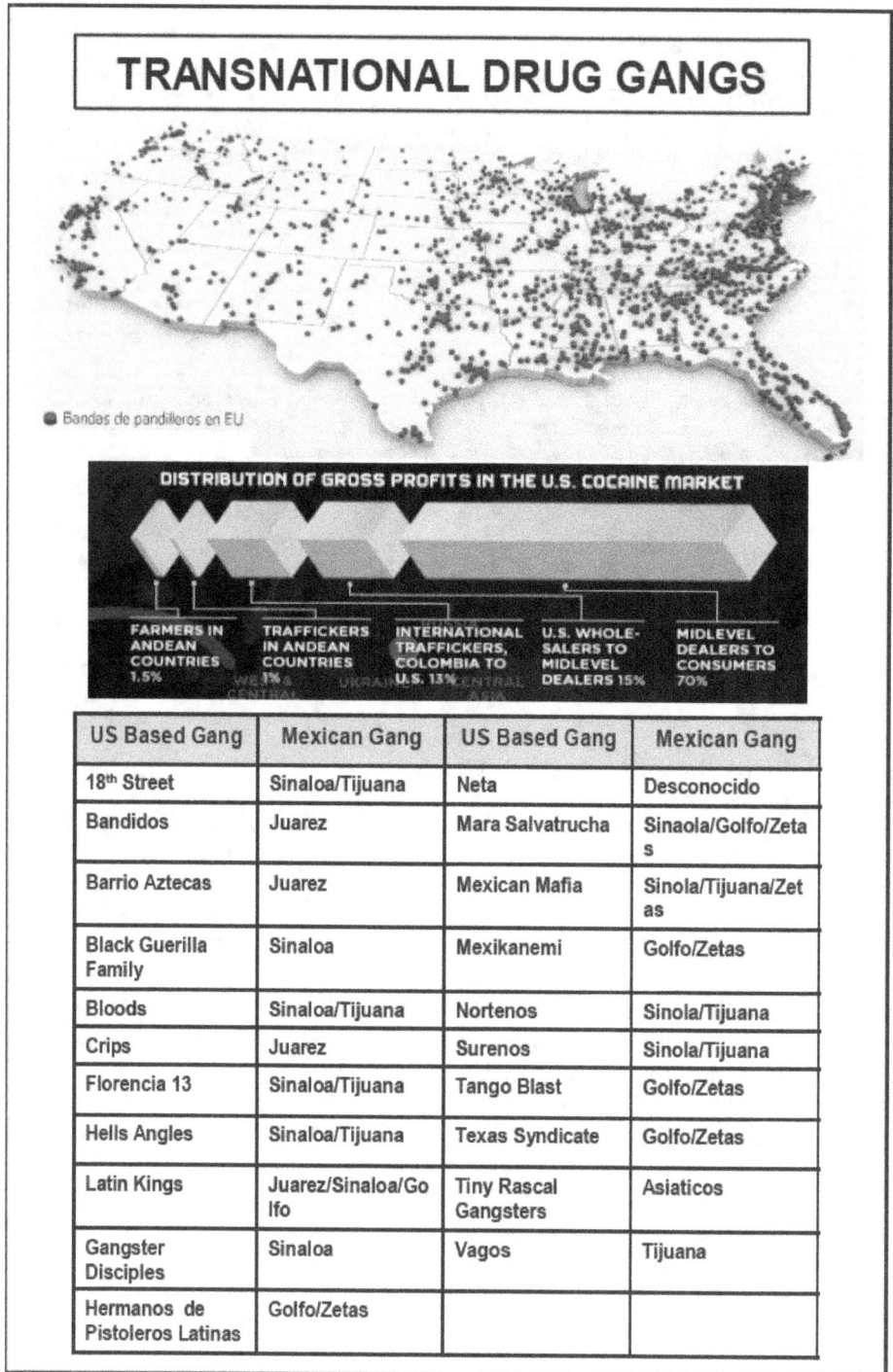

TRANSNATIONAL DRUG GANGS

● Bandas de pandilleros en EU

DISTRIBUTION OF GROSS PROFITS IN THE U.S. COCAINE MARKET

| FARMERS IN ANDEAN COUNTRIES 1.5% | TRAFFICKERS IN ANDEAN COUNTRIES 1% | INTERNATIONAL TRAFFICKERS, COLOMBIA TO U.S. 13% | U.S. WHOLE-SALERS TO MIDLEVEL DEALERS 15% | MIDLEVEL DEALERS TO CONSUMERS 70% |

US Based Gang	Mexican Gang	US Based Gang	Mexican Gang
18th Street	Sinaloa/Tijuana	Neta	Desconocido
Bandidos	Juarez	Mara Salvatrucha	Sinaola/Golfo/Zetas
Barrio Aztecas	Juarez	Mexican Mafia	Sinola/Tijuana/Zetas
Black Guerilla Family	Sinaloa	Mexikanemi	Golfo/Zetas
Bloods	Sinaloa/Tijuana	Nortenos	Sinola/Tijuana
Crips	Juarez	Surenos	Sinola/Tijuana
Florencia 13	Sinaloa/Tijuana	Tango Blast	Golfo/Zetas
Hells Angles	Sinaloa/Tijuana	Texas Syndicate	Golfo/Zetas
Latin Kings	Juarez/Sinaloa/Golfo	Tiny Rascal Gangsters	Asiaticos
Gangster Disciples	Sinaloa	Vagos	Tijuana
Hermanos de Pistoleros Latinas	Golfo/Zetas		

Figure C-1. Transnational Drug Gangs

e. Criminal networks are resilient. The inner core leadership that directs the network is often based on bonding mechanisms including ethnicity, family, and common experience. These mechanisms create high degrees of trust and cohesion and makes infiltration or defection unlikely. The network's rank and file or periphery may not share the common bonds of the inner core but do provide the network with the ability to operate (geographically and socially) well beyond the core's reach.

f. Criminal networks form cooperative alliances to facilitate their operations. Thus Colombia cocaine was distributed in (or shipped through) Russia in exchange for guns. In the US, Mexican and US based gangs facilitate the hemisphere wide drug trade (Figure C-1). These transnational affiliations have tremendous financial rewards for US distributors while providing producers with a reliable market for their product. **These strategic alliances or networks of cooperation can also have a profound effect on regional stability and security issues.** Criminal networks transcend physical, geographic and societal borders into the worlds of government, business and finance. The criminal networks ability to freely operate in the legitimate society increases the likelihood of their survival despite the best efforts of law enforcement. The criminal networks especially focus on members of law enforcement agencies and government officials exchanging information and protection for money. In the case of politicians, the exchange can be about personal gain but might also be about assistance in mobilizing the vote, support for electoral campaigns, criminal assistance in providing information about political opponents, or even in intimidating and, in extreme cases, eliminating political enemies. In the case of law enforcement personnel or members of the judiciary, the aim of the criminals is to minimize risks by undermining enforcement efforts, suborning the judicial process, and neutralizing the criminal justice system.

g. Cooperation among various criminal organizations often involves far more than transferring the proceeds/products of their respective criminal enterprises. As part of their effort to stay ahead of law enforcement, criminal organizations will often share technical resources. For example, the Australian Comanchero biker gang, which imports cocaine from the Sinaloa cartel, has been provided with untraceable, encrypted BlackBerry devices by the Mexican cartel. Because the BlackBerry encryption cannot be cracked by Australian law enforcement, both gangs now have secure communications for the conduct of their activities.

2. Criminal Networks and Militant Political Movements

a. In theory militant transnational political movements and criminal networks have different objectives. In reality political militants need to finance their activities and often carry out criminal activities to do so either by cooperating with existing criminal elements or forming their own. Criminal networks also sometimes find it useful to align with militant transnational movements to gain protection and extend their networks. Mutual cooperation is more common in those situations where the groups are connected by shared nationality, ethnicity, or religious beliefs. Their identity networks – based on preexisting communication networks, shared values, and mutual trust – provide settings conducive to collaborative political criminal activities. A second condition is the occurrence of intra- or inter-state armed conflict. War provides incentives and opportunities for crime, especially weapons smuggling, which facilitates collaboration with militants. Third is the interaction of market opportunities and constraints. Constraints encourage establishment of criminal-militant "marriages of convenience." Cooperative relations reduce constraints on criminal markets. Militants and criminals establish alliances to remove obstacles and expand the possibilities of both power- and profit- seeking. The best example of this alliance is that of the FARC terrorists who forged alliances of convenience with drug dealers (drug producers and traffickers who decided to locate processing facilities in FARC-controlled areas and relied on guerrillas to maintain order and security) in exchange paying protection taxes, thereby not only gaining funds for their insurgency but also turning it into a long-term business activity. Similarly, the Kurdish PKK, which seeks the independence of Kurdistan, is heavily involved in the drug trade to finance their operations.

    b. A detailed JIPOE should consider the possibility of varying degrees of cooperation between the threat networks operating in the operational area. While there may be a principle focus for friendly AtN operations, the JTF should be prepared to focus AtN operations on other major networks in the operational area if they are cooperating with and contributing to the overall capabilities of the principle network.

3. Joint Intelligence Preparation of the Operational Environment Development

    Military analysts are not normally qualified to conduct in-depth analyses of complex civilian criminal networks. They require assistance from interagency and other law enforcement professionals to help define the problem and its nuances. In the development of the JIPOE, analysts must be aware of the wide range of regional security threats posed by transnational gangs which can range from corrupting government officials (which undermines the people's confidence in their legal system encouraging unrest) to co-opting the authority of the existing government (leading to open warfare in the streets). Targeting these networks requires a comprehensive JIPOE that examines, in detail, the intricate links between the network and the societies in which the network operates. The JIPOE must include a detailed societal analysis ranging from the effect of local economic conditions on acceptance of criminal activity to the state of rule of law initiatives on the prosecution of criminal activity for the targeted countries in the region. This information is normally obtained from USG, regional, HN and governmental and civilian sources and will require the assistance of SMEs to frame the material for the military audience. The analysis is complicated by the fact that there is little information on the decision making processes that govern how these networks function. It is not always clear where the network starts and ends and whether an apparently successful attack has actually achieved its objective. JIPOE analysts can employ a variety of link analysis techniques to identify and assess the relationships among the people and organizations that constitute the network. Such network visualization can lead to the identification of the key individuals and nodes and the gateways the network uses to access the society. Identification of these individuals and structures makes it easier to identify potential vulnerabilities that can be attacked. JIPOE analysts need to be familiar with the many international, regional, and national law enforcement and regulatory agencies that have jurisdiction in this area and which, after appropriate coordination, can act as information sources on threat network activities. One useful tool in assessing the transnational organized criminal threat is the United Nation's *Serious Organized Crime Assessment Handbook* which provides tools for assessing immediate threats, the direction of current trends and likely future challenges.

4. Network Attack Considerations

a. Attacking transnational criminal HVIs and structural nodes is only part of the equation. It is also critical to target the boundaries, either from one network to another or from the criminal world to the legitimate world. Particularly important in this connection are individuals who, in effect, straddle the boundary between the licit and illicit sectors and provide an important gateway for the criminals into licit financial, political, administrative, or business institutions. Thus lawyers, financiers, and politicians may be important sources of information as well as exploitable targets for nonlethal engagement. Disrupting these gateways is essential to denying the network access to its support structures. Attacking the network's core personnel is preferred but often difficult. Cores leadership can reconstitute. Attack options include: arrest of network members, seizure of property and financial assets, destruction of infrastructure, disruption/denial of supplies, elimination of safe havens. It is also possible to internally attack a network by creating dysfunctional relationships among its members through misinformation and actions designed to create mistrust.

b. In transnational criminal AtN operations, governments are often hindered by being organized along hierarchical lines, bureaucratic rivalry and competition, interagency antipathies, and a reluctance to share information and coordinate operations. To be as agile as the networks they confront, it may be necessary to form intergovernmental JTFs that pool resources and information (preferably on a regional basis) to pursue the network. In third world countries, governmental cooperation is often complicated by corruption, resource constraints, and a legal structure that is not designed to support comprehensive AtN activities. One approach to dealing with the problem of money laundering and other financial crimes has been in the creation of financial intelligence units (FIUs). The FIU is a central, national agency responsible for receiving (and, as permitted, requesting), analyzing and disseminating to the competent authorities, disclosures of financial information: concerning suspected proceeds of crime and potential financing of terrorism, or required by national legislation or regulation, in order to counter money laundering and terrorism financing. They are able to provide a rapid exchange of information (between financial institutions and law enforcement/ prosecutorial authorities, as well as between jurisdictions), while protecting the interests of the innocent individuals contained in their data.

FINANCIAL INTELLIGENCE UNIT NETWORK

Recognizing the benefits inherent in the development of a FIU network, in 1995, a group of FIUs met at the Egmont Arenberg Palace in Brussels and decided to establish an informal group for the stimulation of international co-operation. Now known as the Egmont Group of Financial Intelligence Units, these FIUs meet regularly to find ways to cooperate, especially in the areas of information exchange, training, and the sharing of expertise.

The goal of the Egmont Group is to provide a forum for FIUs around the world to improve cooperation in the fight against money laundering and financing of terrorism and to foster the implementation of domestic programs in this field. This support includes:

• Expanding and systematizing international cooperation in the reciprocal exchange of information;

• Increasing the effectiveness of FIUs by offering training and promoting personnel exchanges to improve the expertise and capabilities of personnel employed by FIUs.

VARIOUS SOURCES

c. As transnational organized criminals extend their reach around the globe, the rule of law is being challenged, especially in low-income countries and countries in or emerging from conflict. Crime thrives in institutional vacuums, flourishing where justice is weak and lawlessness and instability prevail. When countries lack strong institutions of justice—such as forceful criminal legislation, reliable law enforcement, a fair judiciary and a humane prison system—criminals find opportunities to profit. Strengthening the rule of law and its supporting institutions is a major step in defeating the enemy and the military will often be called upon to support these activities. However, employment of foreign military resources is subject to a number of legislative and perceptual constraints. Thus the use of foreign forces inside a HN, even one where the situation is rapidly deteriorating, requires careful preparation of the local and regional population – a strategic communications initiative. In most instances, the US military will be providing assistance in the form of intelligence collection and analysis, logistical support and training for the HN's security forces. The more active, visible role will be played by other USG personnel including advisors/trainers from the FBI, ATF, Department of Justice, the federal judiciary and their international counterparts.

5. The Columbian Experience

One of the best examples of an effort to eliminate a transnational organized crime network was the USG-Columbian governments' attempt to eradicate the Columbian drug cartels, which was conducted throughout the 1990s. The Columbian example is important for a number of reasons: first, the cartels were well organized, with plentiful resources, and were embedded in the local societal infrastructure; second, despite the levels of governmental corruption on the part of US and Colombian officials, the cooperative efforts of law enforcement, military officials and intelligence analysts from both countries effectively disrupted all of the major cocaine cartels; and third, the lessons learned from the "post cartel" experience demonstrate the adaptive capabilities of these organizations.

THE COLOMBIAN CARTELS

The organizational gestation of the Colombian cartels can be traced back to the 1970s, when ambitious, young criminal entrepreneurs such as Pablo Escobar Gaviria, Gonzalo Gacha, and Gilberto Orejuela sought to exploit the growing demand for cocaine in the US drug markets by transporting relatively small quantities of the illicit drug from Ecuador, Bolivia, and Peru to Columbia, where it underwent further refinement in makeshift laboratories before final shipment northward. Over time and repeated exchange, a number of traffickers developed their operations into transnational networks capable of coordinating numerous multi-ton cocaine shipments annually. These networks contained a core group that coordinated activities among functionally specific nodes, including cocaine base suppliers, processing labs, transportation rings, and distribution groups that delivered cocaine to independent retailers and funneled profits to network leaders and investors. Certain nodes, particularly those engaged in high risk activities such as cross-border transportation or wholesale distribution in consumer markets, were often compartmentalized into discrete cells. Cells maintained close communication with core groups but enjoyed some autonomy in planning and implementing their illicit activities.

Core groups directed the transnational enterprise, providing security and enforcement throughout the network and securing resources from independent investors. With the help of cells and other participants, they also gathered intelligence about government drug enforcement efforts and influence public policy on matters of direct interest, such as the extradition of Colombian nationals to the US.

By the mid-1980s, US and Colombian officials were fully sensitized to the danger represented by the handful of cartels. With US assistance, Colombian officials launched several crackdowns against leaders of these transnational networks destroying processing labs, seizing cocaine shipments, and arresting (and occasionally extraditing) various mid-level leaders. However, network leaders were not greatly affected by these short-lived offensives; sophisticated security arrangements allowed them to continue their smuggling activities relatively unimpeded. Throughout the 1980s, police officials routinely discovered numerous multi-ton shipments, indicating the growing capacity of the Colombian networks. For example, DEA and Customs agents discovered approximately 12,000 pounds of cocaine in a warehouse in Queens, New York used by a trafficking rings affiliated with a Cali-based trafficking network. Throughout the 1980s the estimated average price of cocaine at "dealer" level dropped from $191 per gram to $65 per gram and the purity rose from 60% to 80%. Clearly, a change in the counter-narcotics strategy was needed.

In 1992, the DEA introduced a major initiative that quickly became the agency's primary counter-narcotics program. The Kingpin strategy channeled the DEA's substantial investigative and enforcement resources towards disrupting and dismantling major narcotics networks. A kingpin was defined as the leader of an international trafficking enterprise that directs the production, transportation, and distribution of large quantities of cocaine or heroin, as well as the organization's financial operations. By "neutralizing" kingpins and dismantling their trafficking infrastructure, the DEA claimed it would be able to significantly reduce the availability of drugs in the United States.

The principal targets of the Kingpin strategy included the leaders of the Colombian cartels – Escobar, Orjuela, Gaviria. Working closely with the Colombian National Police, the DEA sought to disable the trafficking networks led by these entrepreneurs by attacking their communications, transportation, and finance systems. Recognizing that the most sophisticated Colombian networks were compartmentalized, the DEA and the Colombians focused on the heads of US based distribution cells and their communications with the kingpins based in Colombia. A critical element of the strategy was the aggressive use of electronic surveillance...Drug enforcers from both countries used the tactical intelligence gathered from wiretaps to identify participants, drug shipments, stash house locations, and other information for conducting raids and other enforcement operations.

The Kingpin strategy produced some noteworthy outputs. A year and a half after implementation, the DEA reported the seizure of $210 million in drug proceeds, the confiscation of 144 aircraft, and 91 boat, trucks and cars and the arrest of over 713 significant traffickers. In Colombia, counter-narcotics units destroyed hundreds of cocaine processing labs, thousands of hectares of coca leaf plantings, and arrested hundreds of traffickers. Following Orejuela's arrest, the Colombian prosecutor general claimed that "narco-trafficking is in the way of disappearing from Colombia".

However, the reports of the death of the Colombian cocaine trade turned out to be exaggerated. Following a brief period of regeneration, hundreds of new and restructured trafficking enterprises emerged to produce greater amounts of cocaine than ever before. Rather than a handful of centralized networks that dominated cocaine production and distribution, the post cartel drug industry was characterized by hundreds of small and medium-sized concerns that stepped into the vacuum created by the downfall of the Medellin and Cali cartels. In addition, hundreds of family based trafficking enterprises that specialized single-phases of production, processing and transportation activities emerged from the shadows of the cartels. These enterprises downsized splitting into hundreds of small, independent firms that specialized in specific activities, such as processing, transportation, and distribution. These new operations were not only smaller but were organizationally "flatter", compromising no more than two layers of management and a dozen participants. Different groups pool their resources and transact ad hoc support networks sometimes composed of members of former competing organizations. These new networks are characterized by flat hierarchies, horizontal accountability, and loosely coupled nodes.

Michael Kinney, The Challenge of Eradicating Transnational Criminal Networks: Lessons from the War on Drugs, 2002

6. Cybercrime

a. Internet-based criminal activity is a well documented phenomena. The internet has provided criminals with an unprecedented degree of anonymity, ready access to millions of potential victims (citizens, businesses, governments), and a law enforcement system that is hampered by geographic jurisdictional issues and a lack of technical resources, knowledge, and training. The internet also provides a communications backbone to facilitate criminal operations. While DOD cyber activities are focused on protecting its own networks from intrusion, as the level of sophistication and range of activities of the cyber criminal's continue to expand, they pose a potential threat to USG (and critical civilian infrastructure) systems. Criminal enterprises who control bot nets (ad-hoc clusters of several thousands of computers that, unbeknown to the user, are being deployed toward some nefarious end) can be hired for almost any purpose. For example, in February 2004, the FBI broke up a bot net ring in which the CEO of a small Ohio-based internet service provider called CIT/Foonet allegedly paid hackers to conduct bot network-based attacks on his business rivals. The attacks cost his rivals $2 million and the CEO is now a fugitive. Bot nets have come to inundate the Internet. On a typical day, 40% of the 800 million computers connected to the Internet are bots engaged in distributing e-mail spam, stealing sensitive data typed at banking and shopping websites, bombarding websites as part of extortionist denial-of-service attacks, and spreading fresh infections. Criminal enterprises may operate their own bot armies or provide the technology to other organizations.

b. There is also evidence that some criminals on the cutting edge are using data harvested by bot nets to send e-mail to specific executives at certain government agencies and large corporations. Carefully crafted to look like they come from a colleague or business contact, the e-mails include a corrupted Microsoft office file. Once opened, the tainted file cloaks itself and installs a tool that monitors incoming and outgoing traffic, collecting clues on ways to drill deeper inside the organization's internal network. The cyber threat is real and there are serious implications for the USG's ability to protect the national infrastructure.

c. While the majority of malicious cyber activity has been directed against individuals and businesses, the use of bot armies to attack government communications infrastructures was amply demonstrated in Georgia and Estonia. Operating on behalf (or at the direction) of their government, Russian computer hackers effectively shut down those governments communications infrastructures – cutting them off from their people during an escalating crisis. A deployed JTF and the HN could be subject to similar disruptive attacks either by insurgents, criminals hired by the insurgents, or by national entity sympathetic to the insurgents. In addition to defending from potential attack, the friendly forces must be aware of the enemy's use of cyberspace, identify potential vulnerabilities, and be prepared to take appropriate action.

d. While the cyberspace threat is real, the use of cyberspace is, like the IED, is a tool employed by the enemy to gain an advantage. Just as friendly forces attempt to leverage the capabilities that cyberspace provide to neutralize various enemy capabilities, a sophisticated enemy will undertake defensive and offensive measures in order to maintain the integrity of their operations. While operations in cyberspace have generally been limited to attacking websites, stealing/corrupting data, and interfering with communications, the potential exists for much wider disruption of civilian infrastructure that could directly impact friendly military operations. **Friendly force planners must anticipate the malicious use of cyberspace and include offensive and defensive cyberspace options into operational plans.**

APPENDIX D
REGIONAL THREATS: SOMALIA AND PIRACY

"We remain resolved to halt the rise of piracy in this region. To achieve that goal, we must continue to work with our partners to prevent future attacks, be prepared to interdict acts of piracy and ensure that those who commit acts of piracy are held accountable for their crimes."

President Barack Obama
January 12, 2009

1. Introduction

a. Failed states provide a number of unique cooperative opportunities for transnational terrorists, local insurgents, and criminal gangs. In the aggregate the activities of these groups can have a destabilizing effect on the surrounding region and beyond. Somalia is an excellent example of such opportunism. Al Qaeda uses the country as a safe haven, staging area and recruiting center; Al Shabab, the local insurgency, is attempting to wrest control of the country from the local warlords; and local Somali criminal gangs who have stepped into the power vacuum to establish a flourishing business as pirates. While Al Qaeda has attracted US military intervention and Al Shabab is battling occasional Ethiopian military forays and African Union forces supporting a transitional government, it is the pirates who have focused the world's attention on the region.

b. After the Somali civil war began in 1991, the impoverished coastal people turned to piracy and achieved phenomenal success. In 2008 alone, Somali pirates made over 125 million dollars in ransom payments. Operating in a target rich environment in which more than 30% of the world's oil passes, the pirates have been able to operate with relative impunity despite the presence of international naval forces. Their impact on the local region is profound – interfering with the flow of humanitarian and development aid to Somalia and other needy countries and increasing the shipping cost for oil and other goods to Europe and the Far East.

c. The pirates have successfully integrated themselves into the entire fabric of the local society. Besides the normal 3d World clan affiliations, there is the pure motivator of economic profit. In the pirate stronghold of Harardhere, small companies like Ganfanji collect venture capital, which they use to buy speedboats, ladders, fuel and RPGs, and send pirates out to sea. Anyone who wants to be a shareholder but has no money can also buy his way in with weapons or provisions. Money also provides security. Along the Somali coast, in these places, the entire local economy revolves around hijacking ships, with hundreds of men, women, and children employed as guards, scouts, cooks, deckhands, mechanics, skiff-builders, accountants, and tea-makers. The prettiest young women in pirate towns dream of a pirate groom; little boys can hardly wait until they are old enough to sling an AK-47 over their shoulder and head out to sea. There is even a functioning pirate stock exchange in Xarardheere, where locals buy "shares" in seventy-two individual pirate "companies" and get a respectable return if the company is successful. According to a convicted pirate, a single armed pirate can earn anywhere from US $6,000 to $10,000 for a US $1 million ransom. This is approximately equivalent to two to three years' worth of salary for an armed guard at a humanitarian agency and much higher than what a local business would pay.

> *"The district receives its share of every ransom, and that goes into public infrastructure, including the hospital and public schools," the deputy security chief of Harardhere recently explained. The leaders of the pirate trade now probably include senior members of the tightly run al-Shabab militias, which dominate large parts of Somalia. In the past, these Islamists were known for their severe punishments of pirates, because they believed that piracy is un-Islamic. Today, however, al-Shabab seems to have adopted the view that it is better not to cut off the hand that feeds you. Clan leaders in Harardhere say that they share ransoms with the militias. In return, a Canadian intelligence report concludes, the Islamists offer "weapons, gun training and local protection."*
>
> **Frank Gardner,**
> **"The Losing Battle Against Piracy"**
> **February 2011**

d. While the problem would seem to be confined to Somalia, in fact, the pirates receive support from a wide spread network of suppliers and financiers in Lebanon, Somalia, and the United Arab Emirates. The nation of Yemen also provides pirate mother ships with port facilities to refuel, replenish and rearm. A UN report said: "Members of the Harardhere pirate group have been linked to the trafficking of arms from Yemen to (the Somali towns of) Harardhere and Hobyo, which have long been two of the main points of entry for arms shipments destined for armed opposition groups in Somalia and Ethiopia." In a region with weak central governments and rule of law, criminal groups have effectively leveraged the situation for their own ends.

e. In addition to local support, the pirates have a number of advantages. These include operating in a lawless country the size of Texas that they can use as a sanctuary and an ocean operating area that covers over four million square miles (Figure D-1); an international community with uncertain laws regarding piracy and equally ill defined rules of engagement; and a reluctance on the part of Western nations to carry the fight to the enemy's land bases for fear of sparking a wider regional problem with Islamist extremists.

f. Some 1,400 Somalis are estimated to be involved in piracy. Two main piracy networks in Somalia have been recognized; one in the semi-autonomous northern Puntland in the Eyl district and another group based in Haradheere in Central Somalia. Smaller pirate groups have been recognized operating from the ports of Bosaso, Qandala, Caluula, Bargaal, Hobyo, Mogadishu and Garad. It appears that a number of groups are organized along clan lines, with the sub-clans of Darood and Hawiye being particularly prominent. Most piracy groups appear to be equal-opportunity employers, seeking recruits in the refugee camps housing some 40,000 internally displaced Somalis. Specific groups mentioned in reports from the region include:

(1) The Somali Marines based in Central Somalia, this group appears to have pioneered the use of mother ships;

(2) The Kismayu group (also own as National Volunteer Coastguard) from Kismayu in southern Somalia, focused on small boats, close to the shore;

(3) The Marka Group operating south of Mogadishu to Kismayo, this small group uses fishing boats with long-range fire power; and,

(4) The Puntland group operating from a small village near Bossaso, using modified fishing vessels and seized vessels for continued attacks.

EXPANSION OF THE PIRATE'S OPERATIONAL AREA

DUE TO COPYRIGHT RESTRICTIONS
SOME OR ALL IMAGES ARE NOT INCLUDED

Figure D-1. Expansion of the Pirate's Operational Area

g. Operating from approximately eight larger (trawler size) mother ships, approximately four to eight skiffs will swarm the targeted vessel, board it, seize the crew, and take it to an Somali port. The ability of pirates to locate target vessels in vast expanses of sea has led some to conclude that pirates are being provided with GPS coordinates by informants with access to ship tracking data. Crews of some hijacked vessels have said that the pirates appear to know everything about the ship on boarding, from the layout of the vessel to its ports of call. Calls made by pirates from captured ships using satellite phones indicate an international network. Once the pirates have seized a vessel, the risk of harm to the hostages is such that the NATO naval force will normally not try to retake the vessel.

2. Addressing the Threat

"...we shall continue to lead and support international efforts to repress piracy and other acts of violence against maritime navigation and urge other states to take decisive action both individually and through international efforts."

"Piracy repression should include diplomatic, military, intelligence, economic, law enforcement, and judicial actions. Effectively responding to piracy and criminal activity sends an important deterrent message and requires coordination by all departments and agencies of the U.S. Government in order to ensure that those responsible are brought to justice in a timely manner."

**Policy for the Repression of Piracy
and other Criminal Acts of Violence at Sea
June 2007**

a. **US and International Response.** The US Secretary of State (SECSTATE) has stated that the US will not make concessions or ransom payments to pirates. SECSTATE also announced four immediate steps the USG is taking in an expanded counter-piracy program: work with international partners to crack down on pirate bases and decrease incentives to engage in piracy; develop an expanded multinational response; engage with the Somali government and regional leaders in Puntland to take action against pirates operating from bases within their territories; and work with shippers and the insurance industry to address gaps in self-defense measures. This reflects a whole-of-government approach which seeks to resolve the situation in multiple levels of engagement to include the **limited application** of military pressure in an international setting.

(1) The US implementing LOE include the participation in an international naval force to counter the immediate threat and longer term initiatives aimed at establishing governance, rule of law, security, and economic development in Somalia. The US action plan consists of three distinct LOE: 1) prevent pirate attacks by reducing the vulnerability of the maritime domain to piracy; 2) disrupt acts of piracy consistent with international law and the rights and responsibilities of coastal and flag States; and 3) ensure that those who commit acts of piracy are held accountable for their actions by facilitating the prosecution of suspected pirates by flag, victim and coastal States, and, in appropriate cases, the United States.

(2) As part of an international response to the piracy threat, NATO conducts Operation OCEAN SHIELD. It is NATO's counter-piracy mission combining at-sea counter-piracy operations while providing (requesting) regional-state entities with counter-piracy capacity building. The US Navy participates in this NATO operation as part of Combined Task Force 151. The task force is responsible for deterring, disrupting, and suppressing piracy (Figure D-2) throughout the Gulf of Aden, Gulf of Oman, western Indian Ocean, and off the coast of Somalia. In addition to the NATO force, a number of nations have independently operating naval units operating off Somalia.

PIRATES CAPTURED BY EUROPEAN UNION NAVAL FORCES

Figure D-2. Pirates Captured by European Union Naval Forces

b. **US Military Options**. The current policy focuses on **deterrence through presence** with very restrictive rules of engagement in those rare instances where pirates are caught in the act. Since it takes less than 30 minutes to seize a vessel, the opportunity for NATO vessels to successfully interdict a pirate in the act is negligible. Under United Nations Security Council Resolution 1816, the Security Council has created conditions for third-party governments to conduct anti-piracy operations in Somali territorial waters, as well as, engaging in on-shore operations with authorization from the Somali Transitional Federal Government. However, while military forces have located the pirate bases, identified (and can presumably track) the pirate mother ships, and have trained forces capable of retaking any vessel, the risk to the hostages and the potential regional political repercussions have precluded the full exercise of the military option. Rather, the approach is to change the underlying circumstances that create the need to become a pirate by international efforts to combat hunger, promote development and bring peace to Somalia – a very long term solution.

c. Nonlethal options also are limited. With the amount of money the pirates are pouring into the local economy and strong tribal ties, there is little chance, in the near term, of convincing the population to adopt an opposed or even neutral position. Even the Shabab and the local elders who are opposed on religious grounds have been seduced financially. Cutting the pirates off from their funds is also problematic. They do not use a formal banking system – preferring the halawa system, most of their money is spent on the spot, and the ship owners would rather pay a ransom in order to get their ships, cargos, and crews back unharmed.

Intentionally Blank

APPENDIX E
ENEMY FINANCE

1. Introduction

Threat networks require operating capital (money, assets, and other financial resources) to function and that operating capital has to be continually generated to sustain continuous and long term operations. Ideology may provide the psychological motivation to take action but money gives the group the capability to take the actions to enact that ideology. Ideology has limited chances of spreading without financial resources. The amount of money the enemy needs to raise will vary greatly by the level of the group's activity. Areas that have a high level of enemy activity will have a large and aggressive fund raising effort.

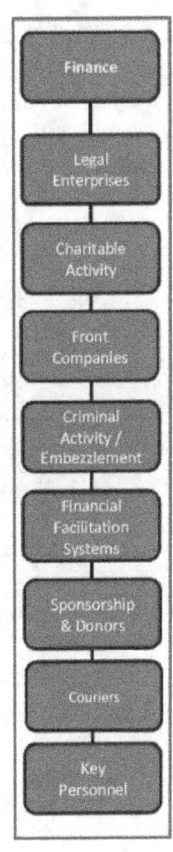

a. Criminal activity that serves as a source of funds to enemy groups includes:

(1) Extortion and protection rackets

(2) Smuggling

(3) Kidnapping

(4) Prostitution rings

(5) Human trafficking

(6) Narcotics trafficking

(7) Credit card fraud and identity theft

(8) Counterfeiting currencies and pharmaceuticals, cigarettes, alcohol and other goods,

(9) Pirating videos, compact discs, tapes and computer software

b. The Madrid railway station bombings in 2004 were supported by the sale of counterfeit music/video CDs. Supporters of Hezbollah were arrested in the US after they purchased cigarettes in North Carolina and then re-sold them in Michigan at a discount, where state cigarette taxes are much higher and the price discrepancy can net smugglers up to $2 million per truckload.

c. Counter threat finance (CTF) operations are complex and time consuming. The military rarely has the lead and is usually contributing to a whole of government effort directed by the State Department or the Department of the Treasury. The military contribution, at a minimum, usually includes intelligence collection support and supporting intelligence analysis. As a situation escalates, US military forces, if deployed, can take a more active role consistent with the direction of the lead federal agency.

2. Fundraising Considerations

a. Threat financial operations may be performed at the international, national, regional, and/or local levels. The locations that a group may raise funds are based on their access to the locations, law enforcement or regulatory enforcement, the number of skilled fund raisers that the group has and the amount of money that the group has to conduct the fund raising activities.

b. Some of the activities that need to be funded include:

(1) Training

(2) Recruitment

(3) Living expenses

(4) Travel

(5) Communications

(6) Operations

(7) Weapons and material

(8) Safe houses

(9) Bribes

(10) Transportation and vehicles

(11) Forged identification and travel documents

(12) Intelligence gathering

(13) Media time / advertising

(14) Paid demonstrations

(15) Payments to families of soldiers and martyrs

c. Fund raising operations at any level require an organization that is well organized and disciplined; has people that are well trained and have excellent political, personal, sales and marketing skills; have a network of illicit personal contacts that are able to identify and target people or groups that have funds; know what themes to use that will motivate people to donate; know where to go to raise funds; know how to dress when soliciting funds; are familiar with law enforcement and regulatory capabilities and personalities; have money that can be used to bribe government officials; understand the financial underground in the countries they operate in and are well versed in fund raising and transfer techniques for the countries they operate in. International operations can provide access to very large pools or money but can also expose the group to greater scrutiny by intelligence and law enforcement agencies that are not sympathetic to their cause.

> *"The chief problems of denying funding to terrorist groups are that the amount of money they use is small, and the networks they rely on are mass market in character, and thus difficult to monitor without specific intelligence. Terrorist cells are unlikely to use large international networks for international funds transfer. Reports are that the Tamil Tigers in Sri Lanka have used on-line eBay and PayPal accounts for money laundering, arms trafficking, and other activities. Such small accounts are very difficult to monitor."*
>
> **Paul Bracken, Financial Warfare,**
> **September 2007**

d. Enemy groups that are able to provide financial support to their communities by providing food and supplies, renting houses, providing medical support, providing education and employing members of the community have a far greater chance of earning the loyalty of the local population versus groups that use violent criminal tactics to raise funds and obtain needed resources.

> *"Blocking bank accounts of key groups and individuals puts the spotlight on them and thereby increases the risks to any company or government doing business with them. Financial sanctions legitimize additional actions, both financial and non-financial, which can ratchet up more pressure. This is where financial warfare and military strategy converge. Most people think of financial warfare as a substitute for military action, which it is, up to a point. But after a point it becomes a complement rather than a substitute."*
>
> **Paul Bracken, Financial Warfare,**
> **September 2007**

e. Adversaries will make every effort possible to exploit, subvert and take control of the local, regional and national economies. Legitimate governments obtain a significant percentage of their income from taxes. When threat organizations are able to take physical control over these areas they are also taking control over the economic and tax base. Local insurgencies will remain local insurgencies unless they receive sufficient income and logistical resources to expand their personnel based and military capabilities. Even a modest increase in manpower or operations can significantly increase the financial burden on small groups. Large scale enemy operations in third world economies will initially require extensive financial and logistical support which will probably be provided by entities outside of the contested country. High operational tempo operations for enemy groups can quickly drain local economies and will create significant public relations problems with the local populace. Most small villages are incapable of providing the flow of money or logistical support that is required to maintain military operations.

3. JIPOE Financial Indicators

When developing the estimate of the enemy's financial activities, analysts should develop information on the local economy, employment opportunities for the local population, the local unemployment rate, typical wages paid in the area, the cost of living, the cost of fuel, the cost of weapons and ammunition, the exchange rate with the US dollar, etc. This information will become invaluable in understanding the relevance of cash seizures; comparing lifestyles of government, law enforcement and military personnel to their income potential (corruption indicators) and the willingness of the local population to either support, cooperate with, or become members of threat organizations.

"Financial warfare complements military operations as well as information operations. When combined with advances in social network mapping, it can give a highly detailed picture of an elite communication and financial structure that can be used for targeting. Communication and software tools now exist to analyze connections in vast networks of heterogeneous information, such as financial transactions, mobile telephone calls, e-mail, and air travel. This gigantic information pool can be a source of knowledge about a nation's elite, where they stash their money, who they talk to, and their position in a social hierarchy. The key to doing this lies in constructing overlays of these datasets to visualize the various connections.

Watching how money flows out of a country in a crisis can be an important tip-off to who is in the know and who is at least partially responsible for national decisions. Carried to the next step, this can be combined with precise military attacks to go after a nation's elite. For example, tracking mobile telephone calls can reveal things like where the elite live, their vacation homes, and their travel patterns. Financial tracking of their bank accounts can reveal where they keep their money and who has access to their accounts. This creates the conditions for potentially ruinous attacks with far-reaching social implications on the national leadership."

**Paul Bracken, Financial Warfare,
September 2007**

4. Disrupting the Financial Foundation

a. Disrupting the external support networks requires detecting, identifying, tracking and engaging their financial systems and funding sources. This is an extraordinarily difficult task since the enemy will normally be firmly emplaced in both legitimate and illegitimate financial enterprises. However, even temporary, localized disruptions – intercepting the weekly payroll – can have an effect. Enemy organizations must be able to establish a reliable and efficient way of raising funds to generate a regular cash flow to increase their credibility with the local populace and within their own membership. Taking excessive amounts of money from the local populace, missing a couple of pay days, not making promised martyr payments or failure to make good on bonus payments makes the enemy organization vulnerable to information campaigns which point out their fiscal weakness because the internal membership is living the pain of not having sufficient funds to operate or to take care of their families. In an irregular warfare environment, the enemy organizations will make efforts to compromise the government and its security forces through bribery and deal making, this is especially true in countries that have high levels of corruption. It is much easier to infiltrate the government by buying your way in than to violently over throw that same government. Enemy organizations will use their ability to blend in with the populace and the criminal element to the fullest advantage. Using criminal activities to mask their fund raising efforts makes it difficult for military commanders to engage their personnel. Enemy organizations will also take full advantage of all relief efforts that are brought into their country. They will take advantage of employment opportunities, use the NGO access to gain information on military operations, divert charitable funds and construction materials and other schemes to raise funds under the guise of charitable efforts. Enemy organizations will use the NGO's good name to raise funds domestically and abroad. Specialized CTF personnel are required to conduct the initial financial evaluation of the operational area in support of JIPOE development; support the identification, development, and on-going targeting of key financial nodes; and provide commanders at all echelons with advice on disrupting enemy financial capabilities.

b. Money laundering (Figure E-1) is the method by which criminals disguise the illegal origins of their wealth and protect their asset bases. It enables criminals to avoid the suspicion of law enforcement agencies; prevents leaving a trail of incriminating evidence; and, protects the money from seizure. Money laundering is a dynamic three stage process that requires:

(1) placement, moving funds from direct association with the crime;

(2) layering, disguising the trail to foil pursuit; and,

(3) integration, making the money available to the criminal, once again, with its occupational and geographic origins hidden from view.

c. Terrorists and insurgents rely on money gathered from a variety of sources to sustain their operations. While these enemies are not concerned with disguising the origin of their funding, they are concerned with concealing its destination and the purpose for which it has been collected. Terrorists and insurgents therefore employ techniques similar to those used by money launderers to hide their money. Unfortunately the globalization of the world's economy now facilitates the rapid transfer of funds across international borders. Fuelled by advances in technology and communications, the financial infrastructure has developed into a perpetually operating global system in which "megabyte money" (money in the form of symbols on computer screens) can move anywhere in the world unhindered. Finding, freezing, and forfeiting criminally derived income and assets is now being conducted on a global scale by dozens of nations.

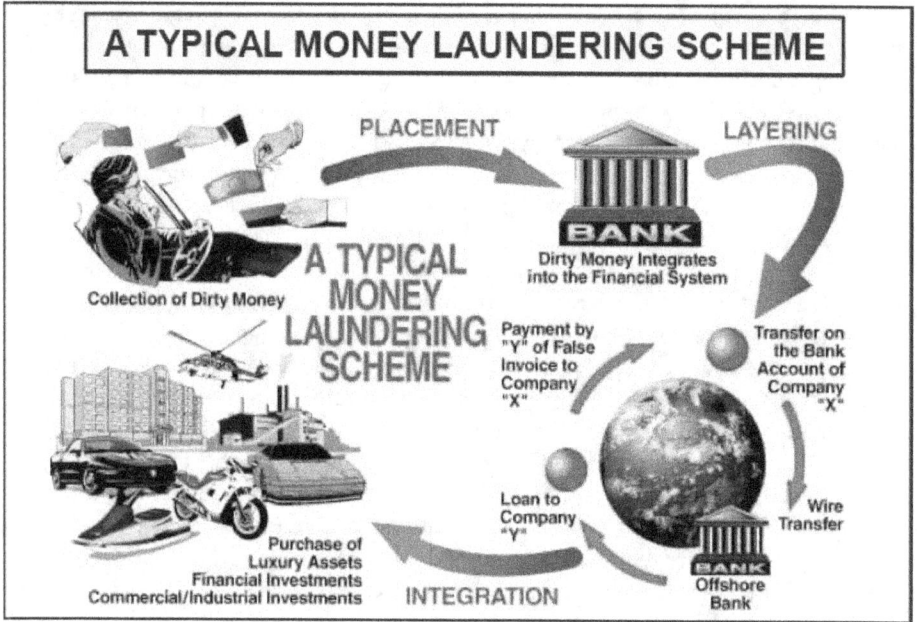

Figure E-1. A Typical Money Laundering Scheme

5. Threat Finance Cells

a. If personnel resources are available, expertise on enemy financial activities should be provided through the creation threat finance cells at division headquarters and higher. The cell would include a mix of analysts and SMEs on law enforcement, regulatory matters, financial institutions that would be drawn from DOD and interagency resources. The cell's responsibilities vary by at the tactical and operational levels.

b. In tactical units, the threat finance cell is responsible for:

(1) Providing threat finance expertise and advice to the commander and staff.

(2) Assisting the staff intelligence officer in the development of intelligence collection priorities focused on enemy financial and support systems that terminate in the unit's area of operation.

(3) Consolidating information on persons providing direct or indirect financial, material and logistics support to enemy elements in the unit's area of operation.

(4) Providing information concerning enemy exploitation of US resources such as transportation, logistical and construction contractors working in support of US facilities, exploitation of NGO resources, and exploitation of supporting HN personnel.

(5) Identifying enemy organizations that are coordinating or cooperating with local criminals or drug trafficking or other criminal organizations.

(6) Providing assessments of the enemy's financial viability – ability to fund and maintain operations – and the implications for friendly operations.

(7) Developing targeting package recommendations for enemy financial and logistics support persons for attack by lethal and nonlethal means.

(8) Notifying commanders when there are changes in the financial or support operations of the enemy organization which could indicate changes in enemy operating tempo or support capability.

(9) Coordinating with and share information with other threat finance cells to build a comprehensive picture of the enemy's financial activities.

c. At the operational level, the threat finance cell is responsible for developing and maintaining an understanding of the economic and financial environment of the HN and surrounding countries. This assists in the detection and tracking of illicit financial activities, understanding where financial support is coming from, how that support is being moved into the area of operation, and how that financial support is being used. The cell:

(1) Works with the J-2 to develop enemy finance related PIR and establish enemy finance all source intelligence collection priorities. The cell assists the J-2 in the detection, identification, tracking, analysis, and targeting of enemy personnel and networks associated with financial support across the operational area.

(2) The cell coordinates with tactical and theater threat finance cells and shares information with those entities as well as the coalition, HN, and USG intelligence community.

(3) The cell establishes a network picture for all known enemy elements in the operational area; establishes individual portfolios or target packages for persons identified as providing financial or material support to the enemy's elements in the operational area; identifies enemy financial TTPs for fund raising, transfer mechanisms, distribution, management and control, and disbursements; and identifies and distributes information on fund raising methods that are being used by specific groups in the operational area. The cell can also:

(a) Identify specific financial institutions that are involved with or that are providing financial support to the threat and how those institutions are being exploited by the threat.

(b) Provide CTF expertise on smuggling and cross border financial and logistics activities.

(c) Establish and maintain information on enemy operating costs in the operational area.

d. Targets identified by the operational level cell are shared with the tactical cells. This allows the tactical finance cells to support and coordinate tactical units to act as an action arm for targets identified by the operational level CTF element, and coordinate tactical intelligence assets and sources against enemy elements identified by the operational level CTF element.

e. Multi-echelon information sharing is critical to unraveling the complexities of an enemy's financial infrastructure. Operational level CTF elements require the detailed financial intelligence that is typically obtained by resources controlled by the tactical elements. Information obtained from tactical sources may require IC or HN sources to gain access to the source of the documents or to financial accounts, communications accounts, etc. Tactical level CTF will require help in identifying and tracking financial support operations that initiate outside of, and terminate in, their operational areas.

f. The operational level CTF cell facilitates the provision of USG and coalition agencies' support at the tactical level. This is especially true for USG agencies that have representation at the American Embassy.

g. Tactical level CTF cells will require support from the operational level to obtain HN political support to deal with negative influencers that can only be controlled or removed by national level political leaders. These include Governors, Deputy Governors, District Leads, Agency leadership, Chiefs of Police, Shura Leaders, elected officials, and others persons serving in official positions; and HN security forces, civilian institutions, and even NGO's/charities that may be providing the enemy with financial and logistical support.

APPENDIX F
ATTACK THE NETWORK ANNEX
TO THE OPERATIONS PLAN

The following is a sample format that a joint force staff can use as a guide when developing an AtN annex for a joint operation plan (OPLAN). The exact format and level of detail may vary somewhat among joint commands, based on theater-specific requirements and other factors. However, joint OPLANs will always contain the basic five paragraphs (such as paragraph 3, "Execution") and their primary subparagraphs (such as paragraph 3a, "Concept of Operations"). This sample format is based on a C-IED network type threat but can be modified to accommodate any enemy.

(U) Copy No. _____

(U) Issuing Headquarters

(U) Place of Issue

(U) Effective Date/Time Group

(U) OPERATION PLAN: (Number or Code Name)

(U) USXXXXCOM OPERATIONS TO . . .

(U) References: (List any maps, charts, and other relevant documents deemed essential to comprehension of the plan.)

1. (U) **Situation**

   a. (U) <u>General</u>. The use of improvised explosive devices (IEDs) has proven to be an effective tactic and weapon of strategic influence. IEDs are complex, adaptive systems. Challenging and unpredictable employment tactics, successful attacks without central direction, the social complexity of IED networks, and the strategic impacts caused by IEDs, create an ill-structured strategic problem- for US forces. Counter-IED (C-IED) is a focus of special effort for the command due to the unique and challenging nature of an IED attack, the extreme difficulty in defeating the IED threat, the adverse psychological effects a successful IED campaign has on our friendly forces and local populations, and the overall confidence of an adaptive enemy. C-IED is a combination of collective efforts and operations that include the offensive and defensive measures taken to defeat the IED network.

b. (U) <u>Purpose</u>. This annex describes C-IED functions and assigns responsibilities for the execution of PLAN XX. It provides the concept for the scheme of C-IED operations, gives employment guidelines, and assigns missions to component command C-IED Task Forces.

c. (U) <u>Enemy Forces</u>. Annex B (Intelligence). Refer to (Intelligence Estimate) for the typical structure of an IED Network (each network is unique yet contains the same functions in varying capacity).

d. (U) Friendly Forces. Annex A (Task Organization)

2. (U) **Mission**

Mission. Basic Plan.

3. (U) **Execution**

a. (U) Concept of <u>Operations</u>. In order to achieve goals outlined in the basic plan, [Combatant Command X] conducts simultaneous C-IED actions coordinated through the six planning phases: Phase 0 – Shape, Phase I – Deter/Engage, Phase II - Seize the Initiative, Phase III – Dominate/Decisive Operations, Phase IV – Stabilize, and Phase V – Enable Civil Authorities. While some Joint Operation Areas (JOAs) are further along in the phases individually, across the whole AOR, we are currently in Phase [X]. [General note: The Combatant Command should establish a core set of C-IED enablers that run through each phase. As the phases progress the enabler will take on more fidelity or responsibility for action. An example would be dynamic network analysis for IED network modeling (non-material solution) or supply chain countermeasures (materiel solution).]

(1) (U) Phase 0 – Shape: This phase will set conditions that provide friendly forces (US and partners) the freedom of action to conduct operations against the enemy and deter the use of IEDs. These activities will be designed to enhance US and partner access to priority and high priority countries and develop the appropriate theater infrastructure required to support C-IED operations against the enemy. By shaping the environment,

(Combatant Command X) will create conditions that inhibit the IED threat from gaining a foothold. This phase will establish an environment hostile to the IED network and establish the battlefield infrastructure required to execute PLAN XX.

(a) (U) Phase 0 Operational Objectives:

<u>1</u>. (U) Shape future behavior within regional area by expanding security cooperation with allies and Partner Nations (PN) to protect US interests and prevent the spread of extremist ideology.

<u>2</u>. (U) Develop relationships with and assure operational access to allies and PNs to enable effective partnerships in times of crisis.

<u>3</u>. (U) Propagate Memorandums of Agreement (MOA) and Understanding (MOU) with the interagency to prevent bureaucratic restrictions.

<u>4</u>. (U) Establish mechanisms through the host nation partner or DOS to leverage commercial supply chains.

<u>5</u>. (U) Establish mechanisms through the host nation partner to leverage local telecommunication networks, and to provide support to the strategic communication plan within the local, national, and regional media sources.

(b) (U) Phase 0 Essential Capabilities:

<u>1</u>. (U) <u>Network Attack</u>. Establish a Federated Node and integrate into the C-IED Federated enterprise for access to C-IED information. Develop a phased ISR plan for multi-layered C-IED operations. Perform military intelligence operations to identify IED networks and their supporters. Conduct dynamic network analysis to define IED network structures and relationships.

<u>2</u>. (U) <u>C-IED Training</u>. Ensure friendly forces are appropriately postured and trained to conduct C-IED operations as Plan XX is executed.

<u>3</u>. (U) <u>International</u>. Establish relationships with partner organizations and nations through embassy and country teams, military attachés, and other multi-agency efforts for

Information and capability sharing to build C-IED capacity throughout the region.

4. (U) <u>Planning</u>. Develop model for a joint C-IED task force if Plan XX enters offensive operations.

(c) (U) Phase 0 End state: This phase ends with providing a security environment favorable to US interests and host nation objectives. The results of the shaping activities will be a favorable environment established for friendly forces to interdict the target set at the place and time of their choosing.

(2) (U) Phase 1 – Deter: This phase will set the conditions required to conduct offensive actions against the IED threat network and achieve decisive results outlined in Plan XX and facilitate the competency of allied and PN C-IED organizations.

(a) (U) Phase 1 Operational Objectives:

1. (U) Bilaterally with HN, conduct direct action against known bomb-makers and facilitators

2. (U) Monitor environment to detect and predict IED trends and attacks.

3. (U) Exploit IED network C2 and decision-making capability.

4. (U) Defend Multinational forces from the effects of IEDs.

5. (U) Develop proper command and control infrastructure with defined command relationships and robust communications to link the strategic, operational, and tactical levels of the C-IED campaign.

6. (U) Establish procedures to collect, consolidate, and disseminate IED and C-IED lessons learned throughout the AOR.

7. Establish procedures to identify capability needs, request for new technologies, and prioritize technology programs.

<u>8</u>. (U) Conduct Joint Intelligence Preparation of the Operational Environment (JIPOE) to identify key sources of IED supplies and critical IED production facilities.

<u>9</u>. (U) Identify existing C-IED organizations within the AOR and establish procedures or coordinated and supported efforts.

<u>10</u>. (U) Protect PNs from the effect of IEDs.

<u>11</u>. (U) Engage PN governments to assist in developing their C-IED capabilities.

<u>12</u>. (U) Conduct joint C-IED exercises and training with allies and PNs.

<u>13</u>. (U) Conduct C-IED strategic communication operations.

<u>14</u>. (U) Use elements of Information Operations targeting AOR populations in order to discredit the use of IEDs as an accepted tactic.

(b) (U) Phase 1 Essential Capabilities:

<u>1</u>. (U) <u>Network Attack</u>. Perform multi-layered, multi-intelligence analysis to identify IED networks. Conduct dynamic network analysis to define IED network structures and relationships.

<u>2</u>. (U) <u>C-IED Training</u>. Ensure friendly forces are appropriately postured and trained to conduct C-IED operations as enemy tactics evolve.

<u>3</u>. (U) <u>International</u>. Share information through Embassy and Country Teams, Military Attachés, and other multi-agency efforts to build C-IED capacity throughout the region.

<u>4</u>. (U) <u>Planning</u>. Implement model for a joint C-IED task force appropriately staffed for the threat level.

(3) (U) Phase 2 – Seize the Initiative: This phase will shift the main effort to the destruction of enemy IED networks, and contain the spread of IEDs throughout the area of operations.

(a) (U) Phase 2 Operational Objectives:

1. (U) Conduct detailed IPB focused upon the specific IED networks the JOAs and conduct tailored Critical Factors Analysis on the networks.

2. (U) Identify effective TTP and technologies to defeat IEDs.

3. (U) Source, in significant quantities, networks proven effective against emplaced devices.

4. (U) Execute the Explosive Remnants of War (ERW) reduction plan to decrease the supply of IED components.

5. (U) Test and develop technologies to defeat anticipated future devices and emplacement tactics.

6. (U) Initiate Joint Interdiction operations that neutralize bomb makers, facilitators and resources.

7. (U) Transition applicable C-IED solutions to PN and Multinational forces.

8. (U) Engage PN governments to assist in developing their C-IED capabilities.

9. (U) Execute Information Operations targeting AOR populations in order to discredit the use of IEDs as an accepted tactic.

(b) (U) Phase 2 Essential Capabilities:

1. (U) Network Attack. Perform multi-layered, multi-intelligence analysis to identify, attack, and defeat IED networks. Conduct dynamic network analysis to define IED network structures and relationships.

2. (U) C-IED Training. Ensure friendly forces are appropriately postured and trained to conduct C-IED operations as enemy tactics evolve.

3. (U) <u>International</u>. Share information through Embassy and Country Teams, Military Attachés, and other multi-agency efforts to build C-IED capacity throughout the region.

4. (U) <u>Planning</u>. Implement model for a joint C-IED task force appropriately staffed for the threat level.

(c) (U) Phase 2 End state: This phase ends with:

1. (U) Effective technologies fielded in significant quantities to defend all Multinational forces in theater against current IED techniques.

2. (U) C-IED Joint Interdiction operations established.

3. (U) ERW reduced to a manageable level. Accountability and security maintained over remaining ERW stockpiles.

4. (U) PN has a trained and ready C-IED Force

5. (U) Focused research and development on anticipated IED techniques.

6. (U) Institutionalize C-IED efforts throughout DOTMLPF.

(4) (U) Phase 3 – Dominate: This phase will focus on defeating IED networks, and reduce IED employment throughout the area of operations.

(a) (U) Phase 3 Operational Objectives:

1. (U) Identify, target, and interdict all elements of the IED network with specific emphasis on critical nodes and commodities of network.

2. (U) Continue ERW reduction plan.

3. (U) Continue to target and neutralize bomb makers and facilitators.

4. (U) Continue to engage PN governments to assist in developing their C-IED capabilities

(b) (U) Phase 3 Essential Capabilities:

1. (U) Network Attack. Perform multi-layered, multi-intelligence analysis to identify, attack, and defeat IED networks. Conduct dynamic network analysis to define IED network structures and relationships.

2. (U) C-IED Training. Ensure friendly forces are appropriately postured and trained to conduct C-IED operations as enemy tactics evolve.

3. (U) International. Share information through embassy and country teams, military attachés, and other multi-agency efforts to build C-IED capacity throughout the region.

4. (U) Planning. Implement model for a joint C-IED task force appropriately staffed for the threat level.

(c) (U) Phase 3 End state:

1. (U) Severely restrict insurgent and terrorist IED networks' freedom of action and movement.

2. (U) Destroy and disrupt IED networks.

3. (U) PN populations unsupportive of IED use within the AOR.

4. (U) IED critical components developed out of theater are tracked and interdicted.

5. (U) ERW reduced to a manageable level. Accountability and security maintained over remaining ERW stockpiles.

(5) (U) Phase 4 – Stabilize the Environment: This phase will shift main effort from US forces defeating IED networks to HN forces responsible for C-IED operations.

(a) (U) Phase 4 Operational Objectives:

<u>1</u>. (U) Protect the US, multinational forces (if applicable), and HN from the effects of IEDs.

<u>2</u>. (U) Develop and share C-IED capability with multinational forces and HN.

<u>3</u>. (U) Transition control of the C-IED effort from US to HN.

(b) (U) Phase 4 Essential Capabilities:

<u>1</u>. (U) <u>Network Attack</u>. Perform multi-layered, multi-intelligence analysis to identify, attack, and defeat IED networks. Conduct dynamic network analysis to define IED network structures and relationships.

<u>2</u>. (U) <u>C-IED Training</u>. Ensure friendly forces, with special emphasis to HN forces, are appropriately postured and trained to conduct C-IED operations as enemy tactics evolve.

<u>3</u>. (U) <u>International</u>. Share information through embassy and country teams, military attachés, and other multi-agency efforts to build C-IED capacity throughout the region.

<u>4</u>. (U) <u>Planning</u>. Implement model for a joint C-IED task force appropriately staffed for the threat level.

(c) (U) Phase 4 End state:

<u>1</u>. (U) PN assumes lead role in executing C-IED efforts.

<u>2</u>. (U) PN manned, trained, and equipped to execute C-IED efforts.

(6) (U) Phase 5 – Enable Civil Authorities: This phase will shift the main effort to support legitimate civil governance in the theater and ensure HN military can effectively and independently perform C-IED operations.

(a) (U) Phase 5 Operational Objectives:

1. (U) Enable viability and provision of essential civil services.

2. (U) Train HN forces.

(b) (U) Phase 5 Essential Capabilities:

1. (U) C-IED Training. Ensure friendly forces are appropriately postured and trained to conduct C-IED operations as enemy tactics evolve.

2. (U) International. Share information through embassy and country teams, military attachés, and other multi-agency efforts to build C-IED capacity throughout the region.

(c) (U) Phase 5 End state: HN conducts C-IED operations autonomously.

b. (U) Tasks

c. (U) Coordinating Instructions. [Expand this section as necessary.]

4. (U) **Administration and Logistics**. [Expand this section as necessary.]

5. (U) **Command and Control**. [Expand this section as necessary.]

APPENDIX G
COMPREHENSIVE APPROACH TO COUNTERINSURGENCY

> *"American counterinsurgency practice rests on a number of assumptions: that the decisive effort is rarely military (although security is the essential prerequisite for success); that our efforts must be directed to the creation of local and national governmental structures that will serve their populations, and, over time, replace the efforts of foreign partners; that superior knowledge, and in particular, understanding of the 'human terrain' is essential; and that we must have the patience to persevere in what will necessarily prove long struggles."*
>
> **U.S. Government Counterinsurgency Guide**
> **January 2009**

1. Introduction

a. Insurgency is the organized use of subversion and violence to seize, nullify or challenge political control of a region. As such, it is primarily a political struggle, in which both sides use armed force to create space for their political, economic and influence activities to be effective. They only need the active support of a few enabling individuals, but the passive acquiescence of a large proportion of the contested population will give a higher probability of success. This is best achieved when the political cause of the insurgency has strong appeal, manipulating religious, tribal or local identity to exploit common societal grievances or needs. Insurgents seek to gain control of populations through a combination of persuasion, subversion and coercion while using guerrilla tactics to offset the strengths of government security forces. Their intent is usually to protract the struggle, exhaust the government and win sufficient popular support to force capitulation or political accommodation. Complex insurgencies, which feature a mix of local insurgents, transnational terrorists, and criminal gangs whose activities threaten the stability of a partner government, pose the greatest challenge for AtN operations. Setting the conditions for achieving stability requires:

(1) Developing and maintaining a highly detailed picture of the OE from the tactical to the strategic level and developing a range of operations that can positively influence and shape that environment and the enemy forces operating in that environment;

(2) Friendly forces to engage the local populace and disengage them from supporting the enemy; and,

(3) Identifying who the true adversaries are, understanding how they function, and leveraging their exploitable vulnerabilities.

b. At each echelon of command, the actions taken to achieve stability vary only in the amount of detail required to create an actionable picture of the enemy and the environment. Each echelon of command has unique functions that it must perform, in synchronization with the other echelons, as part of the overall operation to defeat the enemy. **AtN is woven into the daily routine of achieving stability and the support of the people.** AtN operations contribute to the overall stability goals; they are conducted within the context of the stability campaign and should not be conducted independently of that campaign. However, AtN is not synonymous with, or specific to, the COIN environment.

c. COIN is the blend of comprehensive civilian and military efforts designed to simultaneously contain insurgency and address its root causes. Unlike conventional warfare, non-military means are often the most effective elements, with military forces playing an enabling role. COIN is an extremely complex undertaking, which demands of policy makers a detailed understanding of their own specialist field, but also a broad knowledge of a wide variety of related disciplines. COIN approaches must be adaptable and agile. Strategies will usually be focused primarily on the population rather than the enemy and will seek to reinforce the legitimacy of the affected government while reducing insurgent influence.

d. The overall objective in COIN is to enable the affected government to establish control, consolidating and then transitioning it from intervening forces to national forces and from military to civil institutions. This objective is accomplished through the interaction of five main functional components (Figure G-1):

(1) The **political function** is the key function, providing a framework of political reconciliation, and reform of governance around which all other COIN activities are organized. In general, a COIN strategy is only as good as the political plan at its heart.

(2) The **economic function** seeks to provide essential services and stimulate long term economic growth, thereby generating confidence in the government while at the same time reducing the pool of frustrated, unemployed young men and women from which insurgents can readily recruit.

(3) The **security function** is an enabler for the other functions and involves development not just of the affected nation's military force, but its whole security sector, including the related legal framework, civilian oversight mechanisms and judicial system. Establishing security is not a precursor to economic and governance activity: rather security, economic and governance activity must be developed in parallel.

(4) The **information function** comprises intelligence (required to gain understanding), and influence (to promote the affected government's cause). It is essential that the influence campaign is in tune with the strategic narrative, resonates with the relevant audiences, and is based on genuine resolve by the affected government and that physical actions match. What makes COIN different from other stabilization and humanitarian tasks is that both elements of the information function will be conducted in stark competition with the insurgents' own information functions.

(5) **Control.** The four functions (information, political, security and economic) contribute to the overall objective of enabling the affected government to control its environment. This implies the ability to contain insurgent activity (the tempo of operations, level and intensity of violence, and degree of instability that it engenders) such that the

population will, in the long run, support the government against the insurgents — noting that this "balance" can differ from one society to the next.

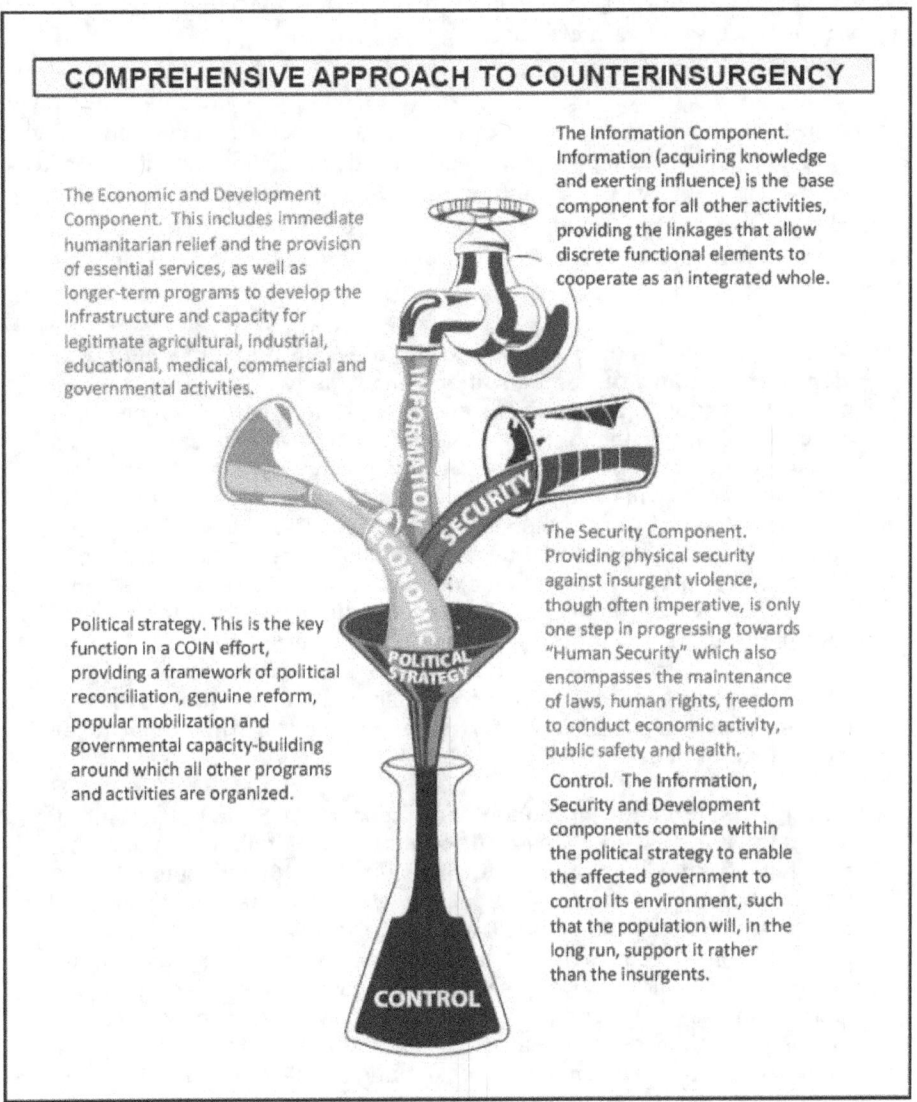

COMPREHENSIVE APPROACH TO COUNTERINSURGENCY

The Economic and Development Component. This includes immediate humanitarian relief and the provision of essential services, as well as longer-term programs to develop the infrastructure and capacity for legitimate agricultural, industrial, educational, medical, commercial and governmental activities.

The Information Component. Information (acquiring knowledge and exerting influence) is the base component for all other activities, providing the linkages that allow discrete functional elements to cooperate as an integrated whole.

Political strategy. This is the key function in a COIN effort, providing a framework of political reconciliation, genuine reform, popular mobilization and governmental capacity-building around which all other programs and activities are organized.

The Security Component. Providing physical security against insurgent violence, though often imperative, is only one step in progressing towards "Human Security" which also encompasses the maintenance of laws, human rights, freedom to conduct economic activity, public safety and health.

Control. The Information, Security and Development components combine within the political strategy to enable the affected government to control its environment, such that the population will, in the long run, support it rather than the insurgents.

Figure G-1. Comprehensive Approach to Counterinsurgency

e. The imperative to achieve synergy among political, security, economic and information activities demands unity of effort between all participants (the affected government, USG agencies and coalition partners). This is best achieved through an integrated approach to assessment and planning. A common interagency **assessment** of the insurgency establishes a deep and shared understanding of the cultural, ideological, religious, demographic and geographical factors that affect the insurgency. Once US assistance is committed, a COIN **strategy** must be devised, ideally in collaboration with the affected government and other coalition partners, since their early inclusion can help mitigate the effects of operational level differences in goals, capabilities and culture. Detailed, **integrated planning** then follows and a process of **continuous monitoring, evaluation** and **assessment** is used to measure progress and identify where changes in approach are necessary to achieve success.

f. A key aspect of AtN in COIN operations requires conducting integrated, synchronized operations against the enemy to achieve the desired lethal and nonlethal effects. This cannot be accomplished without detailed information about the OE and the enemy's activities. Most of this information will be based on tactical reporting painstakingly gathered by individual soldiers at the point of the spear. How well the CJTF organizes this information gathering effort may determine the success or failure of the mission.

Our success in bringing stability to the area did not come without a significant amount of combat. After almost daily, intense, and often prolonged engagements with the enemy starting in late October 2009, direct fire contact with the enemy in the company area of operations (AO) all but ceased after 27 December 2009. On this day, a reinforced and partnered Marine rifle squad battled with organic weapons a reinforced squad-sized enemy force equipped with at least (5) RPK and/or PK machine guns. The fight's results had become common: the partnered Marine-Afghan National Army (ANA) unit closed over 400 meters, killing (2) and wounding (1) enemy fighter. Two PK machine guns, (1) RPK machine gun, and hundreds of rounds of ammunition were seized from the enemy fighters. The patrol leader turned the dead enemy fighters over to the local elder while ensuring that his corpsman treated the wounded fighter. He then called in a MEDEVAC for the enemy fighter while other local nationals watched.

This fight was "heard" throughout the company AO. Equally, if not more important, this fight was "heard" throughout the battalion AO and in the provincial capital in Lashkar Gah, approximately 100 kilometers to the north. In the days following the fight, key elders that had fled in fear the greater Mian Poshteh and Lakari areas for Lashkar Gah when the Taliban assumed control years earlier, returned home. From January throughout the rest of the deployment, these elders, along with other elders, mullahs, and their increasingly confident and bold villagers, voted with their actions to work with their government, each other, the ANA, the Marines, and eventually the Afghan National Police to bring stability to an area that had been among the most dangerous and violent in Afghanistan.

It is important to highlight that all but (2) of the "kinetic" engagements with the enemy within the company AO were prior to 1 January 2010 and more than 90% of the IED attacks and those found within the company AO were emplaced before this date as well. Post 1 January 2010, after successfully "closing with" the people and the enemy, daily activity within the company AO typically focused on how to bring a greater level of stability through shuras, re-construction projects, Afghan National Security Force recruiting, alternative seed programs, etc. More than 95% of the enemy activity from January through May 2010 involved IED finds. And, more than 90% of the finds in this period were directly due to elders, mullahs, and villagers telling us where the IEDs were located, if not digging up and bringing IEDs directly to us for disposal. Additionally, the two main IED cells in the company AO were eliminated after local national tips helped us identify and then kill, capture, or convert those that were in them.

2nd Battalion, 2nd Marine Regiment
After Action Report for OPERATION ENDURING FREEDOM
April 2010

2. Tactical Shaping of the Environment

a. **Lethal Options**. While the tactical level is normally focused on combat and security operations, it is also heavily involved in the nonlethal shaping of the (local) environment through interaction with the enemy and local influence leaders.

(1) The first requirement in COIN operations is to separate the enemy from the local population and the support base. Winning the support of the population for the legitimate government will often entail a breaking of the ideological, financial or intimidation linkages between insurgent leaders and their supporters, perhaps one family grouping or village at a time. Initially "clearing" the enemy from an area – this can be by physically eliminating him or by denying him the freedom of movement and action he previously enjoyed – is a combat operation. In a full scale insurgency the battle must be brought to the insurgent and friendly forces must maintain continuous pressure on the enemy – kill, capture, or convert to the government side. A successful military operation can turn the tide (locally) and permit civilian measures to start the slow process towards stabilizing an area one village at a time.

(2) Successfully closing on the enemy makes it very clear to the innocent people caught in the middle that the multinational forces and HN security forces can protect them and that the partnered units are the so-called "strongest tribe." Within the moral and mental dimensions of the COIN fight, it is critical that the people truly believe that they can pick their government without having to worry about intimidation or worse from the enemy.

(3) While lethal actions will often be necessary to eliminate key individuals in a network, the effects must be carefully considered as lethal actions may alienate portions of the population. An arrest and prosecution can remove an enemy from the battlefield as effectively as a bullet.

b. **Nonlethal Options - Gaining the Population's Confidence**. The people are the prize, and the people are our greatest weapon against insurgents. People have needs that vary from severe medical problems to everyday run-of-the-mill issues. If these problems can be resolved by friendly forces when the insurgent can't, defeating the enemy's cause is much easier. There are a number of simple techniques that can be employed to gain the population's support:

(1) **Establish a working partnership with the local security forces (Army and Police).** Conducting joint patrols, collocating living arrangements, integrate security

forces into meetings and planning sessions for partnered operations, understanding cultural restrictions, all of these contribute to working understanding of the local environment and to setting a positive example for the population.

> From day one in southern Afghanistan, Fightin' Fox, partnered with our Afghan National Army (ANA) brothers and eventually a small Afghan National Police (ANP) force, focused on crushing the enemy's will to fight, while tirelessly engaging all elders, mullahs, and villagers in an effort to bring stability to the area. These daily engagements played a key role in ultimately convincing thousands of Afghans caught in the middle of the fight that the Marines and their ANSF were in their villages to not only hunt the enemy, but just as important, if not more important, to simultaneously do everything that we could to help the innocent. Local elders, mullahs, and villagers became increasingly convinced of our genuine desire to help after partnered Marine-ANA units cleared IED-laden roads for them; helped them fix roads and bazaars that had been destroyed by years of war; precisely killed, captured, and/or converted more than 65 enemy fighters; provided medical assistance to more than 2,300 local nationals (to include formal evaluations and treatment for in excess of 100 Afghan women); helped establish an executive elder shura that connected the people to their legitimate district government for the first time in years; etc.
>
> **2nd Battalion, 2nd Marine Regiment**
> **After Action Report for OPERATION ENDURING FREEDOM**
> **April 2010**

(2) **Conduct Key Leader Engagements (KLE).** Securing the support of the local leadership requires delicate negotiation. They must be convinced that you are stronger than the enemy, can benefit their interests, and are there to stay. While the actual techniques for conducting KLE are situationally driven at the village level, night KLEs should be a daily occurrence. Bring a doctor and/or (in Muslim countries) a female engagement team (FET) to offer medical assistance (elders were grateful when a female corpsman was present to provide medical treatment for their wives and/or children). Also, bring a computer that has the unit's detailed human terrain mapping database on it. Go through every picture with the elder. Ask him to tell you about all individuals, their history, their desires, and, when the time is right, the enemy. Repeat this process frequently with as many elders as possible. Based on collective input from all the elders and from as many villages as possible, information gained from your night KLEs will likely decrease, if not altogether eliminate, the enemy's ability to "hide among the population."

(3) **Support Economic Development Initiatives.** In addition to providing physical security, one of the most effective ways to win people to the government side is to enable legitimate governance by providing tangible economic benefits. A comprehensive COIN program will involve multinational "whole of government" initiatives to stabilize the HN politically and economically. At the local level, these initiatives will feature the employment of experts in development and agriculture, backed by appropriate funding, deployed to district level to assist the HN government in establishing its credibility with the people. Developing and maintaining a close relationship with these (Provincial Reconstruction

or District Support) teams and closely coordinating the military's with this civilian effort are essential to achieving stability.

See also the USJFCOM publication, "Commander's Handbook on Military Support to Economic Stabilization," for a detailed discussion on economic development initiatives.

> **The District Support Team was led by British and US diplomats and supported by development and agriculture experts from the US, Britain, New Zealand, and Afghanistan. Among the District Support Team's many tasks were to assist the district governor in enabling legitimate governance throughout Garmsir District. This was done through a variety of governance, economic, ANSF, and security-related initiatives. For example, the team leader worked closely with the district government leadership to enable key elders to return from Lashkar Gah; to inspire and implement ANSF recruiting efforts; to spread United States Agency for International Development (USAID) agricultural initiatives throughout Garmsir District; and to formalize and oversee a prisoner review shura for all individuals detained by ISAF, ANA, or the ANP... Every elder in the company AO knew him by face and name. He personally proved integral to bringing the AO's main elders home from Lashkar Gah, in getting the police recruiting drive off the ground, in quelling the protests over the falsified Koran desecration stories, and in bringing a school, medical clinic, and police station project to Mian Poshteh.**
>
> **2nd Battalion, 2nd Marine Regiment**
> **After Action Report for OPERATION ENDURING FREEDOM**
> **April 2010**

(4) **Employ Information Operations**

(a) Multi-echelon, synchronized IO is an essential element to gaining the trust of the population and influencing the OE. At the tactical level, the message must be carefully tailored to the local audience, focusing on the community's key influence peddlers and using media (radio, print, clerics) that resonate with the population. Friendly forces must get the message out at every opportunity. The IO messages must tangibly convey to the population that the enemy Taliban truly has nothing to offer the local populace whereas we can, have, and will continue to bring the people legitimate government leadership, security led by the HN security forces, veterinarian assistance, doctors, money, projects, the list goes on. Friendly forces should always support the local government by enabling the friendly tribal leaders to take credit for beneficial development projects.

(b) The enemy also is trying to influence the local power base and it is necessary to identify the TTP the enemy is employing to gain and maintain that influence. At a minimum:

1. Identify what motivated enemy forces (religion, money fear, pride).

2. Determine what goods and services the enemy provides the locals to gain leverage over them. Identify superior alternatives that you can provide.

3. Determine what coercion or threats the enemy uses to gain leverage over the locals. Interdict the communication of the threat or protect them from it.

4. Talk to the locals to identify the hierarchy of needs at their level. Their priorities are rarely the same as ours, or of each other.

(c) Tactical level examples of IO techniques include:

1. Squad leaders often engage with local nationals who have questions about: "what are you (friendly forces) doing for us?" A simple solution is to carry an "IO playbook." The "playbook" enables friendly forces to capitalize on every friendly force/enemy action that you can snap a picture of and turn it into true, physical evidence that you can use to gain the trust and confidence of the locals. Pictures go a long way toward getting a point across. Experience suggests that one can often tell an Afghan everything being accomplished with minimal effects, but showing that individual the physical proof of the effort drives the point home a million times over.

> Many times after showing these IO "plays", we have received tips on IED locations, enemy activity, etc. For example, in one instance where a local doctor questioned Afghan National Army and Marine leadership about how much we'd helped the average Afghan, the ANA and Marine leaders walked the doctor through the IO "playbook" for over 35 minutes. The doctor stopped the ANA and Marine leaders in the middle of going over the IO "playbook" and said the following in English: "Do you have map by my house?" The patrol leader did not have a detailed enough map with him. The Afghan doctor then took out a notepad and drew and talked the Marine and ANA leadership onto an IED location that was confirmed the following morning.
>
> **2nd Battalion, 2nd Marine Regiment**
> **After Action Report for OPERATION ENDURING FREEDOM**
> **April 2010**

2. Small gifts can have far ranging impact. For example providing civilians with combination battery-powered and hand-crank radios is not only a friendly gesture, but it also enables them to listen to the friendly forces sponsored radio programs that are broadcasting the IO messages. It's all about who tells the story first and loudest. Putting the truth on the radio quickly is essential to making sure the enemy can't spread lies about any actions/events that have unfolded.

(5) **Leverage Cultural Sensitivities**. In most third world societies, the women in the family wield enormous power and have access to a great deal of information. Reaching out to these potential sources can be complicated by cultural restrictions. In Afghanistan, US forces have employed female military members as Female Engagement Teams to "win the woman of the house, win the household." In the majority of villages, the women know the insurgents and the foreign fighters, where the IEDs and weapons caches are located, and who is running the local society.

(6) **Leverage Technology**. Biometric recording of the population (enhanced ID cards) robs the enemy of his ability to "hide among the people." In Afghanistan, multiple enemy fighters have been identified through their fingerprints gained from BAT enrollment when compared to IED evidence that was collected and the sent to the combined exploitation cell. Employing portable photographic databases that can be reviewed during KLEs is an essential tool.

> Throughout the deployment, we have routinely gained actionable intelligence from key leader engagements that take place after the final call for prayer. These engagements have lasted anywhere from an hour to throughout the entire night, with Marines, Sailors, and ANA Soldiers sometimes being asked to stay in an elder's guest-house. Afghans are much more comfortable talking with ISAF and the ANA at night, in the confines of their own guest-houses, where no one else is observing. It is often best to set conditions for such engagements by informing the elder earlier in the day that you'd like to visit that night or on a subsequent night, but this is not always necessary. Depending on relationships developed, elders might request for you to visit. If small unit leaders (i.e., squad leaders through the company commander), including the ANA, develop relationships with elders, these engagements will greatly increase a unit's tempo against the enemy, as the elders – who naturally have an informant network that ranges anywhere from 40 to in excess of 100 male villagers, not to mention thousands of tribal members in some cases – will tell you a great deal about who the enemy is, how he operates, and how to counter him. Further, these engagements might lead to the unit gaining information that will lead to detaining an enemy fighter. To lock-up enemy fighters in the Afghan justice system, you will often need witness statements from local elders. We have found that the best way to get these statements is at night, one-on-one, with key elders. In addition to enhancing the unit's understanding of the enemy, night KLEs are also vital in that they help connect ISAF and the ANSF to the local community in ways that are nearly impossible to do during daylight hours. Simple conversations about life in the U.S., a Marine or Sailor's family, goals in life, etc. often set the conditions for the elders wanting to tell you about the enemy – because he realizes that your unit is, indeed, in Afghanistan to help him, his family, and the innocent Afghan people.
>
> **2nd Battalion, 2nd Marine Regiment**
> **After Action Report for OPERATION ENDURING FREEDOM**
> **April 2010**

c. **Reporting and Information Sharing**. The aforementioned techniques are designed to encourage the local population to provide friendly forces with information on: the local society and who the real power brokers are; the needs of the people (i.e., a new well, school supplies, doctor visits, etc); and, on the enemy. At the tactical level, a system should be in place to facilitate the rapid sharing of collected information with all units in the local AO who may organize an AtN response. Specific TTP used to successfully gain information about the innocent and the enemy in one AO can typically be applied across a unit's battlespace. Tactical patrols should provide the following in their situation reports:

(1) Who the patrols spoke to, what were the main points of the conversations, what, if any, assistance did the locals request.

(2) Did the locals provide tips about enemy activity? If yes, why?

(3) Where was the patrol when the locals told them?

Detailed reporting further enhances the unit's understanding of their local environment and facilitates their ability to organize the fight and more effectively manage that environment by employing their enablers to attack the network. For example, if one unit's patrol de-brief commented on a KLE where an elder discussed enemy activity, the commander (or the company staff) then, with a few words on the SITREP, ensured that all positions understood what was being reported and the commander's expectation to find out more details or to act on the information dependent on the initial details.

> On one such occasion, a senior Taliban judge and recruiter came to Marine and ANA leadership one night begging us to allow him to reconcile. He openly admitted to working for the Taliban in the past and said that he wanted to reconcile. When asked why, he said "you know what I've done and now everyone knows what I've done." He further begged us to stop showing his picture to anyone. This particular Taliban leader turned primarily because a partnered squad was told one night by an elder, after seeing the judge's picture in the company's human terrain database, that he was evil. The squad's de-brief was then passed through the company to adjacent units who then applied maximum pressure to the enemy system by ensuring that the judge's picture was included in most every KLE. And, in these KLEs, most elders validated information that we already knew without prodding. We then told the elder that we already knew about the judge and were rapidly closing on him. The judge got the message, came to us for his freedom, and then went to the district governor and requested to officially reconcile with the Afghan government.
>
> **2nd Battalion, 2nd Marine Regiment**
> **After Action Report for OPERATION ENDURING FREEDOM**
> **April 2010**

d. **Attacking the Network Locally**. Gaining the initiative in tactical AtN operations is based on the timeliness and quality of the information gathered by units operating in their respective AOs. At the tactical level, AtN is accomplished piece by piece, cache by cache, fighter by fighter. It involves a steady whittling away at the enemy's infrastructure and support base so that he is denied freedom of action and freedom of movement and is placed permanently on the defensive. By isolating the enemy from the people by countless (but organized) actions at the individual, home, and village level; friendly forces can eventually tear apart the threat network at the local level. Sometimes the best way to crush the network involves going after its leader; at other times, the support network; and still other times, the middle-man. In all cases, **detailed investigative work is required if the friendly forces intend to succeed**. The following is an example of how all these pieces came together.

Recently, Fightin' Fox (2d Battalion, 2d Marine Regiment) detained an IED cell leader after months of detailed investigative work. This work started with detailed human terrain mapping and then a series of night KLEs that identified the IED cell leader as an active Taliban fighter. A few weeks later, a reliable informant that owns a construction shop in a nearby bazaar told our ANA partners that two Taliban fighters recently asked him to make them a few pressure plates, which he assumed were for IEDs. The informant then spent hours looking through our human terrain database to find the two Taliban fighters. Next, multiple local nationals told Fightin' Fox Marines and the ANA about a few recently emplaced IEDs. While they couldn't give us a picture of the Taliban fighter that emplaced the IEDs, they did know one of his names. In cross-referencing our active Taliban fighter database, similar to what cops do in the U.S. and similar to what many of Fightin' Fox's leaders observed on their ride-alongs, we then identified the IED emplacer's name as the same as one of the two Taliban fighters that bought the pressure plates. Then, through a series of night KLEs and medical visits, we obtained six witness statements against the Taliban IED cell leader, all from elders and local villagers who either knew that he emplaced the IEDs and/or that watched him emplace the IEDs. Due to the detailed investigative work, the IED emplacer will now go to jail, likely for up to 10 years. Further, after detaining this Taliban IED cell leader less than 72 hours after he emplaced the IEDs, two more Taliban fighters have approached their elders seeking to reconcile with the government out of fear that the Marines and ANA have already compiled enough evidence to detain them as well.

2nd Battalion, 2nd Marine Regiment
After Action Report for OPERATION ENDURING FREEDOM
April 2010

Intentionally Blank

GLOSSARY
PART I - ABBREVIATIONS AND ACRONYMS

AO	area of operations
ANA	Afghan National Army
ANAT	advanced network analysis and targeting
ANP	Afghan National Police
ANSF	Afghan National Security Forces
ATF	Bureau of Alcohol, Tobacco, and Firearms
AtN	attack the network
AWG	asymmetric warfare group
BCT	brigade combat team
BDA	battle damage assessment
C2	command and control
CA	civil affairs
CALL	Center for Army Lessons Learned
CAP	capabilities
CARVER	criticality, accessibility, recuperability, vulnerability, effect, recognizability
CELLEX	cellular exploitation
CCIR	commander's critical information requirements
CDR	commander
CEXC	combined exploitation center
CFA	critical factors analysis
C-IED	counter-improvised explosive device
CIDNE	Combined Information Data Network Exchange
CITP	counterinsurgency targeting program (formerly the counter-IED targeting program)
CJTF	commander, joint task force commander
CNO	computer network operations
COIC	counter-IED operations integration center
COIN	counterinsurgency
COA	courses of action
COE	center of excellence
COG	center of gravity
COIST	company intelligence support team
COM	Chief of Mission
CONOPS	concept of operations
CONUS	continental United States
CPOF	command post of the future
CTF	counter threat finance
D3A	decide, detect, deliver, and assess
DCGS-A	distributable common ground system – Army
DEA	Drug Enforcement Administration

DHS	Department of Homeland Security
DET	detonation
DIA	Defense Intelligence Agency
DIME	diplomatic, information, military, economic
DOD	Department of Defense
DOMEX	document and media exploitation
EOD	explosive ordnance disposal
EW	electronic warfare
F2T2EA	find, fix, track, target, engage, assess
F3EAD	find, fix, finish, exploit, analyze, disseminate
FARC	Revolutionary Armed Forces of Columbia
FBI	Federal Bureau of Investigation
FET	female engagement team
FIU	financial intelligence unit
FRAGORD	fragmentary order
GCC	geographic combatant commander
GEO	geospatial
GEOINT	geospatial intelligence
GIS	geographic information system
GMI	general military intelligence
GMLRS	guided multiple launched rocket system
GMTI	ground moving target indicator
HUMINT	human intelligence
HET	human environment team
HN	host nation
HPT	high payoff target
HTT	human terrain teams
HVI	high value individual
IA	interagency
IC	intelligence community
IED	improvised explosive device
IGO	intergovernmental organization
IO	information operations
IMO	information management officer
ISR	intelligence, surveillance, and reconnaissance
J-2	intelligence directorate of a joint staff
J-3	operations directorate of a joint staff
JCAST	joint counter-IED analytical support team
JCOE	joint center of excellence
JET	joint expeditionary team
JIACG	joint interagency coordination group
JIATF	joint interagency task force

JIEDDO	Joint Improvised Explosive Device Defeat Organization
JIOC	joint intelligence operations center
JIPOE	joint intelligence preparation of the operational environment
JIWCS	joint intelligence world-wide communications system
JKNIFE	JIEDDO knowledge and information fusion exchange
JSTARS	joint surveillance target attack radar system
JFC	joint force commander
JTF	joint task force
KLE	key leader engagement
KMO	knowledge management officer
LEP	law enforcement professional
LOE	line of effort
LLVI	low level voice intercept
MASINT	measurements and signatures intelligence
MAWS	money as a weapons system
MEDEX	medical exploitation
MISO	military information support and/to operations
MOE	measures of effectiveness
MOP	measures of performance
NAI	named area of interest
NATO	North Atlantic Treaty Organization
NGA	National Geospatial Intelligence Agency
NGIC	National Ground Intelligence Center
NGO	non-governmental organization
OE	operational environment
OPLAN	operation plan
ORSA	operations research/systems analyst
OPSEC	operations security
OSINT	open source intelligence
PA	public affairs
PIR	priority intelligence requirements
PMESII	political, military, economic, social, infrastructure, information
PN	partner nation
PRT	provincial reconstruction teams
RAID	rapid aerostat initial deployment
RFI	request for information
RFS	request for support
ROVER	remote operational video enhanced receiver
SAT	signatures analysis team
SE	site exploitation

SIGACT	significant action
SIGINT	signals intelligence
SIPRNET	SECRET internet router protocol network
SIR	serious incident report
SF	special forces
SJA	staff judge advocate
SOF	special operations forces
SME	subject matter expert
SNA	social network analysis
STT	stability and transition teams
SWEAT-MS	sewer, water, electricity, academics, transportation, medical, safety
TAI	target area of interest
TiGRNet	tactical ground reporting network
TF	task force
TECHINT	technical intelligence
TEDAC	Terrorist Explosive Device Analytical Center
TST	time sensitive target
TM	team
TFE	threat finance exploitation
TQ	tactical exploitation
TSE	tactical site exploitation
TTP	tactics, techniques, and procedures
TTL	tag, track, locate
UGS	unattended ground sensor
US	United States
USAID	US Agency for International Development
USG	United States Government
USAFRICOM	United States Africa Command
USCENTCOM	United States Central Command
USEUCOM	United States European Command
USNORTHCOM	United States Northern Command
USPACOM	United States Pacific Command
USSOUTHCOM	United States Southern Command
UAV	unmanned aerial vehicle
UAS	unmanned aircraft system
UN	United Nations
WebTAS	web-based temporal analysis system
WG	working group
WTI	weapons technical intelligence

PART II — APPROVED JOINT TERMS AND DEFINITIONS

assessment — 1. A continuous process that measures the overall effectiveness of employing joint force capabilities during military operations. 2. Determination of the progress toward accomplishing a task, creating an effect, or achieving an objective. (JP 3-0)

battle damage assessment — The estimate of damage resulting from the application of lethal or nonlethal military force. Battle damage assessment is composed of physical damage assessment, functional damage assessment, and target system assessment. Also called **BDA**. (JP 3-0)

biometrics — The process of recognizing an individual based on measurable anatomical, physiological, and behavioral characteristics. (JP 2-0)

CARVER — A special operations forces acronym used throughout the targeting and mission planning cycle to assess mission validity and requirements. The acronym stands for criticality, accessibility, recuperability, vulnerability, effect, and recognizability. (JP 3-05.1)

cell — A subordinate organization formed around a specific process, capability, or activity within a designated larger organization of a joint force commander's headquarters. A cell usually is part of both a functional and traditional staff structures. (JP 3-33)

center of gravity — The source of power that provides moral or physical strength, freedom of action, or will to act. Also called **COG**. (JP 3-0)

collection — In intelligence usage, the acquisition of information and the provision of this information to processing elements. (JP 2-01)

counterinsurgency — Comprehensive civilian and military efforts taken to defeat an insurgency and to address any core grievances. Also called **COIN**. (JP 3-24)

counterterrorism — Actions taken directly against terrorist networks and indirectly to influence and render global and regional environments inhospitable to terrorist networks. Also called **CT**. See also antiterrorism; combating terrorism; terrorism. (JP 3-26)

critical capability — A means that is considered a crucial enabler for a center of gravity to function as such and is essential to the accomplishment of the specified or assumed objective(s). (JP 5-0)

critical requirement — An essential condition, resource, and means for a critical capability to be fully operational. (JP 5-0)

critical vulnerability — An aspect of a critical requirement which is deficient or vulnerable to direct or indirect attack that will create decisive or significant effects. (JP 5-0)

detection — 1. In tactical operations, the perception of an object of possible military interest but unconfirmed by recognition. 2. In surveillance, the determination and transmission by a surveillance system that an event has occurred. (JP 3-11)

dynamic targeting — Targeting that prosecutes targets identified too late, or not selected for action in time to be included in deliberate targeting. (JP 3-60)

exploitation — 1. Taking full advantage of success in military operations, following up initial gains, and making permanent the temporary effects already achieved. 2. Taking full advantage of any information that has come to hand for tactical, operational, or strategic purposes. 3. An offensive operation that usually follows a successful attack and is designed to disorganize the enemy in depth. (JP 2-01.3)

link — A behavioral, physical, or functional relationship between nodes. (JP 3-0)

measure of effectiveness — A criterion used to assess changes in system behavior, capability, or operational environment that is tied to measuring the attainment of an end state, achievement of an objective, or creation of an effect. Also called **MOE**. (JP 3-0)

measure of performance — A criterion used to assess friendly actions that is tied to measuring task accomplishment. Also called **MOP**. (JP 3-0)

mission — 1. The task, together with the purpose, that clearly indicates the action to be taken and the reason therefore. (JP 3-0) 2. In common usage, especially when applied to lower military units, a duty assigned to an individual or unit; a task. (JP 3-0)

named area of interest — The geospatial area or systems node or link against which information that will satisfy a specific information requirement can be collected. Named areas of interest are usually selected to capture indications of adversary courses of action, but also may be related to conditions of the operational environment. Also called **NAI**. (JP 2-01.3)

node — An element of a system that represents a person, place, or physical thing. (JP 3-0)

nonlethal weapon — A weapon that is explicitly designed and primarily employed so as to incapacitate personnel or materiel, while minimizing fatalities, permanent injury to personnel, and undesired damage to property and the environment. (JP 3-28)

operational area — An overarching term encompassing more descriptive terms for geographic areas in which military operations are conducted. Operational areas include, but are not limited to, such descriptors as area of responsibility, theater of war, theater of operations, joint operations area, amphibious objective area, joint special operations area, and area of operations. Also called **OA**. (JP 3-0)

system — A functionally, physically, and/or behaviorally related group of regularly interacting or interdependent elements; that group of elements forming a unified whole. (JP 3-0)

target — 1. An entity or object considered for possible engagement or other action. 2. In intelligence usage, a country, area, installation, agency, or person against which intelligence operations are directed. (JP 3-60)

targeting — The process of selecting and prioritizing targets and matching the appropriate response to them, considering operational requirements and capabilities. (JP 3-0)

Intentionally Blank

Commander's Handbook for Attack the Network

PART III – ATTACK THE NETWORK
RELATED TERMS AND DEFINITIONS

The following terms, abbreviations, and definitions not present in JP 1-02, *Department of the Defense Dictionary of Military and Associated Terms*, have been developed to support AtN planning, execution, and assessment. They are still in development and some change is expected as the construct is refined.

3d Dashboard — The 3D Dashboard is a tool used by the JIEDDO COIC to view, navigate, and mark 3D map models.

academia — In the SWEAT-MA construct, academia is the life, community, or world of teachers, schools, and education.

accepted as meaningful — For a measure to be meaningful, it must present data that allow us to take action. It must be customer oriented and support the meeting of our organizational goals and objectives. Metrics foster process understanding and motivate action to continually improve the way we do business.

accommodating environment — The tangible elements (such as infrastructure and terrain) and intangible attributes (such as culture and governance) of the environment that allow the adversary network to operate.

activities matrix — The activities matrix determines connectivity between individuals and anything other than persons (interest/entity). The activities matrix reveals an organization's membership, organizational structure and size, communications network, support structure, linkages with other organizations and entities, group activities and operations, and, national or international ties.

Analyst Notebook — Analyst Notebook is a commercial link analysis and visualization tool that quickly turns large sets of disparate information into high-quality and actionable intelligence to prevent crime and terrorism.

analyze — the ability to apply analytical techniques to identify friendly, neutral, and threat network goals, characteristics, members and TTPs and maintain a detailed understanding of the operational environment in which they operate.

analyze the network — To analyze the network is to examine methodologically the various network kinds of networks by separating them into parts and studying their interrelations. It can include comparing and contrasting various networks to each other in order to understand them.

Anti-Armor Analysis Program — is an analytic program run by the National Ground Intelligence Center (NGIC) that analyzes and adversary development, manufacture, procurement and use of anti-armor weapons. Also called **AAAP**.

areas — Areas in the context of the memory aid ASCOPE are localities or physical terrains that have direct impact on the population and its activities. Examples include tribal regions, police districts, political boundaries, religious boundaries, territorial boundaries, military boundaries, polling stations, and government centers.

ARC/GIS — ArcGIS is a system for people who rely on accurate geographic information to make decisions. It facilitates collaboration and lets you easily author data, maps, globes, and models on the desktop   and serve them out for use on a desktop, in a browser, or in the   field, depending on the needs of your organization.

ASCOPE — ASCOPE is a memory aid when evaluating civil considerations during mission analysis: areas, structures, capabilities, organizations, people, and events.

Assess — Assessment is the continuous process that measures the overall effectiveness of employing joint force capabilities during military operations.

assessment working group — The assessment working group is cross-functional by design and includes membership from across the staff, liaison personnel, and other partners outside the headquarters. The assessment working group fuses assessment information to provide a comprehensive assessment of the operation. They consolidate and discuss emerging trends, issues, and impacts relating to events over the various planning horizons.

association matrix — The association matrix displays a relationship between individuals. It reflects associations within a group or similar activity, and is based on the assumption that people involved in a collective   activity know one another. The format of an association matrix is a right triangle; each name requires a row and column. The association matrix shows known and suspected associations.   Analysts determine a known association by "direct contact" between individuals. Direct contact is defined as face-to-face   meetings or confirmed telephonic conversation between known parties and all members of a particular organization (proponent FM TBD). This is depicted as a filled circle and placed in the square where the two names meet within the matrix. An unfilled circle indicates suspected or weak associations. When an individual dies, a diamond is added at the end of his or her name.

Asymmetric Warfare Group — The Asymmetric Warfare Group (AWG) provides operational advisory assistance in support of Army and joint force commanders. The AWG was created by the Army to enhance the combat effectiveness of the operating force and enable the defeat of asymmetric threats to include IEDs. The AWG deploys its forces worldwide to observe, assess, and analyze information regarding the evolving operating environment and the threat. They also assist in the development, dissemination and integration of material and non material solutions including countermeasures. The AWG serves as an agent of change providing key observations and perspectives for leaders when considering policy and resource decisions.

arms control and disarmament — The identification, verification, inspection, limitation, control, reduction, or elimination of armed forces and armaments of all kinds under international agreement including the necessary steps taken under such an agreement to establish an effective system of international control, or to create and strengthen international organizations for the maintenance of peace.

attack — The ability to conduct deliberate and purposeful lethal and nonlethal offensive operations that engage threat networks or achieve the commander's desired effects against elements of the threat network.

attack the network — A focused approach to understanding and operating against a well-defined type of enemy activity—such as terrorism, insurgency ,and organized criminal actions—that threatens stability in the operational area and is enabled by a network of identifiable nodes and links. Also called **AtN**.

attack the network lead — The attack the network lead is that individual whose function is to organize and supervise the attack the network activities within the staff, to include the various fusion cells and working groups. Also called **AtN Lead**.

attack the network training — AtN Training is the instruction of personnel to enhance their capacity to perform specific AtN functions and tasks. It is also the exercise of one or more military units conducted to enhance their combat readiness. Also called **AtN training**.

Automated Information System — An assembly of computer hardware, software, and/or firmware configured to collect, create, communicate, compute, disseminate, process, store and/or control data or information. Also called **AIS**.

Axis Pro — Axis Pro is a JIEDDO COIC tool that links entities to original data sources and enables advanced queries of data contained with separate link nodal projects.

black network — Black networks are formal and /or informal grouping of criminals that are not necessarily adversarial to the friendly networks, but thwart attempts to create stability so that they can further the aims of their criminal enterprises.

blended network — A blended network has a structure that is a combination of hierarchical and non-hierarchical organizations.

blue network — Blue networks are military and government civilian US, allied and coalition forces.

capabilities — Capabilities in the context of the memory aid ASCOPE are key functions and services. They include, but are not limited to, administration, safety, emergency services, food distribution, agricultural systems, and public safety.

capability gap & solutions — Capability gap & solution analysis is a part of the systematic solutions procurement process established by DOD to identify missing or incomplete capabilities and the solutions to provide those capabilities. The functional solutions analysis follows the functional need analysis that identifies the capability requirement in detail.

capture — To capture is to take into custody of a hostile force, equipment, or personnel as a result of military operations.

catalyst leadership — The person or persons who enable the threat network to form, either through their direct leadership or through their ability to mobilize disparate groups.

cause and effect chart — Cause and effect diagram graphically illustrates the relationship between a given outcome and all the factors that influence this outcome, also called a fishbone diagram (because of its resemblance to a fish skeleton) or Ishikawa diagram.

cell — A cell in social network analysis consists of a small group of individuals who work together for clandestine or subversive purposes.

CELLPACK — CELLPACK is a program used by the JIEDDO COIC to analyze and data mine a list of phone numbers in order to return multiple results as a hypertext markup language page.

Center for Army Lessons Learned — The Center for Army Lessons Learned one of the Army's central knowledge management organization that rapidly collects, analyzes, disseminates, and archives OIL, TTP and operational records in order to facilitate rapid adaptation initiatives and conduct focused knowledge sharing and transfer that informs the Army and enables operationally based decision making, integration, and innovation throughout the Army and within the JIIM environment. Also referred to as **CALL**.

characteristics of a network — Characteristics of a network are the discernible physical, operational, and technical features of a network. The common basic characteristics of a network include its structure and its density.

check sheet — Check sheet is a simple form used to collect data in an organized manner.

civil considerations — Civil considerations entails reflecting before the mission how the manmade infrastructure, civilian institutions, and attitudes and activities of the civilian leaders, populations, and organizations within an area of operations will influence the conduct of the mission.

clearly defined — A metric is clearly defined when it is unambiguously presented or explained.

co-adaptive — Co-adaptive systems adapt to something that is adapting to it. These systems must continually evolve to survive, and members must adapt to their changing environment and the forces that counter it.

collect — To collect is the to methodically identify, gather, and process information to gain a detailed understanding of the operational environment and the friendly, neutral, and threat networks operating within it.

collect & analyze metrics — To collect and analyze metrics is to continue to aggregate metric data over time, to examine trends. It also includes investigating common cause effects on the data and comparing the data to interim performance levels.

Combat Hunter — Combat Hunter is a ten-day course provided by the Marine Corps to create a hunting mindset by integrating enhanced observation, combat profiling, and combat tracking skills in order to produce a more ethically minded, tactically cunning, and lethal infantryman that is better prepared to succeed across the range of military operations.

combatant command CIED cell — The combatant command C-IED cell is the counter-IED team command formed and staffed by the combatant command that provides IED analysis, C-IED services, and liaison to other C-IED capabilities.

Combined Explosives Exploitation Cell – The Combined Explosives Exploitation Cell is a US Navy led, unique joint, combined organization composed of personnel from military, EOD, and intelligence and is often augmented by government agencies with subject matter experts in the fields of explosives, ordnance, IEDs, post blast investigation, and terrorism. The cell's mission is the collection and exploitation of technical weapons intelligence and forensic evidence for the purpose of identifying bomb makers and assisting in the development of defensive and offensive C-IED measures. Also known as **CEXC**.

Combined Information Data Exchange Network — The Combined Information Data Exchange Network is the USCENTCOM-directed reporting tool within Iraq and Afghanistan. It serves as the primary bridge between disparate communities who might not otherwise share data by providing a standardized reporting framework across intelligence and operations disciplines. This common framework allows structured operational and intelligence information to be shared vertically and horizontally as part of flexible, user-defined workflow processes that collect, correlate, aggregate and expose information as part of the end-user's individual information lifecycle requirements. Also referred to as **CIDNE**.

Combined Forces Special Operations Component Command — The forward headquarters for SOCCENT and has operational control (OPCON) over SOF units in the USCENTCOM AOR. Also called **CFSOCC**.

commander's guidance — To ensure focused and effective planning, the commander and staff develop and communicate planning guidance that will accompany tentative courses of actions to subordinate and supporting commanders for their estimates of feasibility and supportability. As a minimum, the planning guidance should include the mission statement; assumptions; operational limitations; a discussion of the national strategic end state; termination criteria; military objectives; and the JFC's initial thoughts on desired and undesired effects. The planning guidance should also address the role of agencies and multinational partners in the pending operation and any related special considerations as required.

company intelligence support teams/company-level intelligence centers — A recently developed capability to provide analytical products at the company-level that have typically been resident at the battalion level and higher. Also referred to as **COISTs** or **CLICs**.

complex adaptive system — Complex adaptive systems consist of many diverse and autonomous components or parts which are interrelated, interdependent, and behave as a unified whole in learning from experience and in adjusting to changes in the environment.

Comprehensive Look Team — The Comprehensive Look Team at JIEDDO's COIC provides comprehensive, multi-disciplinary intelligence analysis in support of the C-IED mission and other attack the network operations as required. Also referred to as **CLT**.

control chart — Control chart is a tool used to analyze process variability over time. They measure the process in a time dimension and show movement toward or away from an average. Control charts have statistically calculated upper and lower control limits.

cordon — A cordon is an operation to encircle an area, to prevent entrance and exit, and to secure open areas.

counter-improvised explosive device operations integration cell — The counter-improvised explosive device operations integration cell leverages existing information and provides strategic capabilities in support of offensive operations against IED networks. Its fused intelligence products are released at the collateral level for warfighters at the tactical level. The cell's architecture of partnerships include more than 20 intelligence agencies and other federal agencies supporting this effort. Also called **COIC**.

counter-improvised explosive device support elements — The counter-improvised explosive device (C-IED) support elements are teams designed to assist the maneuver unit in the planning, coordination and integration of their immediate C-IED operations, and they act as a liaison to the C-IED task force. The C-IED support elements also coordinate the unit's IED infrastructure targeting efforts.

COIC Pattern Analysis Team — A group that identifies, analyzes, and resolves tactical patterns in support of JIEDDO/COIC and its partners in the defense, intelligence, and national security communities, and applies tactical pattern analysis methods to other problems in response to requests for support from authorized users worldwide. Operational research and statistical analysis provides a scientific basis to commanders for operational decisions. Also referred to as **CPAT/ORSA**.

Counter-Improvised Explosive Device Task Force Paladin — The counter-improvised explosive device task force (C-IED TF Paladin) is the C-IED task force at the JTF-level in Afghanistan that has primary responsibility for managing the JTF's C-IED assets and coordinating the activities of many of the assigned/attached C-IED enabling organizations. When a C-IED TF is established, the JTF staff resumes a more traditional staff role in establishing policy and general direction for the JTF's overall C-IED effort.

counter-improvised explosive device site exploitation — The site exploitation teams recognize, collect, process, preserve, or analyze information, personnel, and materiel found during the conduct of C-IED operations for follow-on use by the intelligence or warfighting functions of the staff. Also referred to as **C-IED/SE**.

Counterinsurgency Advisory and Assistance Team-Afghanistan — Because there was inadequate visibility for the Commander, International Security Assistance Force (COMISAF), on the implementation of counterinsurgency (COIN) best practices. The Counterinsurgency Advisory and Assistance Team (CAAT) was created to address these problems. The CAAT's mission is to assist commanders in integrating all aspects of COIN operations. Its purpose is to assist Commanders, identify trends, and disseminate lessons learned to facilitate ISAF organizational and cultural change. Also called **CAAT-A**.

Counterinsurgency Targeting Program — The Counterinsurgency Targeting Program conducts WTI-related identity analysis, biometric analysis, and device or component analysis to support the targeting of key individuals in adversary IED networks. They work closely with the NGIC's biometrics effort to rapidly match individuals to specific IED incidents by matching and assessing latent prints, fibers, and other data. Also referred to as **CITP**.

counter threat finance — Activities include, but are not limited to, countering: narcotics trafficking, proliferation activities, WMD networks, trafficking in persons, weapons trafficking, precursor chemical smuggling, terrorist revenue and logistics, and other such activities that generate revenue through illicit trafficking networks. Also referred to as **CTF**.

Criminal Investigative Division and Law Enforcement Programs — The programs bring together experienced law enforcement professionals from the Drug Enforcement Agency, Federal Bureau of Investigation, police departments, and other agencies in order to lend their expertise to teach and support military personnel to investigate bomb-making networks, investigate incidents, question witnesses and suspects, and collect evidence for pending C-IED operations and prosecutions. Also referred to as **CID/LEP**.

critical factors analysis — The methodical examination of the analysis of critical capabilities, critical requirements, specific activities, observable and measureable indicators, and critical vulnerabilities of an adversary. Also referred to as **CFA**.

critical factors analysis comprehensive look team — The critical factors analysis (CFA) Comprehensive Look Team (CLT) analyzes blue, red, green, and white critical capabilities (CC), critical requirements (CR) and deduces critical vulnerabilities (CV) for exploitation to facilitate US force interests against threat networks at strategic, operational and tactical levels.

data tracker — The COIC tool is a web-deployable client application that converts tracking data in MS Excel format to Google Earth.

decide, detect, deliver, and assess — Land and maritime force commanders normally use an interrelated process to enhance joint fire support planning and interface with the joint targeting cycle known as the decide, detect, deliver, and assess methodology. It incorporates the same fundamental functions of the joint target cycle. The methodology facilitates synchronizing maneuver, intelligence, and fire support. Also called **D3A**.

decisive operation — The operation that directly accomplishes the mission. It determines the outcome of a major operation, battle, or engagement. The decisive operation is the focal point around which commanders design the entire operation.

decisive points — decisive point is a geographic place, specific key event, critical factor, or function that, when acted upon, allows a commander to gain a marked advantage over an adversary or contributes materially to achieving success.

defensive operations — Defensive operations are combat operations conducted to defeat an enemy attack, gain time, economize forces, and develop conditions favorable for offensive or stability operations.

define — "Define" is who, what, when, why, and how of this metric in sufficient detail to permit consistent, repeatable and valid measurement to take place. The operational definition starts with an understanding of your customers' expectations. You then "operationalize" the expectation(s) by defining characteristic(s) of the product, service, or process which are internally measurable and which, if improved, would better satisfy your customers' expectations.

deliberate targeting — Deliberate targeting is a category of targeting that prosecutes planned targets. These are targets that are known to exist in the operational environment with engagement actions scheduled against them to create the effects desired to support achievement of JFC objectives.

deployed capabilities — The personnel, tools, services, and material that are with and utilized by a unit in theater versus the personnel, tools, services, and material that are available by reach back to the continental US for support.

describe the network — Describing the network is to characterize and represent a network to others in words and pictures as accurately to reality as possible in order to make estimates of the network and to take actions against it. This is done through various tools and repeatable approaches.

detect — In AtN, Soldiers detect the presence of a network through the analysis of information, signatures, or materials.

deter — To deter is to prevent undesirable action by the adversary by demonstrating the capabilities and resolve of the joint force.

Defense Intelligence Agency DTK Lab — A strategic-level forensics laboratory for IED evaluation. Also referred to as DIA DTK Lab.

develop the measures of effectiveness — Through out an operation, a commander should create measures of effectiveness that are appropriate to his mission. Develop measures of effectiveness early and continuously refine them as the operation progresses. These measures should cover a range of social, informational, military, and economic issues. Use them to develop an in-depth operational picture. See how the operation is changing, not just that it is starting or ending. Typical measures of effectiveness include the following: percentage of engagements initiated by friendly forces versus those initiated by insurgents; longevity of friendly local leaders in positions of authority; number and quality of tips on insurgent activity that originate spontaneously; economic activity at markets and shops.

diplomatic (operational variable) — Integrate/partnering/leveraging host nation (HN) capabilities and political impact of ground commander's/leader's working with HN leaders through KLEs, etc. to legitimize local government. HN entities, not necessarily government: include elders, local, tribal, governmental, NGOs, regional leadership.

disseminate — the ability to share information, analytical products, TTPs, etc., in a timely manner across the strategic, operational, and tactical levels within the joint, interagency, intergovernmental, and multinational environment.

division counter-improvised explosive device support element — The element coordinates and integrates C-IED operations within the division operational area, and integrates C-IED enablers, analysis, and products into the division targeting process in order to support the division in maintaining freedom of action and defeating insurgent networks. The division C-IED support element is comprised of a mix of specialized C-IED personnel such as CEXC, CITP, intelligence analysis, operations research/systems analyst, LEP) along with intelligence and operations staff. Also referred to as the **DSE**.

document and media exploitation — The document and media exploitation center is responsible for the rapid and accurate extraction, exploitation, and analysis of captured enemy documents, media, and material collected during operations. Also referred to as **DOMEX**.

dominate — To dominate is to break the enemy's will for organized resistance or, in noncombat situations, to control the operational environment. Success in this phase depends upon overmatching joint force capability at the critical time and place.

drive appropriate action — Metrics that drive appropriate action should be aligned to organizational objectives and identify which processes are targeted for improvement through their application.

dyad — A dyad in a social network analysis consists of two nodes and a single link. Individuals in a network are called actors or nodes. (Actor and node are often used interchangeably.) The contacts between nodes are called links. The basic element of a social network graph is the dyad.

economic (operational variable) — Economic variables are those operational variables that encompass individual and group behaviors related to producing, distributing, and consuming resources.

electricity — When used in the SWEAT-MS construct, electricity infrastructure consists of the power stations and conduits necessary for delivering electric power to a society.

ELISRD — An intelligence, surveillance, and reconnaissance (ISR) analysis tool used by the JIEDDO COIC that automatically correlates ISR coverage with user driven points of interest or key events in theater to highlight "exploitation opportunities."

embassy team — The embassy team is the group of political, economic and cultural experts at the United States Mission in country and operates under the oversight of the Department of States.

emergent — Emergent systems display characteristics that are ambiguous, that cannot be anticipated from the properties of its components or parts.

enemy — An enemy is a party identified as hostile against which the use of force is authorized.

enable civil authority — To enable civil authority in an operation or campaign is to take those actions that support legitimate civil governance in theater.

enforcement of sanctions — Enforcement of sanctions is the application of military force, or the threat of its use, normally pursuant to international authorization, to compel compliance with resolutions or sanctions designed to maintain or restore peace and order.

establish baseline — Baseline data is metric data that is captured at the beginning of an operation in order to compare it to metric data collected over time.

evaluation — Evaluation is the appraisal of the effectiveness (MOE) and performance (MOP) of the friendly network's actions.

event matrix — A description of the indicators and activity expected to occur in each named area of interest. It normally cross-references each named area of interest and indicator with the times they are expected to occur and the courses of action they will confirm or deny. There is no prescribed format.

event template — An event template is a guide for collection planning. The event template depicts the named areas of interest where activity, or its lack of activity, will indicate which course of action the adversary has adopted.

event/trends/predictive analysis — Various analytical methods that attempt to anticipate enemy behavior based on past behavior.

events — Events in the context of the memory aid ASCOPE are routine, cyclical, planned, or spontaneous activities that significantly affect the operating environment.

exploit — the ability to recognize, collect, preserve, process, and analyze information, personnel, and materials found during the conduct of operations to support further success.

find, fix, track, target, engage, and assess — A dynamic targeting process. Also called **F2T2EA**.

find, fix, finish, exploit, analyze, and disseminate — A subset of the targeting process, may be used in the AtN context to engage selected high-value individuals (HVIs) or activities (caches, bomb making facilities). It incorporates the same fundamentals of the joint target cycle and facilitates synchronizing maneuver, intelligence and fire support. It features massed, persistent ISR cued to a powerful and decentralized all-source intelligence apparatus. The goal is to find an HVI or activity (weapons cache, bomb factory) in the midst of civilian clutter and fix its exact location. Also called **F3EAD**.

family network — A family network is a series of direct and indirect ties among various actors that belong to the same family. These can be cross-generational.

feasible to collect — A metric is feasible to collect when it is economical (in dollars and manpower) to collect over time.

finalize metric presentation — To finalize the metric presentation is to present the metric externally. The metric descriptors will provide enough information to communicate the appropriate details of the metric to your customer.

flow chart — Flow chart is a graphic, structured representation of all the major steps in a process.

freedom of navigation operations — Freedom of navigation operations are planned actions to demonstrate US or international rights to navigate air or sea routes.

friendly networks — Friendly networks are networks that are sympathetic to or assisting directly or indirectly with our mission. They include the military and civil components and non-governmental organizations associated with allied coalition forces and host nation forces. They are characterized as green or blue.

functional analysis — In network nodal analysis, functional analysis is the examination of the purposes of the network and its components.

fusion cells — Theater level fusion centers, known as Joint Intelligence Operations Centers (JIOC), are a DOD and combatant command level organization. The JIOC mission is to seamlessly integrate all DOD intelligence functions and disciplines, ensuring all sources of information are available across the DOD, and improving the integration of intelligence with traditional operations and plans functions to increase the speed, power and combat effectiveness of DOD operations.

generate new metrics — One generates new metrics when measurements used in the past were not process oriented.

GEO browser — GEO browser is a tool used by the JIEDDO COIC for situational awareness and data mining tool. The tools displays and correlates the COIC Multi-INT Core both spatially and temporally.

global name system — Commercial product recognition used by the COIC that constraints the best of breed technologies designed to address specific needs and demands of managing, searching, analyzing, and comparing multicultural name and data fields.

Global Name Reference Encyclopedia — is a JIEDDO COIC tool that includes much of the detailed information that one needs in order to perform name analysis work on networks. Also called **GNRE**.

green networks — Green networks are military and government civilian host-nation forces.

hierarchical — Hierarchical networks have a well-defined vertical chain of command and responsibility. Information flows up and down organizational channels that correspond to these vertical chains, but may not move horizontally through the organization. This is more traditional, and is common of groups that are well established with a command and support structure. Hierarchical organizations feature greater specialization of functions in their subordinate cells (support, operations, intelligence).

histogram — Histogram is a bar chart used to depict the average and variability of a data set.

historic considerations — Includes the cultural norms, religious beliefs, and past military and political events of a region as they impact the adversary's capabilities and should be considered in operational planning.

host nation special forces engage — The deliberate employment of host nation special forces in an ATN operation to render the enemy's personnel or equipment ineffective.

host nation/partner targeting guidance — Targeting guidance from host nation/partners is the general or specific guidance parameters given by a host nation or partner to direct the activities, the decisions, or the desired outcomes of the person or group that is executing the targeting process.

host nation information requirements — An intelligence requirement, stated as a priority for intelligence support, that the commander and staff need to understand the host nation's government, defense, or intelligence agencies or their respective activities. Also referred to as **HNIRs**.

host nation legal considerations — Accounting for the laws and the considerations jurisprudence of citizens of the host nation when planning for the prosecution of targets.

human terrain element — A group of civilian anthropologists attached to brigades and battalions. This team helps the unit understand local cultures. These social scientists aid leaders in better understanding relevant cultural history, engaging locals in a positive way, and incorporating knowledge of tribal traditions to help resolve conflicts.

human terrain system — A proof of concept program, run by the U.S. Army Training and Doctrine Command (TRADOC), and serves the joint community. The near term focus of the program is to improve the military's ability to understand the highly complex local socio-cultural environment in areas where they are deployed. Also called **HTS**.

identify collection capabilities — To determine the methods of intelligence collection, both organic and inorganic to a unit, that are necessary and available.

Information Dominance Center — supports Army commands and units worldwide through G-2 channels for intelligence-reach operations. The center can provide tailored intelligence products to the field to meet their operational requirements on a quick response basis. The center monitors potential trouble spots, preparing to support contingency operations with intelligence related products. The center continues to explore new analytical technologies and emerging concepts to support Army warfighters. Also called the **IDC**.

identify purpose — To identify purpose is to first align your purpose with your organization's mission, vision, goals, and objectives. These should be inextricably linked to meeting customer needs and serve as a foundation for accomplishing and sustaining continuous, measurable improvement.

identify instacheck — A COIC tool that provides identity resolution support and analysis by massing and fusing sources of contextual data and results of biometric matches.

individual component — When conducting nodal analysis, a component is a constituent part of the network.

influence neutral networks — To influence neutral networks is to sway allegiance and support of the neutral network away from the threat network(s) and/or towards the friendly network.

information engagement — Information engagement is the integrated employment of public affairs to inform U.S. and friendly audiences; psychological operations, combat camera, US Government strategic communication and defense support to public diplomacy, and other means necessary to influence foreign audiences; and, leader and Soldier engagements to support both efforts.

informational (operational variable) — Informational variables are those operational variables that whereby individuals, organizations, and systems collect, process, disseminate, or act on information.

infrastructure (operational variable) — Infrastructure variables are those operational variables that comprise the basic facilities, services, and installations needed for a society's functioning.

integrate enablers — To integrate enablers is to blend efficiently and effectively the necessary organic and inorganic experts, tools, and material for attack the network activities.

integrate host nation capabilities — To integrate HN capabilities is to blend efficiently into attack the network operations the relevant national assets and services of the host nation where the US and its coalition are operating. These assets and services span the diplomatic, intelligence, legal, law enforcement, informational, military, and economic functions of commercial, government, and non-government organization.

integrate US/partner capabilities — To integrate US/partner capabilities are to blend efficiently into attack the network operations the relevant national assets and services of the US and its coalition partners. These assets and services span the diplomatic, intelligence, legal, law enforcement, informational, military, and economic functions of commercial, government, and non-government organizations.

integrate intelligence — Leveraging traditional and non-traditional information resources, such as human intelligence (HUMINT). Integrating central and local government intelligence apparatus; quasi-governmental institutions such as tribal affiliations, ethnic affiliations, religious, professional affiliations to legitimize government.

intelligence, surveillance, and reconnaissance tasks — are the actions of the intelligence collection effort. These actions synchronize or integrate the planning and operation of sensors, assets, and processing, exploitation, and dissemination systems in direct support of current and future operations. Also called **ISR tasks**.

Joint Center of Excellence — The execution arm of JIEDDO's C-IED training program. JCOE is located at Fort Irwin, Ca. and has been operational since April 2006. Together with the four service-specific centers of excellence (COEs), JCOE provides deploying forces with training on rapidly fielded C-IED equipment and capabilities. JCOE and the service COEs facilitate individual, collective, and unit C-IED training; develop and publish IED defeat tactics, techniques and procedures; and make available to deploying units C-IED lessons learned from those returning from theater. Also referred as **JCOE/Service COEs**.

Joint Expeditionary Team — Supports all echelons of the joint force, interagency, and multinational partners. Its purpose is to train, advise, observe, analyze, and to collect and disseminate tactics, techniques, and procedures (TTPs), lessons learned, and best practices to mitigate the IED threat. They will normally operate in two to three man teams and be placed OPCON to the TF's C-IED commander. Also called a **JET**.

Joint Knowledge and Information Fusion Exchange — Acts as the DOD central repository for IED related information. Its primary purpose is to exchange information, consolidate best practices and respond to requests for information related to the asymmetric application of IED related TTPs by both enemy and friendly forces. Also called **JKnIFE**.

Joint Training Counter-IED Operations Integration Center — Organization mission is to ensure Army and joint organizations are aware of and able to employ rapidly fielded counter-IED capabilities. Established as a partnership between JIEDDO and TRADOC, the state-of-the-art center combines the operational focus of the Department of Defense's lead counter-IED organization with the training resources and expertise of the Army's premier training command. Also called **JTCOIC**.

Joint Urgent Operational Needs Statement — An urgent operational need identified by a combatant commander involved in an ongoing named operation. A JUONS main purpose is to identify and subsequently gain Joint Staff validation and resourcing of a solution, usually within days or weeks, to meet a specific high-priority combatant commander need. Also referred to as a **JUON**.

law enforcement capabilities — Law enforcement capabilities are those police faculties that are not organic to the unit and must be requested from the continental United States such as small-unit tactics, special weapons employment, convoy escort, riot control, traffic control, prisoner and detainee handling and processing, police intelligence, criminal intelligence, criminal handling, stations management.

lethal — Lethal targets are best addressed with operations to kill, damage, disrupt, or capture. *It is important to understand that lethal does not necessarily equate to fatal. Lethal refers to the potential effects of targeting, fire, and maneuver.*

line of effort — A line of effort is a line that links multiple tasks and missions using the logic of purpose—cause and effect—to focus efforts toward establishing operational and strategic conditions.

link analysis — link analysis is an analytical method for determining the relationships between critical personalities and members within their network.

link diagram — A link diagram depicts the linkages in a network between actors, their interests, entities, events, organizations, or other factors.

medical — The range of professional services that provide medical care to a society. The nature and extent of this infrastructure and the implications to AtN planning must be understood when conducting operations.

military (operational variables) — Military variables are those operational variables that includes the military capabilities of all armed forces in a given operational environment.

mission variables — Mission variables are those aspects of the operational environment that directly affect a mission. They consist of mission, enemy, terrain and weather, troops and support available, time available, and civil considerations.

money as a weapons system — Money as a weapon system is designed to leverage money to positively influence the host nation populace (e.g. commander's emergency response program). Also called **MAWS**.

multinational capabilities — Capabilities of the multinational participants (civil and military) within the operational area (e.g. law enforcement, health professionals, engineers, etc.) that can be applied in support of ongoing operations.

national caveats — National caveats are general or specific parameters given by the US national leadership team to direct the activities, decisions, or desired outcomes of a person or group that is executing the operation process – usually includes specific limitations on targeting.

national assistance (host nation support) — National assistance is civil and/or military assistance rendered to a nation by foreign forces within that nation's territory during peacetime, crises or emergencies, or war based on agreements mutually concluded between nations. Nation assistance programs include, but are not limited to, security assistance, foreign internal defense, other US Code Title 10 (DOD) programs, and activities performed on a reimbursable basis by Federal agencies or international organizations.

Network — That group of elements forming a unified whole, also known as a system.

North Atlantic Treaty Organize Attack the Network enablers — The enablers are personnel, services, tools, and material from NATO partners that are used to supplement, enhance, and complement US and coalition forces capabilities for conducting attack the network operations. Also referred to as **NATO AtN enablers**.

North Atlantic Treaty Organization counter-improvised explosive device cell — The cell is the counter-IED team provided by the North Atlantic Treaty Organization that provides C-IED analysis, C-IED services, and liaison to other C-IED capabilities. Also called **NATO C-IED cell**.

network components — Network components are the elemental parts of a network when graphically mapping a social network

network formation conditions — Network formation conditions are those existing state of affairs in the operational environment that allow a series of direct and indirect ties from one actor to a collection of others (a network) to generate.

network/nodal analysis — Nodal analysis is a qualitative examination of the interrelationships and interactions among multiple target systems to determine the degree and points of interdependence and linkages of their activities. Nodal analysis results in the identification of the specific functional nodes that empower that network.

network templating — Network templating is identifying and representing a threat networks critical capabilities so that analysts and action officers can understand its critical requirements and critical vulnerabilities in order to exploit its vulnerabilities through operations.

network tools — Network tools are the various collection and analytical systems that enable a network analyst to represent, analyze, and make estimates on networks.

neutral network — Neutral networks are networks that are not hostile to, or in any way supportive of any one of the forces in a hostile environment. Sometimes characterized as White networks.

nodal component analysis — Nodal component analysis is the analysis of how nodes of a designated system function in relation to one another.

non-hierarchical — Non-hierarchical networks are any decentralized decision-making structure.

observables — Observables are indicators that can be directly or indirectly observed through collection.

offensive operations — Offensive operations are combat operations conducted to defeat and destroy enemy forces and seize terrain, resources, and population centers.

operational variables — Operational variables are those general factors within an operational environment or situation around which a unit, system, or individual is expected to operate and which may affect performance.

organizational risk analyzer — Organizational risk analyzer is a dynamic meta-network assessment and analysis tool. It contains hundreds of social network, dynamic network metrics, trail metrics, procedures for grouping nodes, identifying local patterns, comparing and contrasting networks, groups, and individuals from a dynamic meta-network perspective. It has been used to examine how networks change through space and time. Also referred to as **ORA**.

organizations — Organizations in the context of the memory aid ASCOPE are groups of individuals that have associated themselves around some purpose or interest. They can be religious, fraternal, criminal, media, patriotic or service, and community watch groups. They include media, IGOs, NGOs, merchants, squatters, and other groups.

organize for the attack the network fight — To organize for the fight it to identify those organic and inorganic experts, tools, and material that are needed for conducting attack the network operations.

organize the staff for attack the network — To organize the staff is to define the structure, roles, and responsibilities of a unit and its leadership in order to conduct attack the network operations. Organizing the staff is different at the theater, division, and tactical levels because their missions, their composition, and the enablers available to them are different.

Palantir — Palantir is a commercial tool used by the JIEDDO COIC that integrates, visualizes, and analyzes various data, to include structured, unstructured, relational, temporal, and geospatial data.

Pareto Chart — Pareto Chart is a bar graph used to separate the "vital few" from the "trivial many." Based on the Pareto Principal which states that 10-20 percent of the problems have 80-90 percent of the impact.

pattern analysis — Using prior actions and activities to identify trends in activities or behaviors. Once identified, these patterns can be used to predict future enemy actions, plan intelligence, surveillance, and reconnaissance (ISR) activities.

pattern analysis plot sheet — A pattern analysis plot sheets helps distinguish patterns in activities associated with particular days, dates, or times when they are depicted graphically. Analysts may choose to modify this product to track longer or shorter period as appropriate.

people — In the context of the memory aid ASCOPE, all nonmilitary personnel in the area of interest.

police intelligence — Police intelligence results from the application of systems, technologies, and processes that analyze applicable data and information necessary for situational understanding and focusing policing activities to achieve social order.

political (operational variable) — Political variables are those operational variables that describe the distribution of responsibility and power at all levels of governance.

prepare the organization (for AtN) — Political variables are those operational variables that describe the distribution of responsibility and power at all levels of governance.

process improvement — In the context of metrics, process improvement is using the data to effect change within your organization.

prosecution based targeting — Prosecution-based targeting is a form of nonlethal targeting against an adversary by removing him from the battlefield by using intelligence collection and analysis to build a case that will effectively prosecute him in a host nation's criminal system.

prosecution working group — The threat working group is cross-functional by design and includes membership from across the staff, liaison personnel, and other partners outside the headquarters. This working group identifies, prioritizes, and coordinates actions regarding targets for nonlethal targeting by removing him from the battlefield by using intelligence collection and analysis to build a case that will effectively prosecute him in a host nation's criminal system.

protection of shipping operations — Protection of shipping is the use of proportionate force by US warships, military aircraft, and other forces, when necessary for the protection of US flag vessels and aircraft, US citizens (whether embarked in US or foreign vessels), and their property against unlawful violence. This protection may be extended (consistent with international law) to foreign flag vessels, aircraft, and persons.

proximity network — A proximity network is a series of direct and indirect associations among various actors due to the geographical ties of its members (ex. past bonding in correctional or other institutions, or living within specific regions or neighborhoods). Members may also form a network with proximity to an area strategic to their criminal interests (ex. a neighborhood or key border entry point). There may be a dominant ethnicity within the group, but they are primarily together for geographical reasons.

raids — Raids are operations to temporarily seize an area in order to secure information, confuse an adversary, capture personnel or equipment, or to destroy a capability. It ends with a planned withdrawal upon completion of the assigned mission.

rate metrics — To rate a metric is to judge a created metric against the eight characteristics of a good metric: meaningful to the customer; tells how well organizational goals and objectives are being met through processes and tasks; is simple, understandable, logical and repeatable; shows a trend; is unambiguously defined; is economical to collect; is timely; drives the "appropriate action."

reach-back capabilities — Those experts, tools, equipment, services, or material that are provided by organizations that are not forward deployed.

receptive audience — A receptive audience is a body of persons each of whom feels that he has something to gain by engaging in the activities of the network.

red networks — Red networks are formal and/or informal grouping of adversarial actors that are in opposition to the friendly networks. Red networks are the adversary network(s) identified in the commander's intent.

Red Team — The mission of the Red Team at JIEDDO's COIC is to provide its parent organization with a continuous process of analysis and counter-analysis that assesses: the likely enemy operational and tactical TTP innovations; countermeasures; wargaming the effectiveness of those countermeasures. The Red Team also identifies gaps, challenges assumptions and predicts 2nd and 3rd order effects. The Red Team does that through adversarial emulation, independent analysis, and critical review in support of current operations, plans, and capabilities for committed units and JIEDDO in order to enhance the counter-IED fight.

regenerative — A regenerative systems is a complex, adaptive system that can rebuild itself after attack. Removal of a single node has minimal impact on the system as a whole.

request for support tracker — The tracker is a database created in-house at the JIEDDO COIC to document and track requests for support from the warfighter. Also referred to as **RFS**.

restated mission — The mission statement after operational planning that is short sentence or paragraph that describes the organization's essential task (or tasks) and purpose — a clear statement of the action to be taken and the reason for doing so. The mission statement contains the elements of who, what, when, where, and why, but seldom specifies how. It forms the basis for planning and is included in the planning guidance, the planning directive, staff estimates, the commander's estimate, the concept of operations (CONOPS), and the completed plan.

route clearance patrol — Route clearance is the detection, investigation, marking and reporting, and neutralization of explosive hazards (EH) and other obstacles along a defined route to enable assured mobility for the maneuver commander. It is a combined arms operation that relies on a reconnaissance of the route to be cleared. The goal of route clearance is to detect and neutralize EH and improve and know the route to be able to conduct future change detection operations.

run chart — Run chart is a graph of a process measurement over time.

safety — In the SWEAT-MS construct, the range of services that protect the people in a society from fire and crime or that respond to disasters. The nature and extent of this infrastructure and the implications to AtN planning must be understood when conducting operations.

Signatures Analysis Team — Provides predictive analysis of both terrain and force oriented problems via signatures analysis. Also referred to as the **SAT**.

scatter diagram — Scatter diagram is a type of graph used to reveal the possible relationship between two variables.

seize the initiative — To seize the initiative is to execute offensive operations at the earliest possible time, forcing the adversary to offensive culmination and setting the conditions for decisive operations.

self-organizing — Self-organizing systems operate without a central authority or external element imposing structure upon it. This is basically a 'bottom up' developed organization.

Service knowledge management — Service knowledge management encompasses the various electronic repositories of organized information that are relevant to AtN operations and are maintained by the various services to include the Army Center for Lessons learned and the Marine Corps Lessons Learned Center.

Service tools — Service tools are the various collection and analytical systems procured by a service (Air Force, Navy, Army, or Marine Corps) that enable a network analyst to represent, analyze, and make estimates on networks.

sewer — In the SWEAT-MS construct, sewer infrastructure is an artificial usually subterranean conduit to carry off sewage and sometimes surface water (as from rainfall).

shaping operations — A shaping operation is an operation at any echelon that creates and preserves conditions for the success of the decisive operation.

shows trends — To show trends is to demonstrate a measurement over time extending in a general direction.

signatures — Signatures are indicators that can be inferred through measurements.

social network analysis — Social network analysis is a tool for understanding the organizational dynamics of an insurgency and how best to attack or exploit it. It allows analysts to identify and portray the details of a network structure. Also referred to as **SNA**.

societal — Societal variables are those operational variables that describes societies within an operational environment. A society is a population whose members are subject to the same political authority, occupy a common territory, have a common culture, and share a sense of identity.

Special Operations Force-Task Force — Provides multi-discipline intelligence analysis, fusion and integration to support USSOCOM operations. Also called **SOF-TF**.

specialized network — In a specialized network, individuals come together to undertake activities primarily based on the skills, expertise or particular capabilities they offer.

structures — Structures in the context of the memory aid ASCOPE are existing important infrastructure. Examples include hospitals, bridges, communications towers, and power plants.

support friendly networks — To support friendly networks is to provide material support, personnel, guidance, or public affirmation to network that is sympathetic to or cooperating in support of US interests.

support to host nation operations — Support to host nation operations is providing material support, personnel or guidance to a host nationals planned operation.

support to insurgency — To provide aid or comfort to an insurgency, which is an organized, protracted politico-military struggle designed to weaken the control and legitimacy of an established government, occupying power, or other political authority while increasing insurgent control.

supports objectives — A metric must directly support corporate goals or objectives because it is built from the strategic and business plans. All efforts to evaluate your current situation and steps taken to improve your processes will be in vain unless the end result is the advancement of the organization toward successfully meeting corporate goals.

sustaining operations — An operation at any echelon that enables the decisive operation or shaping operations by generating and maintaining combat power.

tactical AtN capabilities — Tactical AtN capabilities are the personnel, tools, services, and material that are with and utilized by forces at the brigade/regimental combat team-level and below versus those that are at the division-level and above.

Tactical Conflict Assessment and Planning Framework — The Tactical Conflict Assessment and Planning Framework was a practical framework designed to assist commanders and their staffs identify the causes of instability in an area of operation, develop activities to diminish or mitigate them, and evaluate the effectiveness of the activities in fostering stability. Also called **TCAPF**.

tactical exploitation teams — Tactical exploitation teams deploy from the C-IED task forces on short-notice to provide site exploitation, which are those activities that recognize, collect, process, preserve, or analyze information, personnel, and materiel found during the conduct of C-IED operations.

tactical patience — Tactical patience is the intentional delay of the execution of an operation against a target to allow a more fully developed picture of the operational environment or network. Tactical patience requires balancing the operational risk of not acting now with opportunities for intelligence gain and greater operational effects in the future.

target assessment — A target assessment is a broad assessment of the overall impact and effectiveness of the full spectrum of military force applied against the operation of an enemy target system or total combat effectiveness (including significant subdivisions of the system) relative to the operational objectives established.

targeting board (lethal/nonlethal) — A targeting board is a temporary grouping of designated predetermined staff representatives with decision authority to coordinate and synchronize the targeting process.

targeting guidance — Targeting guidance describes the desired effects of lethal and nonlethal fires. It is expressed in terms of targeting objectives (limit, disrupt, delay, divert, or destroy) or IO effects (destroy, degrade, disrupt, deny, deceive, exploit, or influence).

Team–L — Team L is a Comprehensive Look Team at the JIEDDO COIC that supports offensive operations focused on attacking networks as part of the overall Joint Improvised Explosive Devise Defeat Organization (JIEDDO), Counter-IED Operations Integration Center (COIC) C-IED support structure.

Team Phoenix — Team Phoenix integrates intelligence, operations, and technology with training to enable pre-emptive analysis to attack networks.

terrain & weather — Identifying the terrain and weather before a military action is to determine the natural features (such as rivers and mountains) and man-made features (such as cities, airfields, and bridges) that will affect the mission as well as the effect of the weather on the mission.

Terrorist Explosive Device Analytical Center — The center is responsible for the prevention of potential improvised explosive device (IED) attacks by coordinating and managing the unified efforts of law enforcement, intelligence, and military assets to technically and forensically exploit all terrorist IEDs worldwide of interest to the US government. The information and intelligence derived from the exploitation of terrorist IEDs is used to provide actionable intelligence to anti-terror missions and to help protect the US military and coalition assets around the globe. Also known as **TEDAC**.

theater forensics — Theater forensics labs include Joint Expeditionary Forensic Facilities (JEFFs) and the Combined Explosives Exploitation Cell (CEXC). A JEFF is a modular and scalable deployable forensic laboratory designed to support targeting, sourcing, prosecution and detainment and interrogation operations. CEXC is an enduring in-theater laboratory whose mission is the collection and exploitation of technical weapons intelligence and forensic evidence for the purpose of identifying bomb makers and assisting in the development of defensive and offensive C-IED measures.

threat networks — Threat networks are networks that are in opposition to the friendly networks. They are characterized as red or black.

time available — Identifying the time available before a military action is to assess the time available for planning, preparing, and executing the mission. This includes the time required to assemble, deploy, and maneuver units to where they can best mass the effects of combat power. Commanders also consider how much time they can give subordinates to plan and prepare their own operations.

to be determined — In the context of capabilities, capabilities that will be needed in the future, but at the current time are indeterminable. Also referred to as **TBD**.

transportation — In the SWEAT-MS construct, the range of infrastructure (rail, car, air, etc,) that moves people, property, and commerce within a society. The nature and extent of this infrastructure and the implications to AtN planning must be understood when conducting operations.

troops — Identifying the troops before a military action is to determine the number, type, capabilities, and condition of available friendly forces and support that are required for the given mission. These forces include resources from joint, interagency, multinational, host-nation, commercial (via contracting), and private organizations. It also includes support provided by civilians.

United States Agency for International Development — An independent federal government agency that receives overall foreign policy guidance from the Secretary of State. It supports long-term and equitable economic growth and advances U.S. foreign policy objectives by supporting economic growth, agriculture, and trade; global health; and democracy, conflict prevention, and humanitarian assistance. Also referred to as **USAID**.

user defined operational picture — A JIEDDO COIC tool that provides situational awareness environment and rides on top of Google Earth. Also known as **UDOP/Google Search**.

understand the commander's intent — Understanding the commander's intent is to comprehend the concise expression of the purpose of the operation and the desired end state delivered by the commander. It may also include an assessment of where and how much risk is acceptable during the operation. See also assessment; end state.

understanding the operational environment — Understanding the operational environment is to comprehend the "composite of the conditions, circumstances, and influences that affect the employment of capabilities and bear on the decisions of the commander.

understand the mission — In an attack the network context, understanding the mission means to comprehend the AtN task, together with the purpose, that clearly indicates the action to be taken and the reason therefore.

understand the network — Understanding the network or local cells means having an appreciation for the nature of adaptive networked threats, their structure, characteristics, dynamics, and purpose.

understand network concepts — Understanding network concepts means to comprehend or perceive the general ideas around the nature, purposes, and activities of the various kinds of networks in one's area of operations.

universal needs statement — An official request submitted to a service's requirements process by which a unit makes a request for current and future wartime capabilities. Also called **UNS.**

virtual network — A virtual network is a series of direct and indirect associations among various actors that may never physically meet, but work together through the Internet or other means of communication (ex. networks involved in online fraud, theft or money laundering).

wargaming — Requires the development and employment of a standing, on-demand wargaming capability to enhance AtN strategy development using threat scenarios and modeling and simulation resources to assess future operations in the context of friendly and enemy courses of action (COA), concepts of operations (CONOPS), tactics, techniques, and procedures (TTP), and emerging technologies.

warrant based targeting — Warrant-based targeting is a form of nonlethal targeting against an adversary that uses intelligence in concert with hosts-nation law enforcement and judicial capabilities to generate a warrant against the adversary in order to arrest him and remove him from the battlefield.

water — In the SWEAT-MS, construct, water infrastructure refers to a source, means, or process of supplying water (as for a community) usually including reservoirs, tunnels, and pipelines.

web threads — Web threads is a JIEDDO COIC tool to assist counter-threat and force protection analysts corroborate human intelligence reporting of terrorist/force protection threats through the fusion of space systems-generated data.

web based temporal analysis system — A government off-the-shelf (GOTS) software toolkit providing visualization, integration and analysis of disparate data in a service oriented architecture (SOA) compliant platform. Built using non-proprietary software, it provides both Java thick client and web browser-based access, visualization and analysis capabilities. Also known as **WebTAS.**

weapons intelligence team — The weapons intelligence team or C-IED teams are assigned to the C-IED TF. Normally an EOD company, with a direct support WIT, will be placed in direct support of each brigade combat team. They will be placed OPCON to the TF's C-IED commander. Also known as **WIT**.

weapons technical intelligence — A category of intelligence derived from the technical and forensic collection and exploitation of IEDs, associated components, improvised weapons, and other weapon systems. Also called **WTI**.

white network — see neutral networks.

www.ingramcontent.com/pod-product-compliance
Lightning Source LLC
Chambersburg PA
CBHW080249290526
45790CB00005B/1748